Beauty Unleashed

Transforming a Woman's Soul

Heidi McLaughlin

VMI PUBLISHERS
Sisters, OR

Scripture quotations marked "NIV" are taken from the Life Application Bible, New International Version, Zondervan Publishers, copyright© 1988, 1989, 1990, 1991.

Scripture quotations marked "MSG" are taken from The Message. Copyright © by Eugene H. Peterson 1993, 1994, 1995, 1996, 2000, 2001, 2002. Used by permission of NavPress Publishing Group.

Scriptures marked "TLB" are taken from The Living Bible Paraphrase, Tyndale House Publishers, copyright © 1971, 1973.

Published by
VMI PUBLISHERS
Sisters, Oregon
www.vmipublishers.com

13-digit ISBN: 978-1-933204-40-6
10-digit ISBN: 1-933204-40-0

Library of Congress Control Number: 2007924529

Printed in the United States of America

Cover design by Joe Bailen

Heidi uses her passion and gifts of speaking and writing in her ministry called "*HEART CONNECTIONS.*" You can contact her through her web page: www.heartconnection.ca or write to her at:

Heidi McLaughlin
1529 Chardonnay Place
Kelowna, British Columbia
Canada
V4T 2P9
250-470-9299

This book is dedicated to the man who has gently taught
me to let God unleash all the beauty in my life:

My darling Jack

CONTENTS

ACKNOWLEDGEMENTS

*B*EHIND EVERY RESTLESS desire, certain people are needed to stand on the sidelines to cheer us on and encourage us to put our inspiration into action. Thank goodness for those people who love us enough to believe in us and validate the unusual stirrings in our spirit—who listen and hope with us against all odds.

When I told my two accountability partners that I was thinking about writing a book but that the odds of getting published were probably 1%, my friend Joanne confidently responded, "Heidi, that is all God needs." This is the type of person we all need in our lives to help us realize our dreams.

My husband Jack spent hours with me on the patio deck outside our home in the summer of 2006, answering my endless questions such as, "What do *you* feel like when you are disappointed?" and "What does a scarcity mentality look like to you?" He never tired of my passion or ever grumbled when I asked him to read another chapter—again.

When I told my children that I was writing a book, my son Donovan immediately replied, "Mom, I would love to be your reader." I told him that it would be a book for a female audience, so he just wistfully smiled and shrugged. Whenever I needed a second set of women's eyes and ears, I e-mailed the chapters to my daughter Michelle, whose comments were always so insightful and honest. My stepchildren, Jennifer, Janice, and David, and their families were so generous in their praise by letting me know how proud they were of me. When Janice came to visit in the summer of 2006, I sat her down, and we spent hours talking about the joys, pain, and expectations of friendships.

My mother, sisters, and many friends who prayed for me always asked, "How is the book going?" I thanked them for joining me on this exhilarating journey. It is a magnificent gift when people share our joy.

Mark Buchanan, the author of *The Rest of God*, gave me my best advice. He told me that while I was writing this book, I should write every word as an "act of worship" to God. That wisdom was imprinted in my mind and poured out of every prayer and sentence which I put down on paper. Consequently, every word in this book is an offering of praise and an *act of worship* meant to unleash women's beauty and bring glory to our God.

INTRODUCTION

*T*HERE IS NOTHING MORE beautiful than a woman who knows that she is loved. She is the one who glows with energy and confidence when she walks into a room. Everyone yearns to be this kind of woman, but many just can't seem to find the magic formula. Never before in our society's history have we been able to access more information, technical advice, and "how to" steps to make over every area of our lives. Yet, our souls are emptier than ever as we hide behind our masks of frantic activities and silent fatigue.

I love to sit across from a woman whose eyes beg to discover her own beauty and to find ways to bring fulfillment and purpose to her life. So often, however, when the mask comes off, those same eyes are filled with pain and despair. That woman knows there has to be more passion and value in what she does, but she doesn't know how to find it. She thinks the rest of the world has it, so she can't understand what is wrong with her. In fact, many women confess their feelings of hopelessness and anxiety, often turning to anti-depressants so they can "just get through this rough spot."

What has happened to the innocent laughter and beauty that came from within us as little children? Girls giggle and laugh when we make faces at them, their eyes sparkling with glee. They adorn themselves in princess dresses, twirl, and dance uninhibited in their bare feet. Because everything delights and fascinates them, they engage their world with creativity, joy, and the giddy anticipation of a great adventure. Little girls spread their unconditional love wherever they go and eagerly accept it in return. They are carefree because they believe life is like the fairy-tale stories in which they always become the beautiful princesses who are rescued by handsome princes.

Now that we are women, I fear that we have become too smart and busy for this uninhibited kind of joy. Who will rescue us and make us feel beautiful once again?

- Have we been hurt so many times that we've learned to shut off our feelings?
- Have we perfected the art of pretending to be the woman everyone expects us to be?
- Are we so busy with our endless "to do" lists that we have no time to "just be"?
- Is life just a series of "shoulds," "coulds," and "have-tos?"
- Do we feel that we do not even *deserve* abundant joy in our lives?
- Does our self worth come from our accomplishments rather than who we are?
- Has anyone ever taken the time to help us connect with God to find our true self?

We have not lost our beauty. It is right where God placed it on the day He created us in our mothers' wombs. Our life struggles, disappointments, and humiliations have taught us to lock beauty away, hiding and protecting it from the world. Many women do not enjoy their beauty because they don't feel worthy enough to even acknowledge that it is there.

I need to know how to use each day of my life the way God has intended for me to live it. I don't believe I was meant to aimlessly survive each day at break-neck speed. God tells us in His Word to "be still and know that I am God" (Psalm 46:10 NIV). By staying quiet, seeking Him, and experiencing the beauty of God's magnificent, unconditional love and kindness toward us, we will begin to discover and identify the unique beauty that is within each of us.

Let's look at our modern-day crisis of too many choices, hectic lifestyles, and the resulting emptiness through the eyes of the one who created us and knows us better than anyone else—our rescuer, God's Son Jesus. He walked and talked with His twelve disciples and taught them how to live through stories, object lessons, and a lot of love. I believe stories are powerful ways to teach truths so that we can comprehend confusing and difficult situations.

As you read each of the following chapters, I encourage you to imagine me sitting across from you, gently urging you to soften your heart and connect it to God so that He can speak to you. Then, anticipate His answers to give you new hope and wisdom for obstacles you face each day.

Each chapter starts with my personal story of the mistakes and challenges I have encountered over the years. Life can be hard, but I want you to know that you are not alone with your disappointments and confusion. Then, I invite you to explore with me the pressures that enter our daily lives and rob us of this beauty. Each chapter ends with a reminder of the ways God can unleash your beauty.

Stop and ask God to Unleash Your Beauty

S: **Scripture verse** will be available here for reflection.

T: **Thanksgiving.** Thank God for the beauty He has placed in our souls.

O: **Observation.** What would we like to ask God to do in our lives?

P: **Pray.** Ask Him.

My Prayer for You:

I will end each chapter praying with you because I am passionate about God transforming your life into the most magnificent beauty you have ever known. I may have never met you, but I have ministered to women like you for many years, and I love you dearly. I have seen God change women's lives right before my very eyes. I know He can do it, because He is your creator, as well as the King of kings and Lord of lords. He has been pursuing you your entire life, so let Him because He wants to. The King is enthralled with your beauty.

1

UNLEASHING THE BEAUTY OF PURPOSE
Like an Ant

The trouble with so many of us is that we underestimate the power of simplicity. We have a tendency, it seems, to overcomplicate our lives and forget what's important and what's not. We tend to mistake movement for achievement. We tend to focus on activities instead of results. And as the pace of life continues to race along in the outside world, we forget that we have the power to control our lives regardless of what's going on outside.

—ROBERT STUBERG

MY FEET HIT THE GROUND running as the alarm went off at 6 a.m. There was no time to think about anything except being the first one in the bathroom for my coveted long, hot, luxurious shower. This would probably be the only pampering and quiet time I would get all day, so I wanted to make it last as long as possible. It was just another frantic day in the Conley household, with a mental "to do" list that had me on the verge of tears just thinking about it.

The day started with a warm, sit-down breakfast for my two children, Michelle and Donovan. Then, I needed to pack the lunches, feed the dog and cat, water the plants, and check the priority calendar that glared at me with all of its obligations. What else? Check the fridge to see if there is something to prepare for supper. Oh, and by the way, don't forget to fit in that work-out in the gym during lunch hour. Even though it was just another typical day, I could barely face it. As I drove down the highway on the way to my job at the law firm, tears streamed down my face. I was already crying, and the day hadn't even officially started.

HOW HAD THINGS gotten so frantic in my life? I knew this was not the abundant living that Jesus was talking about: "I have come that they may have life, and have it to the full" (John 10:10 NIV). I was caught up in a lifestyle that was flying by at Mach 2 speed, but I didn't know how to change it. I felt overburdened, tired, and sad. I knew that I had to find ways to change it; otherwise, the speed would crush me and destroy the people I loved most of all.

I was beginning to dislike my constant feelings of irritation when things did not go according to my clearly defined daily plans. I wanted to be a woman who had joy written all over her face—not one with a forced smile, gritted teeth, and a mind constantly occupied by the next task. Living out the image of my perfect family life was destroying my soul, so I knew it had to stop. I didn't know how, so I prayed and asked God to help me slow down.

THERE IS NO BEAUTY IN SPEED

This typical day I just described happened about fifteen years ago. Since that time I have done a lot of praying, researching, and studying about ways to live the abundant life in this fast-paced world. I wanted to be one of those women who get up joyfully each morning, kiss each one of her children, and adoringly greet them as they came to sit down at the breakfast table. I envisioned a table laden with freshly baked bread, hot Cream of Wheat, and fresh fruit all arranged on a table covered in a newly ironed tablecloth. The kids' lunch bags would be sitting on the counter with their names written on them and love notes thoughtfully tucked inside. They would wear clean, ironed clothes. Their shoes would wait for them neatly arranged by the back door, along with their gym clothes, freshly washed and folded in their backpacks. All the while, we are chatting cheerfully about the upcoming events of the day as I sit peacefully at the kitchen table sipping a steaming cup of coffee, just brewed from my favorite freshly ground coffee beans. I then kiss my handsome husband as he leaves the house to go to his job that provides sufficiently for our perfect little family.

This is probably the fantasy morning of almost every mother on earth, filled with images of perfection in her dreams. Most of us fail miserably, however, when we compare our actual lives to those ideal ones we envision. We are moving so fast that we can hardly think, and each day feels like a struggle just to survive. Hundreds of years ago, the battle to live consisted of scrounging around for enough food to eat. Today, our subsistence depends on navigating the maze of constant busyness and dealing with the overwhelming burden of too many choices. It is a dreadful social disease that is killing our spirits and crushes our desire to get up each morning to start a new day all over again.

In an article in *The Globe and Mail,* I read, "'What do I feel about my work and my life? Who has the luxury or time to think about it? I don't feel like I'm living my life. I feel like it is living me.' Not surprisingly, this can also lead to depression. People experience an erosion of self-esteem as they feel they are not accomplishing anything. And it is, after all, the sense of accomplishment that contributes to our sense of competence."[1]

We cannot find God when we are moving at such a hectic pace in our lives that we don't have time to see or hear the beauty He wants to show us. Have you ever tried to focus on the beauty of a waterfall or read the expression on someone's face from a train moving at 180 kilometers per hour? We just can't do it. In the same way, we cannot locate the beauty in ourselves or in God when we are moving so fast that life is just a blur.

WHY DO I MOVE SO FAST?

This is how our world functions today, but I don't need to join in that pace. Why do I choose to be so busy?

- I have too many demands on my life.
- I need to feel needed.
- I need the approval of others.
- When I am busy, it gives me an excuse to say "no" to things I don't like to do or things I know I need to do.
- I feel guilty and useless if I am not busy.
- I feel like I am a "somebody" when I say that I am busy.
- I am afraid to say "no."
- I want to be like everybody else.
- I know no other way.
- I don't know how it got this way.
- I can't seem to stop.
- If I don't do it, who will?
- Busyness gives me the things I enjoy.

WE PLAY THE COMPARING GAME

Comparing ourselves to other women and the rest of the world just makes us feel inadequate. There will always be someone who has a better career, bigger house, nicer husband, and more friends than I do. There will always be someone whose children are smarter or more athletic. We can constantly compete with those who read more books, go to more conferences, and get asked to sing more, speak more, write more, or teach more. I'll meet others who decorate more, travel more, and who seem to have everything I don't have. The more we compare, the more we fall short, so let's find our own unique way in this world.

I started to discover my own uniqueness when I learned to let go of something that I loved to do but didn't do well: singing. I have always loved to sing and once had dreams of learning to sing so beautifully that people would be moved to tears. I remember singing in the kitchen and my son putting his hands over his ears and pleading, "Mommy, please stop singing!" On the day when my best friend went to sit in another spot in choir because my unprofessional singing voice irritated her, I realized that God did not give me the voice that I had yearned for. I was finally able to accept my voice for what it was—one that God had given me for speaking, encouraging, and teaching, but not for singing.

Most of us don't have brilliant careers as artists, musicians, or talented professionals in some visible area. We compare ourselves to the people with accomplishments and sell ourselves short, but we are wrong when we do this. Each one of us has natural talents that are unique to you and me. It may not be singing, painting, or making the headlines of some famous magazine, but it rather may be preparing a beautiful home, sewing, remembering numbers, or teaching pre-schoolers. God has given every one of us a unique talent, and we need to starting recognizing and enjoying it.

When I started learning to cultivate the unique strengths and gifts God had given to me, I began that wonderful journey of delighting in my individual identity, instead of constantly comparing myself to others.

We listen to shoulds.
The word "should" to a woman is like saying "sic 'em" to a dog. It doesn't take much for the guilt factor to crop up in our lives, and there is nothing that makes it appear faster than the word *should.* The burdens get heavier on us as we try to live up to the expectations of what it takes to be the right kind of woman, mother, wife, friend, and employee. How many of these "shoulds" are on your shoulders?

- You should make your children take swimming lessons; after all, you live near the water.
- You should lose weight.
- You should have an hour of "quiet time" with God in the morning.
- You should go to this retreat or conference.
- You should stay home with the children.
- You should go to work and help with the finances.
- You should learn how to use the Internet.

- You should get that college degree.
- You should take that course on parenting.
- You should have all the family over for Thanksgiving.
- You should exercise.
- You should floss every morning and every night.
- You should put cuticle oil on your nails every night.
- You should get cosmetic surgery!

In order for something to really change in our lives, most of us need to come to a point of crisis where we are forced to make critical and life-changing choices. For some, this crisis involves "burn-out." For others, it means deep depression, or the profound feeling of hopelessness. For others, traumatic events initiate the crisis. Others may feel that they are simply tired of the dreary sameness of their lives. For me, the crisis came with the death of my husband.

When Dick died suddenly two weeks before Christmas in 1994, all my perfect holiday events and carefully orchestrated life plans went flying out the window. Nothing mattered at this point, except finding the will just to eat, sleep, and breathe. I was helpless and did not even have the energy to pray. My family and friends did everything for me: they cooked, prayed, ran errands, answered the phone, bought groceries, and helped me survive those dark days. Life lost its urgency; nothing mattered to me except the basic chores of daily survival.

Traumatic events can shift our values and priorities in life. What may seem so critical yesterday suddenly means absolutely nothing. As our whole world is turned upside down and our schedules, tasks, and "to do" lists are thrown into a state of complete chaos, our real priorities rise to the top and become crystal clear. When all our perfectly planned schedules fall apart, it makes us realize how little control we really have in this life.

WHERE ARE SERENITY AND PEACE IN THIS BUSY WORLD?

For thousands of years throughout the history of the Bible, no one seemed to be too busy, but there are many, many places in God's Word where it tells us to "be still." Psalm 46: 10, for example, says, "Be still and know that I am God" (NIV).

Most of us would never commit a sin such as murder, theft, or adultery, and Satan knows he can't entice the majority of us with these "big" sins. He realizes the only way for us to know God is to be still and seek after Him. As long as we move too fast, our relationship with God will never become the powerful, intimate source of joy and peace that it was meant to be.

The first step we need to take is to find a way to slow down. We can do this by focusing on what we really want to build our lives around. One of the most practical verses in the Bible dealing with this issue is, *"Go to the ant, you sluggard, consider its ways and be wise"* (Prov. 6:6 NIV). What is an ant going to teach me about finding my purpose and serenity?

Have you ever watched ants building an ant hill? They take one grain of sand, or one piece of a twig, and carry it from here to there. They do this one after the other, one at a time: slowly and not running. It seems as though they are hardly working at all, but as time goes on, we see the ant village beginning to take shape. They seem to have a methodical plan, carrying it out slowly, day after day, with a distinct purpose.

We need to decide in our own lives what that particular "ant hill" is that we want to build. Ask yourself, "What do I want to accomplish so that when I look back at my life, I know it had value, not just for this time, but for the generations to come after us? How can I use my time to build an "ant hill" that will endure right into eternity?" The Bible gives us a lot of wisdom on this topic:

"God in his kindness has taught me how to be an expert builder. I have laid the foundation and Apollos has built on it. But he who builds on the foundation must be very careful. And no one can ever lay any other real foundation than that one we already have—Jesus Christ. But there are various kinds of materials that can be used to build on that foundation, some use gold and silver and jewels; and some build with sticks, and hay or even straw. There is going to come a time of testing at Christ's Judgment Day to see what kind of material each builder has used. Everyone's work will be put through the fire so that all can see whether or not it keeps its value, and what was really accomplished" (1 Cor. 3:10 TLB).

I know that I want to use my time on this earth to build a foundation of beauty in my life and in the lives of my family members. My desire is to create a foundation that will not only survive the fires but also grow more beautiful while it is *in* the fire. More and more, I realize that the only things which have lasting value are the love and relationships that I have nurtured over the years. Where is that designer suit I worked so hard for? It went to the second-hand store many years ago. How about my flashy red car? It's someone's old, beat-up piece of junk now. But meals together, laughter, and helping someone in need are memorable moments that occurred because I slowed down long enough to spend time with others. I took the time to place beauty and love of God in the centerpiece of my relationships.

Looking back always gives us clearer perspective. In the spring of 2006, I had the amazing privilege to fly over my former home in Lethbridge, Alberta, where I spent the busiest years of my life. Those were my children's growing-up years of school activities which appeared to have no end. As I sat looking out the window of the little airplane, I craned my neck, searching for old, familiar spots. There was the University of Lethbridge, and over there was Nicholas Sheron Park where we played in the summer and ice-skated in the winter. Then I spotted it—our first home at the end of the cul-de-sac on Seneca Place. My heart pounded as I tried to identify my former home from 10,000 feet. With a smile on my face, I caught glimpses of the driveway and the back yard. I could not tell if our old basketball hoop was still hanging above the garage door because the plane was too high.

For the rest of the flight, my mind raced with memories of the years spent in that home. Ten thousand feet up and sixteen years later, so many things had lost their urgency:

- Fussing over having a clean house
- Involving my children in so many activities
- Silly arguments about the yard, the dishes, and the laundry
- Late nights spent sewing outfits for me and my two children
- Constant running back and forth between commitments
- Filling in all the boxes for the week in my "Priority Planner"
- Being involved in too many activities at church

- Dog hairs on the carpet
- Spending too much energy trying to impress people and pretend to be something I was not
- Reading too many romance novels

My heart warmed as I remembered the things that still mattered sixteen years later:

- Meals around the dinner table with each of us laughing and sharing the "best part of our day"
- The basketball challenges in the driveway
- Dinner parties with friends and neighbors
- Teen-age energy filling our home
- Laughing
- Canning peaches with my mom and dad
- Friday "family nights" of movies and junk food
- The family coming to visit
- Getting to know who God really was

I realized then what I deeply valued was the development of my relationships spending time to connect with family, friends and God. At 10,000 feet, everything looks so much clearer. Let's make it even clearer by asking the one who can see our life even beyond that: from the beginning to the end:

"If you want to know what God wants you to do, ask him, and he will gladly tell you, for he is always ready to give a bountiful supply of wisdom to all who ask him; he will not resent it" (James 1:5 TLB).

and

"And this is my prayer: that your love may abound more and more in knowledge and depth of insight, so that you may be able to discern what is best and may be pure and blameless until the day of Christ, filled with the fruit or righteousness that comes through Jesus Christ—to the glory and praise of God" (1 Phil. 1:9 NIV).

We cannot live this life by depending on our foolish wisdom; instead, we need God's wisdom, along with the discernment of the Holy Spirit to tell us which is the best course for us to take. There is a world of "good" out there for us, but we need God's discernment in order to experience the "excellent."

UNLEASHING THE BEAUTY OF OUR LIFE'S PURPOSE

1. Know what we are building.

The beauty in our soul will be unleashed when we find the "ant hill" that we know we want to build. There is nothing more beautiful than a woman who is so focused on where she is going in this life and what she wants to build upon that the world cannot seduce her. We begin to find our unique purpose as we explore our priorities and passions and eliminate those things that cause us unnecessary pain and waste our precious time. Begin by asking yourself some questions:

Priorities:

- When I look back on my life twenty years from today, what do I want it to look like?
- Who are the most important people in my life?
- When they read the eulogy at my funeral, what do I want to be remembered for?
- God, family, friends, career, church, and recreation. What order are these items in?

Passions:

- What fills my soul?
- What brings laughter into my life?
- What keeps me awake at night dreaming about it?

- What did I love to do as a little child?
- Which passionate people do I know?
- What would I pay *anything* for?
- Do I work out of a sense of duty or passion?

Frustrations:

- Am I always tired?
- Do I constantly get irritated?
- What makes me sigh?
- Do I make irrational decisions?
- What robs my peace?
- What makes me angry?

When we begin to ask ourselves these hard, honest questions, we will be able to start distinguishing those things which have true value from those merely consuming our time and leaving us feeling empty and tired.

Katie Brazelton speaks about passion in her book, *Pathway to Purpose*. "What God's gift of passion will do for you, though, is set you free to live without guilt or uncertainty about what you should or should not do to please God. If you simply do what he designed you to do and be, you will find significance beyond measure." [2]

We need to find out what we were created to do so that it can fill our soul. Otherwise, we are simply running around on empty.

2. Say "no."

Many women are people-pleasers, afraid to say "no". We don't like the look of displeasure on someone's face when we say that we can't do something. Our desire instead is to live up to everyone's expectations so that people will brag about us as we keep pretending to be the wonderful women we have led the world to believe that we are. This week, I spoke to a woman who felt crushed because someone told her that she had let them down. She knew that she was being held up to an unrealistic expectation, but her "failure" still left her feeling sad and incompetent. To say "no" without guilt, condemnation, or regret, we must know our order of priorities in life.

When we know what we want to accomplish in our lives, it is much easier to say "no" to those things that are not part of the "ant hill" we are building.

3. Live for delayed gratification.

Most of us want approval right here and now because we need affirmation that we have value. When we know that there are crowns waiting for us in heaven, we can suspend our need for instant gratification, knowing that someday we will receive applause in heaven. If we live this life to please God, His words, "Well done, good and faithful servant," will echo throughout all eternity. A woman of beauty is too wise to throw that eternal expectation away in this lifetime by filling up moments trying to live up to everyone's expectations. She has her eyes set toward heaven, where she knows her heavenly reward is waiting for her.

4. Stay focused on our goals.

I encourage women to write out a mission statement for their lives. I equate going through life without one to going to the grocery store without a shopping list. When I forget my list I usually end up with a pile of items I really do not need and may end up wasting them. Also, I fail to get those essential ingredients for the menus I've prepared.

A mission statement is a simplified version of our spiritual life. If we have a mission for how we chose to live this life for God, it will be much easier to say "no" to those activities that are simply not part of the plan. In the book of Psalms, David describes his many experiences of trouble and anguish and acknowledges God as his only rescuer:

> "Help me to know that I am here for but a moment more. My life is no longer than my hand! My whole lifetime is but a moment to you. Proud man! Frail as breath! A shadow! And all his busy rushing ends in nothing. He heaps up riches for someone else to spend. And so, Lord my only hope is in you" (Psalm 39:5-7 TLB).

Our time here on earth is very short. We have to know what we are working toward, or else we'll end up with nothing. If we don't take the time to enjoy life today, everything we stress about or wear ourselves out for will end up being riches for someone else to spend.

5. Know that there are seasons which will be busy.

There are certain times in our lives when we know our daily schedules are going to be busy and out of control for a while. This can happen when we have a new baby, move, start a new job, or experience a crisis point in our lives. A woman of beauty sees those seasons for what they are: seasons. God has promised that as long as the world exists, the seasons will always come and go. Understanding that truth, a wise woman hangs on until the next season, which brings new life and hope.

6. Realize that we can't do it all.

For some reason, as women, we feel that we have to do it all—everything people ask of us, in addition to our own personal "to do" lists We want our family to love us, and we want everyone else to like us and speak well of us. We have to realize, however, that there are simply not enough hours in the day to accomplish everything on our "to do" lists, let alone satisfy everyone else's expectations. I regularly remind myself of the old saying: "You can please some of the people all of the time, and all of the people some of the time, but you cannot please *all* of the people *all* of the time." Yet we keep trying, don't we?

In her book, *Lies Women Believe and the Truth That Sets Them Free,* Nancy Leigh DeMoss tells us about a common lie that we believe:

> "By the way, there is another, related lie that women in our generation have bought into. In a sense, it is the opposite of the lie that we don't have enough time to do everything we're "supposed" to do. It is the lie that '*I can do it all—that* I should be able to be an ideal wife and mother, keep my house clean and organized, prepare healthy meals for my family, be active in my kids' school and my church and community, stay physically fit, keep up on

current events, *and* have a full-time job outside my home.' Women who subconsciously believe they are supposed to be able to juggle all these roles are likely to end up exhausted and over-whelmed by all the demands on their time. The Truth is, no woman can wear all those hats effectively. Sooner or later, some-thing (or someone) is going to suffer." [3]

I have one daughter, two stepdaughters, and two daughters-in-love who are all extremely busy with their children and careers. As I listen to them describe their daily routines and frantic activities, I recall those times when my children were little, and I was working full time. The demands were endless. Knowing that "we can't do it all" still does not take away all the daily responsibilities that this world seems to thrust upon us each day. On most days, we don't even *want* to do it all; we just want to hide away somewhere we can find some peace and quiet. I will share five words with you that I tell my daughters: *Take care of your heart.* Listen to your heart saying that you *can't.* Listen to your heart when it tells you that *it is not your responsibility.* Listen to your heart when it tells you that *it won't matter fifteen years from now.* And listen to your heart when it tells you that *it's not part of the ant hill that you are building.*

7. Rest.

We are privileged today to have so many time-saving devices that give us more opportunities for leisure and recreation. Our washing machines, dishwashers, refrigerators, and computers allow us to do daily tasks quicker, which get us out the door faster. We are the first generation to indulge ourselves in every recreational sport imaginable. We have some-how confused rest, however, with a leisure *activity,* such as playing golf. Instead of using the Sabbath as a *day of rest,* for example, we choose to fill it with chores and outings—with *shoulds.* As wonderful as these activ-ities may be, they do not help us rest our bodies. Rest is rather simply doing *nothing.*

Gordon MacDonald talks about this situation in his book, *Ordering Your Private World.*

"I am not by any means critical of the pursuit of fun-filled moments, diversion, laughter, or recreation. I am proposing that these alone will not restore the soul in the way that we crave. Although they may provide a momentary rest for the body, they will not satisfy the deep need for rest within the private world." [4]

When did we get so much smarter than God? God created heaven and earth; then, He needed to rest. "On the seventh day God had finished his work. On the seventh day he rested from all his work. God blessed the seventh. He made it a Holy Day because on that day he rested from his work; all the creating God had done" (Gen. 2:2, 3 MSG).

Because we are working and creating all the time, we also need to rest on the seventh day if we want our bodies to function the way they were meant to. In my own life, I know when I am overwhelmed with weariness: I get weepy, irritable, and unable to cope with all the demands in my life. When my tolerance level starts hitting the "red danger zone" my words become fewer and less kind. My compassion level drops because I don't have the energy to help others when I cannot even help myself.

A woman will be more beautiful when she gets the rest that she needs. Her eyes will sparkle, and her words will be kinder and gentler. Her actions will draw people into her circle of love rather than push them away. God has given us permission to seek rest because He actually commanded it. This is one day of the week when we can "rest from our work" without feeling any guilt or obligation. (I do not believe it has to be Sunday. It can be the seventh day of whatever work week we have, just as long as it is one day a week.)

In his book, *The Rest of God,* Mark Buchanan says, "We have forgotten the ancient wisdom, rooted in God's own rhythm of work and rest, of Sabbath. Sabbath is elixir and antidote. It is a gift for our sanity and wholeness—to prolong our lives, to enrich our relationships, to increase our fruitfulness, to make our joy complete. Sabbath restores our bent and withered parts." [5]

Imagine the beauty that can be released in us when we rest from all of our obligations, activities, demands, break-neck pace, and confusion. The rest we experience in our souls will restore the beauty to our faces.

7. *Spend time on our knees.*

Most of us find it difficult to fill the twenty-four hours in our day with activities based on the godly values we have chosen. Thus, we need direction and wisdom from the One who created us to tell us how to rightly prioritize our daily schedule. Even Jesus, the Son of God, prayed all night before He chose His twelve disciples. "One of those days, Jesus went out to a mountainside to pray and spent the night praying to God. When morning came, he called his disciples to him and chose twelve of them, whom he also designated apostles" (Luke 6:12, 13 NIV).

We also need to be on our knees, looking up to our heavenly Father to ask Him for daily wisdom, guidance, and Holy Spirit power, so that our days will have eternal value and we can slow down long enough to see the beauty in the world around us. One of my beloved authors, A.W. Tozer, made this insightful statement in 1948: "The simplicity which is in Christ is rarely found among us. In its stead are programs, methods, organizations and a world of nervous activity which occupy time and attention but can never satisfy the longing of the heart. ...Again, he recommends that in prayer we practice a further stripping down of everything, even our theology....The man who has God for his treasure has all things in One." [6]

When our eyes are focused on God, we'll go to Him for wisdom and direction. He is the only one who can rescue us from our frenzied obligations by filling our lives instead with things that have lasting value. God will show us how to build our very own *ant hill,* one piece at a time. Each one of our *ant hills* are meant to look different because God has a different purpose for each of our lives. We cannot compare our hills because that will only defeat the purpose; instead, we have to slow down long enough to pursue our own passions and set our own unique priorities.

Stop and ask God to Unleash Your Beauty

Begin by asking: God, what makes me unique?

S—Scripture: "For we are God's workmanship, created in Christ Jesus to do good works, which God prepared in advance for us to do"(Eph.2:10 NIV).

T—Thanksgiving: I praise You, God, that I am Your workmanship, your masterpiece, created for a specific purpose. Thank You for giving me gifts that will bring me pleasure and abilities that can be used to bring hope and joy to the people in my area of influence.

O—Observation: What things do I enjoy doing? What makes me laugh? What gives me fulfillment? What makes me frustrated and weepy? These could be the ways God has given me to find my unique purpose.

P—Prayer: Father, I thank You for each one of my days, because I know that they are a gift to me. Teach me to live my days wisely. Teach me how to build a foundation that will not only produce fruit in my life today, but in the lives of the generations to follow me. Teach me to sift through the daily rubble of activities to find those things and events that will have value. I ask You to cultivate the fruit of the Spirit within me so that I can find blessing in my life, as well as bless everyone around me. I ask You, God, to empower me to use the word "no" for those activities that distract me from You and the people I love. Thank You for telling me to ask for wisdom, so that You may pour it out on me freely. Thank You that I can come to the throne of grace so freely, with hands wide open, asking for help. Thank You for the power of prayer. Amen.

2

UNLEASHING THE BEAUTY
OF FRIENDSHIP
Heart Connections

*The greatest sweetener of human life is friendship. To raise this to
the highest pitch of enjoyment is a secret which but few discover.*
—JOSEPH ADDISON (1672-1719)
BRITISH ESSAYIST, POET, AND STATESMAN

I WAS DOUBLED OVER, and the tears
were streaming down my face. The laughter was coming so fast and hard
that I was gulping to catch my breath. It was the second night at a
women's retreat, and it was almost 2:30 in the morning. My new friend
Bea and I should have been asleep, but we had found a common ground
in our conversation and did not want to lose the magic of the moment.

One of the reasons Bea Stinner and I had come to this retreat weekend was that we were both looking for a new Christian friend. By
coincidence, we ended up sharing a room. What a surprise to learn that

we both were the products of a traditional German upbringing. Vivid memories of our childhood returned as we shared hilarious stories and mimicked the different German accents. Once the laughter had simmered down, we discovered that both of us had a longing to develop knowledge and experience in our spiritual journeys. Amid the silly laughter and the authenticity of our shared spiritual longings, we discovered the embryo of a *heart-connection* friendship.

Fourteen months later, we doubled over again, but this time it was with the sobs of disbelief, brought on by grief. When the policeman showed up at my door in the middle of the night to tell me that my husband had died on the basketball floor, one of the first things he said to me was, "Mrs. Conley, you have to call a friend. You need someone to be with you and drive you to the morgue." This is one of those crisis points in our lives when we discover the reality of our friendships. Who do you call in the middle of the night when you have received the worst news of your life?

During that entire night and the days to come, I learned the value of friendship. Bea never left my side for that entire night. She insisted that I call my children right away, despite my concerns about awakening them, because she knew it was the right thing to do. It was comforting to know that someone was doing my thinking for me. She brewed tea, held my hands, and wiped away my tears while we waited for the sun to come up.

In the days that followed, other friends from all over Alberta and British Columbia showed up at my door with tears, hugs, and words of love. After the funeral service, our best friends served as the pallbearers who carried Dick's casket out of the church. His dearest friends who carried him through many turbulent times in his life now lovingly carried him to his final resting place. My two darling children never left my side, and together we watched the power of love pour from our friends and family. It is absolutely true that during those times in our lives when we are bereft of all comfort and consumed with anguish, our friends become the manifest loving and comforting arms of God.

There is a powerful drive within women to have intimate, loving friendships. God created us to have deep, close relationships, and our hearts yearn for them because there is a void within us that needs to be filled. While we are living in our human bodies, it makes sense that the ones who can satisfy that emptiness are the ones who are wired the same as we are: other women. Our brains function the same way, and it is almost like we even have a secret language. We can ask our girlfriend, "How are you today?" and she will answer, "Fine." By the expression on her face and the tone of her voice, we can tell what that word "fine" really means. It can mean any of the following:

- My life is crazy, but I'm holding it together.
- I've just about come to the end of my rope.
- I'm just so-so.
- I had the most amazing thing happen to me today.
- I'm depressed.
- Things have never been better; I'm on top of the world.

No one else in the world is able to de-code one word and receive that many different messages, but women can. A landmark UCLA study suggests that friendships between women are indeed special and have more power than we ever imagined:

"Friendships are also helping us live better. The famed Nurses' Health Study from Harvard Medical School found that the more friends women had, the less likely they were to develop physical impairments as they aged, and the more likely they were to be leading a joyful life. In fact, the results were so significant, the researchers concluded, that not having close friends or confidants was as detrimental to your health as smoking or carrying extra weight.

And that's not all. When the researchers looked at how well women functioned after the death of their spouse, they found that even in the face of this biggest stressor of all, those women who had a close friend and confidante were more likely to survive the experience without any new physical impairments or permanent loss of vitality. Those without friends were not always so fortunate."[7]

This is the kind of friendship we are all looking for—something so beautiful and intimate that it will make us laugh and cry until the tears are rolling down our faces. We long for it to heal us during our pain, affirm our self-worth, allow us to share those dirty, ugly secrets that we can't tell other people, and stick with us through our joyful times. We need a friendship that eliminates isolation and loneliness and keeps us sane by allowing us to be who we need to be at every stage of our lives.

Every person shares these three deep, inner longings:

1. I wish somebody would listen to me without giving me a solution.
2. I wish someone would believe me. Don't judge me to see if I am lying; just believe me and validate my feelings.
3. I wish someone would be there for me. No matter what I am going through, I need to know I have someone at my side.

We want someone we can have a rapport with; be ourselves with; share our trust, values, and dreams; and who will love us anyway.

I call this a *heart-connection friendship*.

HEART-CONNECTION FRIENDSHIP

The word friendship in Greek is philia, which involves "the idea of loving as well as being loved." [8]

When my children were lonely, they would ask me how to find a new friend. To their chagrin, I always quoted Ralph Waldo Emerson who said, "*The only way to have a friend is to be one.*" [9] They would groan and walk away, hoping each time that I would come up with an easier solution. The fact is, however, that there is nothing easier. In order to have the loving, intimate relationship we are looking for, we need to go out of our way to search for it and cultivate it. We like the idea of *being loved in a friendship*, but how do we find it?

1. Pray, watch and listen.
Whatever stage of life you are at on your life's journey, what you love to do in your free time and what makes you laugh are two factors that will

determine who your new friends will be. Make it a top priority to find a new friend. We all hope for that magical moment when we meet our new friend without any effort on our part. This can happen in ways we don't anticipate, such as sharing a common experience like a disaster. After I moved to Kelowna, I *prayed* that God would give me new friends in this unfamiliar city. When I heard there was a women's retreat coming up, I registered for it right away because I wanted to grow in my spiritual journey. I also knew that this would be a good place to find a friend with whom I could share common interests. I actually made several friends that weekend who are still a part of my life to this day.

Watch the women around you. Who laughs at the same things you do? Who is in the same stage of life as you are? Who loves to read the same books or watch the same movies as you? If you are a runner or hiker, a writer or golfer, or a mother or grandmother, eventually you will find those other women who are passionate about the same things you are. Never forget the fact that God may have placed a friend right under your nose. She may have been there all along, but you did not even realize that she could be your dearest friend. Now, it just takes some extra initiative to go after her and get to know her even better.

Listen to what women are saying about their heritage, values, stage of life, or what they do in their spare time, along with how they are saying it. Listening can be one of our most valuable tools for finding a new friend.

When we focus on the interests and feelings of other women, they will stop long enough to take a second look. Dee Brestin tells us in her book, *The Friendships of Women,* "...women who have contagious laughs, words of encouragement, and warm and caring smiles are the ones who find themselves magnetically drawing others." [10]

Unfortunately, some women immerse themselves in so many social activities, Bible studies, church ministries, or a whirl of parties that there is never an opportunity to establish a close relationship. We need to devote ourselves instead to cultivating deep friendships.

To this end, we must intentionally focus on *loving others as well as being loved.* By *praying, watching, and listening,* we will draw women to us so that we can develop beautiful friendships.

2. Be authentic.

I believe a lack of authentic transparency is our biggest obstacle to developing strong friendships. We want the intimacy, but, at the same time, we are afraid to let people know who we really are. We can't have intimacy, however, without authenticity. In order to have a *heart-connection friendship,* we have to allow ourselves to be transparent enough for someone to see our *hearts.* Many of us are afraid that we will be rejected if people find out what we are really like. We are afraid that they will discover that we are not as smart as we've pretended to be, that we have things we are ashamed of, or that we have other deep-seated issues of insecurity.

What if we take off our masks and disclose ourselves, only for that friend to walk away?

But, we still have to let down our defenses of shyness and fear, and feelings of unworthiness, stupidity, shame, or guilt. When we put away our pretenses, eliminate the empty small talk, and remove the fake smile, we are drawn to each other. Finally, we have found someone who has the same insecurities we are experiencing, so we can begin to share our life stories with them. As we laugh, cry, and hug, we will create authentic friendships.

Being authentic also gives the other person permission to be vulnerable. Dee Brestin says in her book:

> "Vulnerability not only hastens bonding, it can embolden a hurting person to open a festering wound that needs to be opened. A godly woman told me, 'Sometimes, when I am aware that it would be helpful to a friend to open up to me about a problem, but sense hesitancy, I'll lead the way by making myself vulnerable. I'll share where I am hurting or failing.'" [11]

I strongly believe strong friendships are forged more often during painful times or disasters because they are periods during which no one has the time or energy to pretend. We can wail in pain, show our anger, and share the common goal of helping each other. By showing who we really are, a *heart-connection* is formed.

3. Time.

Even though time is our most valuable commodity these days, it is also the enemy that prevents our friendships from being formed and nurtured. A recent UCLA study arrived at this insightful conclusion:

> "'Every time we get overly busy with work and family, the first thing we do is let go of friendships with other women,' explains Dr. Josselson. 'We push them right to the back burner. That's really a mistake because women are such a source of strength to each other. We nurture one another. And we need to have unpressured space in which we can do the special kind of talk that women do when they're with other women. It's a very healing experience.'" [12]

We absolutely have to make time for our friendships. It has to be an intentional, uninterrupted period of time when we are not feeling rushed, or not always checking for messages on our cell phone or BlackBerry. In order for us to share deep matters of the heart, it has to be a safe place where we can hear each other, look into each other's eyes, and communicate without feeling like we are taking time away from their next appointment. It also has to be a two-way street, with both of us sharing in each other's lives.

In today's hectic world, where we feel pulled in so many different directions and sometimes even feel overwhelmed with all of our responsibilities, we need to get serious about setting time aside for people if we want to cultivate meaningful friendships.

Make a commitment with your girlfriends to spend some time together. Perhaps you can agree to meet for dinner or lunch once or twice a month. How about planning a weekend away, or a retreat? E-mail can be a solution when personal contact is not possible, but embraces and eye-to-eye conversation are still the most powerful ingredients to keep a friendship vibrant and healthy.

4. Bring out the best in each other.

Friends have the ability to empower each other in ways that no one else can. Once we have reached that place where we can be authentic and trust each other, we have reached a pinnacle of power in our relationship. This is a place of safety where we can kindly point out each other's faults without feeling destroyed. Wise King Solomon tells us that, "As iron sharpens iron, so one man sharpens another" (Prov.27:17 NIV).

Friends have the power to *sharpen* each other in many ways:

- They can encourage us to pursue our creativity.
- They affirm our hopes and dreams.
- They warn us when we are going down the wrong path.
- They validate our feelings when we are feeling exhausted or overwhelmed.
- Friends pray for each other to bring out God's best in their lives.
- Friends bring an added sharpness or clarity to new ideas or passions.
- They stimulate and challenge us to grow in our spiritual journey.
- They are the ones who can assure us that we are not horrible mothers.
- They can tell us when our egos are getting in the way.
- Friends can instill self-confidence and affirm our self-worth.
- They can stick with us despite our mistakes and failures.
- Friends can gently point out our faults.
- They see the potential of who we can become in the Lord.

Ghandi inspired millions of people to go beyond their human limits to accomplish unheard-of feats. In his book, *The Friendship Factor,* Alan Loy McGinnis observes, "He refused to see the bad in people. He often changed human beings by regarding them not as what they were but as though they were what they wished to be, and as though the good in them was all of them." [13]

We need for someone to tell us when we are doing something well so that we will be inspired to go further. We also require a second set of eyes on our spiritual journey to warn us when we deviate from our path of obedience to God, admonish us when we have spoken unkind words, or remind us when we need to forgive. I believe that often God uses our *heart-connection* friends to reveal truths to us that we are too proud or blind to see. True friends are the ones who use this power to help us—not destroy us.

5. Commitment.

When I ask women what they long for in friendships, they tell me over and over again: trust and loyalty. *Loyalty* is defined as, "Faithful to one's oath, commitments, or obligations; faithful to any person or thing conceived of as deserving fidelity or imposing obligations." [14]

This is something we all need in our friendships because we can't find it in the world around us. When we find someone who cares enough to call us a friend, do we not *deserve* her loyalty?

I also treasure this quality and am blessed to have several loyal friends. One of these friends is my dearest Fran. We met in Africa in 1981 while on a business trip with our husbands. (It was one of those divinely appointed times that we could never fully understand. We felt something tugging at our hearts and found ourselves being propelled toward a relationship that we knew was meant to be magnificent.) It started with light-hearted bantering back and forth as so many friendships do, but soon all this changed. As we explored the rustic, enchanting countryside of Africa, we also took bold and exciting steps of faith to venture into each other's hearts. As we began to explore our spiritual beliefs, our children, and our passions, our hearts started to connect.

After the trip was over and we landed at the Calgary, Alberta, airport, we all enthused about what a wonderful time we had and that we should get together again. How many times have we heard those words? "Hey, let's do lunch some time," or "You know, we should get together soon." Fran's greatest gift in her friendship to me is loyalty, and she did make that promised phone call.

When my husband died, Bob and Fran, of course, were the first people on my doorstep. Before they left to fly back to their home in Calgary, Fran assured me: "Heidi, I am far away and I don't know how else I can help you, but I will call you every day." The phone rang every day for an entire month. Sometimes when I answered the phone, all she would hear was my sobbing, so she wept with me.

There is no greater gift we can give our friends than our loyalty to them through both the good times and during adversity. We need our friends to put us first by allowing us to share our deepest longings and wildest fears and then trust them with that information. We need someone to stick with us like Ruth in the biblical story.

Naomi, her husband Elimelech, and their two sons had to move to the foreign country of Moab because there was a famine in their own land of Judah. While living there, her two sons married Moabite women. Over the course of time, Naomi's husband and two sons died. Now, she was in a foreign land, all alone except for her two daughter-in-laws. When Naomi said she was going back to her homeland of Judah, her daughters wanted to go with her. She protested with both of them and told them to stay in Moab. Orpah agreed and remained in Moab, but Ruth would not leave Naomi all alone. I believe that Ruth's response has ignited the hearts of women everywhere:

> "But Ruth replied, 'Don't urge me to leave you or to turn back from you. Where you go I will go, and where you stay I will stay. Your people will be my people and your God my God. Where you die I will die, and there I will be buried. May the Lord deal with me, be it ever so severely, if anything but death separates you and me'"(Ruth 1:16, 17 NIV).

When any of us are in a difficult situation, we want someone who will walk alongside of us and say, "I'll be there for you." We long to have someone that committed to us. This is the kind of loyalty that both empowers us to survive adversity and forms life-long friendships.

6. We need a third person.

I suggest that the third person in our relationships needs to be God. A deep friendship involves *hearts connecting*. Who can connect hearts other than the one who created them, knows what is in them, and knows how to fill them with love and restore their pain? For us to have that *heart-connection friendship,* we need a third person. On our own, we are not able to be loving, loyal, trustworthy, and forgiving. When three people are involved, there is more help and power available to help us in our pursuit and maintenance of that great friendship. King Solomon reminds us again:

> "Two can accomplish more than twice as much as one for the results can be much better. If one falls, the other pulls him up; but if a man falls when he is alone, he's in trouble. Also, on a cold night, two under the same blanket gain warmth from each other, but how can one be warm alone? And one standing alone can be attacked and defeated, but two can stand back to back and conquer; *three is even better, for a triple-braided cord is not easily broken*" (Eccles. 4:9-12 NIV).

When we have the ingredients of a deep friendship and add the power of the Holy Spirit to it, we have a *triple-braided cord that cannot be broken*. We need to possess spiritual grace that will help us overcome misunderstandings, rejections, betrayals, harsh words, and competition. We need to be able to go to God in prayer when we go through difficult times such as misunderstandings or feeling betrayed. One of us may be struggling through depression or some kind of a deep loss in their lives, and we may not be able to pick each other up unless we have the power of God to pull us through that time. We need God's love to affirm our self-worth and help us fend off the insidious enemies of comparison and jealousy. We need God's mercy when our friend has said hurtful words that just want to make us walk away forever. We need God's forgiveness when we have turned our back on our friend, and she in turn has stabbed us. We cannot do a *heart-connection friendship* alone. We need a third person with us: God.

WOULDN'T IT BE NICE if we could stop right here and soak in the warmth and love of discovering and savoring that perfect friendship? Unfortunately, that is not a reality in this life. There is no way to have an authentic, close relationship without some conflict along the way. We are women with deep longings and different personalities who are all trying to establish our sense of significance. We all bring old garbage into our relationship. Even though we may hide it inside our beautiful designer Prada baggage, it is still garbage nonetheless. This unwelcome intruder will emerge during times of stress, miscommunication, and complete openness, when we are laying our hearts on the table. Part of the beauty of becoming vulnerable and authentic can also be the very thing that can destroy a relationship. Once we are aware that conflict is simply part of life, we don't need to run away from it, but rather embrace it to help us grow stronger. We all need to feel safe in every aspect of our lives. Once something happens in any relationship to threaten that safety, we'll experience conflict.

HEART CONNECTIONS

1. The comparing game.

It's one thing to say that we want to bring out the best in each other, but beware when one person accomplishes more than you. We may not be aware that we have feelings of jealousy until something brings them out of the dark shadows that they were lurking in. One of the things that help our friendships to grow are common experiences and shared interests. We like it best, however, when we are all on the same level. Jealousy can rise up when our friend experiences blessings such as new job promotions, economic successes, improvements in looks, more dating prospects, achievements of their children, and growth in their spiritual journey. This toxic feeling will destroy a relationship if it is not discussed and dealt with.

When we were growing up, we were all taught to compete. We were told to get the best grades and excel in athletics. On top of that, we desired to be the most popular and prettiest girl in our class. There is a difference, however, between competing *for something* or competing *against someone*. Immaturity and jealousy comes when we direct our energies to compete *against someone*.

Jealousy can destroy our friendship, but it can also destroy our own soul. Proverbs 27:4 warns us that "jealousy is more dangerous and cruel than anger" (TLB).

Jealously is the same right-brain emotion that springs from feelings of compassion and affection. These originally good feelings become dangerous when they shift into negative emotions so ugly that they keep us awake at night, put poison into our words, cause us to gossip, and ultimately destroy the relationship. We all know what jealousy feels like because at some point in our lives, we have all experienced its bitter taste.

David Foster, in his book, *The Power to Prevail*, explains jealousy this way:

> "Jealousy is like a low-level hum in your ears, like hearing voices of dissatisfaction deep down in your soul that refuse to be stilled and cannot be satisfied. At times, jealousy will feel like a low-grade fever; at others, like a raging paranoia that robs you of rest. It creates a restless tension full of whispered lies that, if repeated often enough, sound real. Sometimes it sounds like a background noise, faint and constant, but other times it erupts like a marching band blaring our Dolby stereo, 'You deserve more and they deserve less!'" [15]

How do we get rid of this ugly, all-consuming toxic bile?

First of all, we need to be honest about how we feel. Until we accept the fact that we are jealous, we cannot see the ugliness of it. I believe most of all jealousy arises because we perceive that someone has an advantage over us. Jealousy also indicates that we are feeling insecure in our relationship with that person, as well as in our relationship with God. When we have a beautiful, intimate relationship with our heavenly Father, we are aware that God works differently in people in various times. We understand that *our time will come*. This is not our time for a raise, a special appointment, or financial success. God works everything out according to His timetable, not ours.

We have to show wisdom in how we disclose our feelings of jealousy to our friend. I am not sure there is ever a time in our lives when we are completely healed from this ugly disease. On several occasions, friends have confided that they *were* jealous of me, but they are no longer. This was one of those times when a friend's feelings were probably better left unshared because from that point on, I have felt like I am walking on eggshells whenever I am around them. Those jealous feelings may have departed for a while, but knowing our sinful human nature, I realize that there will be an event when that green-eyed monster will appear once again. I just don't know where or when.

The power of jealousy dissipates only when we are secure in our identity and relationship with God. I personally know that I do not want to feel any jealousy about anything or toward anyone. In order to accomplish this, I have to remind myself that God has a perfect plan for *my* life, and it doesn't look the same as the one for my friends. God knows what is best for us, and maybe we are just not ready to receive what our friend just got. You might even feel that your friend did not even *deserve* this wonderful thing that has happened to her. We have to trust that God knows what He is doing and that His timing is always perfect.

In his book, *Love Beyond Reason,* John Ortberg says, "I do not like the envy in me. I would make it go away if I could. But I cannot stop envying by trying harder. Envy can only be healed when we live as one who has been chosen by God." [16]

You and I need to realize that God chose us even before the foundations of the earth were laid. Knowing about that kind of love is the power that sustains us when we want to compare ourselves with others. If we get caught up in comparisons, we are really asking God who He loves more: you or me. When we are secure in our love relationship with our heavenly Father, we begin to realize that there is enough love to go around. Let's not hold back, but rather rejoice when our friends are blessed.

It seems that it is easier to mourn with our friends rather than to be happy with them, but the Bible tells us to rejoice with our friends. "When others are happy, be happy with them. If they are sad, share their sorrow" (Rom. 12:15 TLB). If you find this difficult to do, pray and ask God to help you.

2. Expectations.
Hope plays a huge part in relationships. From the moment our friendship begins, each person involved has different expectations. Every morning that you and I wake up, we hope for something good and wonderful to happen. Friendships are the one place where we feel we can expect to find some of that hope fulfilled.

We need to be realistic about our assumptions of what the other person can bring into the relationship. Nothing will turn a person off faster than voicing premature expectations of life-long commitments and activities. It is imperative, however, that we express differing personal views before going on a trip or a shopping spree, doing a Bible study together, or even incorporating her into our own family dynamics. We need to make sure, for example, that she is not going to flirt with our husbands, fight over religion, or expect to be invited to all the family gatherings. When we have expectations that the other person does not know about, or is unable or not interested in fulfilling, it will quickly cause us to feel unloved and build resentment.

You also have to be bold and honest enough with your friend to find out what type of expectations she holds for the relationship. These may be ones that you are unable or unwilling to fulfill.

- She may be expecting you to mentor her.
- She may be looking to you to fill a God-void in her life.
- She may be looking for a mother figure.
- She may be expecting you to spend more time with her than you are willing to give.
- She may be looking to you to fill neediness in her life that comes out of a wounded heart.

Some expectations within a friendship are simply not healthy. When you realize that someone demands that you do things which are morally wrong, such as taking drugs or going to R-rated movies, or tries to force you to give them constant attention that you are unable to provide, this is a good time to sever the relationship. Letting unhealthy relationships continue will only cause a lot of unnecessary disillusionment and pain.

3. Betrayal.

The things that we desire the most will hurt us the most when we don't get them. One of the things that women need most in a friendship is our loyalty. When we invest our time, emotions, and love in a person, we need to know that we can trust them. This is probably why we are so hurt by betrayal. We feel that we *deserved* to be treated better than that.

When I speak to women about pain in their girlfriend relationships, the common thread is that *"trust was broken."* This can be due to your friend breaking a confidence or a promise, flirting with your husband or boyfriend, spreading gossip, lying to you, or saying something that was inappropriate. We also feel betrayed when we are criticized or judged. The emotional pain that this can cause is excruciating; subsequently, the friendship will need a lot of repair. In order to bring healing into this relationship, we need to accept the fact that because we are all still sinners, we will all fail each other at one time or another.

Jesus had spent three years with His twelve disciples. When He needed them the most, some of them betrayed Him. His disciple Judas actually kissed Him on the cheek before turning him over to the authorities for a few pieces of silver. This is a man whom Jesus taught and with whom He shared His passions and even His last meal.

Betrayal is part of life, but humanly, it is not easy to overlook. Forgiveness is supernatural and only flows from the power of the Holy Spirit working it out in us. Betrayal must be dealt with through supernatural powers of forgiveness; there is simply no other way to heal that kind of hurt.

FIGHT THE GOOD FIGHT

It puts a smile on my face to know that at my age I am going to be a bridesmaid *again.* My best friend Shaunie is getting married for the first time, and I have been chosen to be her matron of honor. I am so proud of her, and I consider it to be such an honor to be a part of her wedding party. If this wedding had happened five years ago, I may not have been chosen.

Shaunie and I met in 1993, and our relationship has been one that is so deep and beautiful that we've called it a *heart-connection friendship.* It has all the right ingredients, so we realize that it has been a gift from God and ordained by Him. One of the things that attracted me to her right away was her laughter, her love for God, her loyalty, kindness, and fun-loving spirit.

This is what Shaunie has to say about our friendship:

"True friendship has involved the offering of unconditional love. It has been the acceptance of who I am as an individual and the encouragement to be the best that I can be. It has been a relationship of trust—both given and received. With trust as a key component, only on that basis can we embrace the times when accountability is necessary. It is the excitement of seeing each other's visions, dreams, and desires come to fruition. It is the times of laughter—sometimes when we're not even sure about what— and the times of just listening to each other and often crying together. It is that listening ear and the words of wisdom. *It is that commitment to pray for each other.*"

It was that last sentence which saved our beautiful relationship in August of 2001. While we were having lunch in a quaint Victorian restaurant in Langley, British Columbia, Shaunie said words to me that were unkind and very hurtful. Realizing I was deeply hurt, she promised to call me that night. Her promise helped somewhat, but my trust was destroyed when she did not call that night. As a matter of fact, I did not hear from her for two and a half weeks. By then, anger had started to burn in my heart, and I was at the point of letting the friendship dissolve. I knew I needed to forgive because that was not an option, but first I needed to get over my anger and get on with living.

When we finally talked on the phone, we decided to give each other more time. Soon after that, we made an agreement to start communicating by e-mail. We made a decision to work this out, not by fighting with each other, but by *fighting the good fight.* There is a huge difference. We need to be able to make the same declaration as Paul when his life was finished here on earth: "I have fought the good fight, I have finished the race, I have kept the faith" (2 Tim. 4:7 NIV).

In order to *fight the good fight* in our friendship, we had to:

- Step into each other's shoes to feel each other's pain.
- Confront and be honest about what hurt us.
- Continue loving each other unconditionally.
- Give each other time.
- Both stay committed to this process.
- Realize we could not change each other. We each had to change.
- Make it our goal to save our friendship, not to make accusations about who was wrong.
- Pray and ask God to remove my anger.
- *Forgive.*

We knew we had to forgive, not just from the head, but also from the heart. When we forgive with just words, it is just an intellectual response to hurt; instead, we need God's help when we are involved in a heart matter. I asked God to help me to forgive Shaunie in the same way that He forgave all of mankind: "Jesus said, "Father, forgive them, for they do not know what they are doing" (Luke 23:34 NIV).

We frequently say and do things from our own wounded hearts that hurt others, so we must be aware of our own painful emotional experiences when betrayal and rejection come our way. Sometimes our wounds are still so raw that the hurtful words that blurt out of our mouth are simply an overflow of that pain. When we ask God to heal our past pain, however, He can turn our anger and despair into a miracle.

God is the only one who can help us forgive, but it takes our prayers to accomplish that, along with the determination and communication of all parties involved. In time, healing *will* come.

Almost five months after our devastating luncheon, Shaunie came to Kelowna to visit. As we looked into each other's eyes, we knew the forgiveness process had been completed. There was no anger and no residual hurt. There was forgiveness, new joy, and a deeper love, as well as real appreciation for what might have been discarded. To this very day, we still treasure and guard our friendship with respect, honesty, and unconditional love. Keeping a relationship going can be hard work at times because it doesn't always come naturally, but in the end, the rewards can be *priceless.*

Seasons of Friendship

I believe that some friendships are meant to last for a lifetime, while others are meant to be in our life for only a season. God knows when we need something, so He uses human beings to be His hands and feet on this earth.

It is true that women's priorities change, people move away, and occupations disrupt the flow of time spent together, so we may feel that a friendship has run its course. There are also times when one person loses interest and is no longer committed to the relationship. Sometimes people just drift apart for no apparent reason. There are times to let friendships go, but before we let them go, we must always check our motives. If there is unresolved hurt or anger, it must be dealt with before we separate. We are all going to stand before our holy God someday to account for all our words and actions, so we must be certain that we are ending a friendship with a pure heart.

We never want to stand before another human being or God with regret in our hearts. We need to make sure we live life without regrets. Two of the saddest words that I often hear are, *"If only..."* If you can bless that person as you are letting them go, then I believe that friendship season has come to an end.

Unleashing the Beauty of Friendship

For a woman, there is nothing more precious and valuable than a *heart-connection friend*, and we all long for one. I believe that God has placed us in relationships so that we can learn to become more like His Son. God uses other people in our lives to not only bring out the beautiful aspects of our lives, but our ugliness as well.

A woman of beauty allows the difficult seasons of friendship to make her even more beautiful. In order for *iron to sharpen iron*, sparks have to fly, due to the great amount of heat that is necessary to bring about the desired result. When these sparks start flying, however, many want to run away as fast as they can, but a woman of beauty sees this as an opportunity to allow

God to teach her and change her. This is also how great friendships are strengthened and forged.

Most of us are afraid of conflict of any kind because we know it will involve emotional pain. In every conflict situation where people are fighting against each other, there is always a winner or a loser: somebody will get hurt.

As a woman of beauty, you have the courage to be all who God created you to be: loving, kind, forgiving, and full of His marvelous grace. With that kind of Holy Spirit-power in your life, you do not have to win the arguments in your friendships. You can be the one to mercifully let it go and desperately run after God's grace instead. You're through with getting caught in the comparison trap that forces you to compete and be jealous because you now value relationship over winning.

Difficult times of suffering teach us to accept God's grace and forgiveness for ourselves, but we have to remember that it is not just for us. Believe it or not, it is also for the ones who betray us, reject us, and talk behind our backs.

I long for you to emerge from your pain and struggles the same way a beautiful butterfly comes out of its chrysalis. Often early in the morning, *light* stimulates the butterfly to begin its struggle to escape from its gossamer cocoon. This painful process strengthens the butterfly and enables it to fly.

I am asking you to allow the *light* (the radiant love and grace of God) to stimulate you amidst your struggles so that you will be *strengthened* and become more beautiful over time with each relationship you form.

A woman of beauty also acknowledges that in friendships:

- She may only have one or two intimate friends in her entire lifetime.
- There is risk involved.
- Her greatest relationship will be with Jesus.
- Reconciliation takes two people.
- She has a lot to offer other women.

While we are living our lives here on earth, God is preparing us for heaven. I truly believe that life is not about accomplishing things, but rather how much we learn about unconditional love in our relationships. Our friendships become the greatest opportunities to know and experience God's love and grace in our lives.

I trust that we will treasure each other on the journey. Our friendships are gifts from God: you are a gift from God to someone else. Two hearts connecting with God make for a *heart-connection friendship*.

Stop and ask God to Unleash Your Beauty

Begin by asking: God, where I have allowed comparisons or envy to cause pain in a relationship? God, how do I make this right?

S—Scripture: "Most important of all, continue to show deep love for each other, for love makes up for many of your faults" (1 Peter 4:8 TLB).

T—Thanksgiving: Thank You, God, that love and laughter cover so many faults. Thank You for being such a kind, merciful, and forgiving God. Help me to show a dark and hurting world the power of forgiveness in friendships. Thank You for being the author and teacher of forgiveness. Make me Your most eager and successful student.

O—Observation: We live in conflict every day. Everyone does things in different ways, and people have irritating faults. Forgiveness and loving one another is not an option. We need to be obedient to God and forgive every time someone hurts us.

P—Prayer: God, thank You for making women such amazing, delightful, and fun creatures. Thank You for the joy and laughter of relationships. Thank You for tears that can express pain or triumph. God, teach me to be a great friend. I have so much to learn about relationships, such as overcoming comparisons and allowing You to work goodness out in everyone's life in Your timing. Thank You for loving us all equally and pouring Your blessings out on us in different ways and at different times.

I ask that You would reveal to me the natural talents You have given me so that I can begin to enjoy them and share the delight of them with other friends. Help to bring beauty into relationships and not pain. Quicken my heart and hold me accountable when I am about to break a promise, say an unkind word, make a judgment, or criticize. Help me to bring out the best in each woman that crosses my path. Amen.

3

UNLEASHING THE BEAUTY OF LOVE
Annoying People in My Mirror

"Our love to God is measured by our everyday
fellowship with others and the love it displays."

—ANDREW MURRAY

CAN STILL REMEMBER where I was sitting and what my voice sounded like when I prayed, "God, draw me closer into Your presence. Make me more like You. Teach me to love others with the unconditional love that only comes from You." Since that time, I've discovered that this is a dangerous prayer. We need to be very bold when we pray these words and get ready to put on our hiking boots, because we are going on a field trip over unknown terrain.

I had no qualms about praying that prayer with such courage, because I felt very confident about the way I loved everyone in my life: the employees at my office, the people in my church, the friends in our neighborhood, and, of course, the easiest—my family and intimate friends. I was in safe territory, just as long as I did not have to talk to any car salesmen.

Months passed by since I prayed that prayer. During that time, we were being transferred from Lethbridge, Alberta, to Kelowna, British Columbia, so I had to leave the comfort and security of my loving circle of friends. When I arrived and settled into my new home in Kelowna, I was shocked to discover that I could not find an equivalent career as a legal administrator, so I contracted myself out for a three-month position as a controller in a car dealership. After all, I thought, *three months is not a long time. I will be busy with numbers, anyway, not car salesmen.*

Three months turned into six months, and the lines of my contract blurred. Soon, I realized that I was a full-time employee, and this was my new career. At the time, I was not aware that this was the beginning of a long and treacherous field trip, during which God would teach me to love everyone in His creation. The trip started, as all of them do, with the first few inches, right in front of my nose: the car salesmen. Over the years, I have learned that my personality is completely opposite from that of the car salesmen's. As a logical thinker, my word is as good as gold. I've never considered myself "ego-driven," and I could never even sell an igloo to an Eskimo. I considered car salesmen to be nothing but ego-driven, arrogant, greedy, and prideful people and liked to think that I had none of those characteristics. Oh my, how easy it is to point a finger when sometimes we are actually looking into our own mirror.

At the same time I was trying to figure out how God could love car salesmen, I found another annoying person.[17] Kathy was a tiny, little thing who worked next door. She was one of the employees who regularly came into our building to use the washroom facilities, so I would bump into her occasionally. The first time I encountered Kathy, she looked at me with such contempt and wariness that it almost made me reel. Even though I did not even know her name yet, somehow I knew that I did not want to spend any time with her. Everyone else seemed to like her, but there must have been something about me that caused her to hate me at first sight. *No worries,* I thought, *she was not going to be a problem.* I would stay out of her way and have nothing to do with her. Whenever I caught a glimpse of her, I would quickly turn the other way to avoid any contact.

Isn't it amazing how we can convince ourselves that we are living a spirit-filled Christian life, and yet God's love is not evident in us? God clearly pointed this out to me as I was reading the book of John, who was the beloved disciple of Jesus:

> "Anyone who says he is walking in the light of Christ but dislikes his fellow man is still in darkness. But whoever loves his fellow man is "walking in the light" and can see his way without stumbling around in darkness and sin. For he who dislikes his brother is wandering in spiritual darkness and doesn't know where he is going, for the darkness has made him blind so that he cannot see the way" (1 John 2:9-11 TLB).

Then I read further: "Little children, let us stop just saying we love people; let us really love them, and show it by our actions" (1 John 3:18 TLB). *Where did those words come from?* It was as though God hit me with His words right between my eyes.

I had been praying and asking God to make me a more loving person at my workplace, but my actions clearly showed that I did not know the first thing about love. If Kathy could look at me with such hate, there must have been something in my spirit that made her feel rejected every time she looked at me. It was time to wake up and learn to love those annoying car salesmen and that teeny woman with the contempt in her eyes. I was beginning to wonder if I was radiating even a shred of God's light on the job.

I began by humbly confessing to God my inadequacy to love others. I knew it was time to allow God to really teach me how to love, so that I could be a light so radiant that it would cause people to question its source. That is what I longed for. I started to pray, *"God, teach me to love the people around me, especially that little woman that I have been ignoring for such a long time. Teach me to see them all as Your creation. Right now, I am unable to love them. Help me to see them through Your eyes, and I ask the Holy Spirit to love them through me."* I prayed this over and over again. My mission right now was to ignite some love in my angry co-worker. I waited with anticipation to see how God was going to work this out, but nothing much happened for a long time.

Whenever I passed her in the building, I would intentionally look into her eyes and say "hello." No response. I asked her how she was. No response. Most of the time, she would not even lift her head to acknowl-edge my presence. This pattern continued for a couple of years. Eventually, she looked at me now and then, but she still refused to talk to me. One day before a long Easter weekend, I walked right up to her, hugged her, and wished her a wonderful weekend. Still no response.

On another occasion, I handed her a dozen roses. Another time, I offered her some chocolates. Now she was looking at me; even once in a while I would ask her how she was and she would mutter "fine." Time passed, and I continued to pray and shower her with love. She was beginning to smile at me, and occasionally she would even ask me how I was. I began to tease her a little and ask how her little girls were.

One day we both happened to be using the technicians' change room to wash our hands. She looked at my hands, and then hers, and said, "My hands will always be dirty—not white and clean like yours." From that moment on, I began to see the world through her eyes. In her mind, her career as a painter in a body shop would never measure up to my nice, clean controller's job, so she would always feel inferior to me. God was clearly showing me that what I had perceived as anger spewing from her heart was, in fact, her perceived reaction to my superiority. I probably made her feel unloved and insignificant, so I was even more determined than ever to show her that she was loved.

About this time, we had an incident in our kitchen at home. Someone had accidentally sprayed oven cleaner on a piece of black-painted metal in our microwave. The spray literally burned the black paint off, and it looked horrible. I thought that if body repair shops could paint cars, they could certainly paint strips of metal. The next day I took my ruined metal strip to be painted. The receptionist at the counter said they would be happy to do it, and she took it from me.

Days and weeks passed, and it seemed that my strip of metal had dis-appeared into thin air. One day I went over to the body shop to inquire about my piece of metal to see if they had gotten an opportunity to paint it. From the blank looks on their faces, I was afraid that I would never see this accessory again. *Oh well, I'd better figure out some other way to replace this microwave accessory,* I thought.

A few days later, I was coming back from lunch. Standing against the glass door to my office was my piece of metal, beautifully painted. It looked brand new! I was elated, but could not figure out how it got there. I went into the lunch room and asked everyone there if they knew who had found the piece of metal and painted it for me. They all pointed to Kathy. She looked up at me, our eyes met, and she smiled. Without saying a word, I ran out of the lunchroom and went back into my office, tears welling up in my eyes. She overheard that I had been looking for this piece of metal and needed it painted, so she took it upon herself to paint it and bring it back to me. Realizing this was her gesture of love, I was so overcome with the emotions of praise and thanksgiving for the rest of the day that I could hardly concentrate. God's power expressed through my love still leaves me standing in awe of what He can accomplish when I am willing to let Him.

It is true that the power of love always wins. The love of the Holy Spirit flowing through us can change lives one by one; however, the life that changes the most is me. Through the experience of seeing an angry heart transformed before my very eyes, I was able to see every human being in a completely different way. From that point on, God changed my perspective of everyone around me. This experience showed me that the most important thing we can do is see each person as one of God's beautiful creations. He didn't die on the cross just for me, but for everyone.

Also, why did I think that car salesmen were arrogant, prideful, and rude? I had so much to learn about myself, and these men were the mirror for me that allowed me to change. It was ugly looking in that mirror at first, but beauty began to emerge as I learned about my own selfishness and arrogance, and then let the Holy Spirit teach me how to love.

Love Is Not Fair

We want everything in life to be fair. If you hit me, I'll hit you back. If you are angry with me and don't want to have anything to do with me, that's fine; I won't have anything to do with you.

The stories of Jesus in the Bible provide us with the greatest examples and guidelines for living our lives here on earth. When I read about Jesus in the Garden of Gethsemane in Mark 14:32-42, I am shown the greatest example of love. Jesus knew that He had to go to the cross the next day to die for you and me. He pleaded with his Father, "'Father, Father," he said, "everything is possible for you. Take away this cup from me. Yet I want your will, not mine.'" Mark 14:36 TLB). Jesus died for you and me even though He did not want to. What greater example of love is there? For someone who lived a sinless life and never did anything wrong, what was fair about being put to death?

He was "doing the will of his Father." In order for us to do the will of our heavenly Father, we are instructed to love each other. It is not merely a nice option or a good idea, but a commandment. For God knows that the only way we can live an abundant life on earth is to love one another.

LOVE OTHERS DESPITE REJECTION

We can also learn another very hard lesson from Jesus' Garden of Gethsemane experience. This is especially crushing for us as human beings because rejection is one of the most painful emotions that anyone can ever experience.

Jesus invested three years of His life with the twelve disciples. He was with them twenty-four hours a day, 365 days of the year. He poured His life into them by teaching them, giving them life examples, walking with them, talking with them, admonishing them, and loving them. Then, when He needed them the most, they simply could not stay awake for Him. We are told in Mark 14:41 that He asked them three times to stay awake and pray with Him, but each time they fell asleep: "Are you still sleeping and resting? Enough! The hour has come" (NIV).

The disciples had let Him down, and now it was over. Morning had come, and it was time for Jesus to go to the cross. They had failed Him.

Whenever I read those verses, I feel like someone has punched me in the stomach. We all know that feeling, don't we? When we truly need someone at a crucial point in our lives, they let us down. We have all been rejected at one time or another and it always leaves us in excruciating emotional pain. Which of these have you experienced?

- I told my parents the awful truth, but they did not believe me.
- I had the courage to lay my hopes and dreams on the table, but the friends whom I thought would support me ridiculed me and stomped on my heart.
- I stood up for something that I believe was morally right, but it seemed that everybody went against me.
- I poured my life into my husband and family, but they left me.
- I spent my whole life supporting and helping other people, but when I really needed someone, there was no one to be found.
- I was depressed and lonely, but everyone just told me to "buck up."
- I came home and showed my parents the report card I was so proud of, but they asked why I didn't do better.
- I invited my parents to my school production, and looked for them, but they never came.

We want to run and hide from that kind of pain, but Jesus did not run. He climbed up Calvary's mountain to the cross, and died there for you and me so that we would have hope for something better—both for now and all eternity. He said, "Father, forgive them." We also have to say, "Father, forgive everyone in my life who has hurt me or rejected me." Through this supernatural power of forgiveness, we will be empowered to love in ways we never thought possible.

Rejection is not a good enough reason to run away and stop loving. In fact, being rejected just gives us even more motivation to love others. There is nothing fair about rejection, but loving against all odds is the greatest grace that we will ever experience in this life. Forgiving those who have hurt us will enable us to overcome the horrible sting of rejection. This power will set us free and give us new life.

LOVE IS UNSELFISH

So how do we love those who hurt us, reject us, glare at us, or simply don't like us? How do we love those whom we find irritating and annoying? How do we love the ones who don't look or act like the way we think they should? How do we love the ones whose personalities are so fundamentally different from our own that every time they say or do something it just makes us want to run? How do we love the ones who are dirty, mean, or don't meet our expectations of manners or social skills? Isn't it a whole lot easier to simply stay away from them? Oh, how many times in my life have I just wanted to turn around and walk the other way, look the other way, or at least avoid eye contact. That way, I just don't have to deal with the fact that I am unable to love them.

In 1 Corinthians 13: 4-6, the apostle Paul gives us a practical definition of love:

> "Love is patient, love is kind, it does not envy, it does not boast, it is not proud. It is not rude, it is not self-seeking, it is not easily angered, and it keeps no record of wrongs. Love does not delight in evil but rejoices with the truth. It always protects, always trusts, always hopes, always perseveres" (NIV).

In our human state, it is impossible to love like that because we are too selfish. Every one of those traits can only be attained when we lay down our own ego and love through supernatural means. It is a love that is received from God and flows through us by the power of the Holy Spirit.

We need to understand that apart from the power of the Holy Spirit, we just can't love like that. The word "love" in the verses that I have mentioned above is agape love. This is what the Vine's Dictionary has to say about this Greek word:

> "Christian love, whether exercised toward the brethren, or toward men generally, is not an impulse from the feelings, it does not always run with the natural inclinations, nor does it spend itself only upon those for whom same affinity is discovered.
>
>   "In respect to Agape as used of God, it expresses the deep and constant love and interest of a perfect Being towards entirely *unworthy objects* (italics mine), producing and fostering a reverential love in them towards the Giver, and a practical

love towards those who are partakers of the same, and a desire to help others to seek the Giver…it is an unselfish love, ready to serve."[18]

Loving another person whom we consider an "*unworthy object*" is not natural for us. We need the perfect love from God to flow through us to love like this. But we must do it, because this is the only way that the world around us will ever be illuminated with the knowledge of God.

As I journey this earth during my (hopefully) eighty or ninety-year stay, the people whom I come in contact with have the potential to know God because of the way I love them. That is an incredible thought. As a matter of fact, for me this concept is so big that it brings me to my knees in humility and reverent fear. Oh, that I may never, never miss an opportunity to pour God's love out on anyone.

Just like Jesus went to the cross to die for my sins, I realize that I need to let my ego die regarding my selfishness in letting people irritate or annoy me. I must see each person on this planet as one of God's magnificent creations who needs to know and receive love. I am so grateful that God has taken me on a field trip in my workplace to teach me about love.

Every single day that I work and live on this earth, I am called to love everyone around me—not just to talk about it, but to actually do it.

Love Changes Lives

Whenever we love in the face of rejection, unfairness, or unworthiness, lives are changed. In Kathy's story, I could see the change in her towards me in a very concrete way, as well as feeling the change in myself. The more I prayed for God to love her through me, the more I could feel myself loving her more. It is so strange, yet so magnificent, that when love changes *us,* the other person actually looks different and acts differently.

There is a world all around us that is hurting. Every human being on this planet yearns to be loved. Everyone looks for something real and tangible: unconditional love. You and I have the opportunity to change the world, one person at a time. How humbling, and yet how glorifying, is that?

Unleashing the Beauty of Love

I believe there is nothing more beautiful than a woman who knows she is loved. A woman of beauty will become more beautiful each day as she seeks to live a good, moral life, but nothing will make her more radiant than knowing she is loved by God.

A woman of beauty understands that Jesus died on the cross for her and that all her sins are forgiven. This gives her joy and freedom by first allowing her to love herself, and then to love others. God first revealed and expressed His love through His Son Jesus and is now calling on us to continue with this mission of love on earth. It is the very best thing we can commit our whole life to.

Love is a language that the whole world understands. It doesn't matter where we live, travel, work, or vacation; people will comprehend our language of love. Wherever we are, our love can melt the hardest heart, heal wounded hearts, show compassion, or quiet an anxious or fearful heart. When you and I pour out this kind of love wherever we go, we will be amazed at the blessings that will begin to flow back to us. We will also be amazed how it will soften our hearts and open our eyes to be more compassionate toward the rest of the world.

When we pour out love on others, beauty unfolds in our own lives. There are several ways we can do this:

1. Love with our thoughts.

We can begin to learn how to love by asking God to change our thoughts about life. Every action that we take is always preceded by a thought. If you and I harbor unkind thoughts in our hearts towards others, our actions will become unkind, but if we think loving thoughts, our actions too will become loving. Thus, you and I must carefully choose our thoughts before we open our mouths to speak or move our bodies to act.

We have the power to do this. The apostle Paul exhorts us to take our thoughts captive:

"We demolish arguments and every pretension that sets itself up against the knowledge of God, and we *take captive every thought to make it obedient to Christ*" (2 Cor. 10:5 NIV).

When we walk around looking at people with critical, judgmental thoughts, they will sense our judgmental attitude and respond by rejecting us or getting angry. If we begin to ask God to change our thoughts toward them to ones of love, he will change our hearts so that we will start to look for the good in them.

2. Love with our words.
Words have the greatest power to change lives. If our words of love are spoken with pure, godly motives, they have the power to bring life and hope into people's lives. On the other hand, our words of hate, anger, judgment, criticism, and jealousy have the power to destroy a person's soul, or crush another's hopes and dreams. The writer of Proverbs wisely says, "The tongue has the power of life and death, and those who love it will eat its fruit" (Prov. 18:21 NIV).

A woman of beauty will choose her words carefully before they come out of her mouth. When we begin to see how God's words of love to us have changed us, we will use this same concept to speak words of love to those around us.

It is exhilarating to watch people's responses when we speak words of love to them. We can see them brighten up before our very eyes. Who would want to miss out on opportunities like that?

3. Love with our actions.
We have been told by the apostle John that we are not just to love with words, but also with our actions. How can we do this in a practical way?

- *We can love others by giving them our time.* I believe that time is our greatest commodity these days. When we give other people our time, we are giving them our most treasured possession.

  Author and pastor Rick Warren declares, "The most desired gift of love is not diamonds or roses or chocolate. It is *focused attention.* Love concentrates so intently on another that you forget yourself at that moment. Attention says, 'I value you enough to give you my most precious asset—my time.' Whenever you give your time, you are making a sacrifice, and sacrifice is the essence of love." [19]

- *We can love them by sharing our possessions.* As I am writing this, we are hosting a house guest for an entire month. This particular man had no place to live, and we have a large house with extra bedrooms. It doesn't take a rocket scientist to do the math, but it does take God's selfless love to help us to see the need with eyes of compassion.
- *We can love them by helping them financially in a time of need.*
- *We can give them practical help* such as cutting the grass, watering their plants, giving them a ride, feeding their dog, or even something as simple as sharing a breath mint. It doesn't always take something huge to make someone feel loved. As strange as it seems, sometimes the smallest actions of love with the right motives will speak the loudest.

Let's be generous with our actions and our possessions. We must remember that words with intentions but no actions are useless and empty. Let us remind ourselves to hang onto possessions loosely. We came into this world naked, and we leave with only the clothes on our bodies. So, why not be generous with what God has given us?

4. Love by seeing everyone as God's creations.

John Ortberg recounts a story about a rag doll called Pandy who was loved by a girl named Barbie. She loved this doll even when the doll became raggedy and lost her beauty.

He explained, "But, we are all God's rag dolls. He knows all about our raggedness, and he loves us anyhow. Our raggedness is no longer the most important thing about us. We were not created ragged. From the beginning there was a wonder about human beings that caused God himself to say, "Very Good" as he looked at them in the department store window." He goes on to say, "There is a wonder about you. Raggedness is not your identity. Raggedness is not your destiny, nor is it mine. We may be unlovely, yet we are not unloved." [20]

God allowed me to start seeing Kathy not as an ugly, raggedy doll, but as someone who was angry because she did not feel loved by me. By teaching me how to love her, He not only brought a light into her eyes, but he also unleashed the beauty in *my* own heart. I pray that this happens to each one of us so that God can unleash the beauty in all of our hearts.

5. Love others, realizing that we know Someone who understands rejection.

We learned that while Jesus was in the Garden of Gethsemane He experienced:

- *Betrayal*—Judas Iscariot, one of the Twelve, went to the chief priests to betray Jesus to them.
- *Rejection*—At the most crucial time in his life when Jesus needed his friends to pray with Him, they slept.
- *Surrender of His will*—Jesus prayed for His Father to take the cup from Him: "Yet not what I will, but what you will" (Mark 14:36 NIV). He had to go to the cross anyway.

The harsh reality that Jesus, the Son of God, experienced all that anguish gives us hope when we feel those painful emotions that go with rejection. At one time or another in our lives, we will love deeply, but we *will be betrayed and rejected, and have to surrender our will.* When we feel alone and lose hope, we can look up to heaven and pray with confidence, knowing that there is someone who *understands.*

Stop and ask God to Unleash Your Beauty

Begin by asking: God, what does the love in my heart look like?

S—Scripture: "How great is the love the Father has lavished on us, that we should be called children of God. And that is what we are" (1 John 3:1a NIV).

T—Thanksgiving: Thank you, God, that as my heavenly Father, You want to lavish love on me. Thank You for giving us the Holy Spirit, who is love and will teach us how to love the world around us. Thank You for helping us to overcome irritations and selfishness.

O—Observation: Do I see every person in my life as a child of God—as one of His magnificent creations?

P—Prayer: First of all, thank You, God that You love me so much that You went to the cross to die for my sins. You were like a lamb that went to the slaughter as the sacrifice for me. Help me to comprehend such a love. Thank You: because of Your sacrifice, I am able to learn about Your great love, and, in turn, love others.

God, sometimes loving is so hard. Sometimes it is just easier to hang around with people who are easy to love. But as I get older, I realize more and more that nothing really matters in any situation but how much I am able to love. Teach me more and more each day how to love unconditionally without *my* hidden agenda, but rather with pure motives and eyes that see the whole world as Your magnificent creation.

I ask that I would be a dispenser of love absolutely everywhere I go, whatever I do, and whomever I speak to. When I die I want people to be able to say, "She loved others!" Be my teacher. Show me how to love with every breath I take. Amen.

UNLEASHING THE BEAUTY OF HOPE
Three Quarters

If I can stop one heart from breaking, I shall not live in vain.
—EMILY DICKINSON, AMERICAN POET

WHEN I WAS A LITTLE GIRL, I was invited by my cousins to go to the fair. This was not just any invitation, however. I looked up to my older and adventurous cousins because they had their very own shiny, red and white 1957 Pontiac. The night before they picked me up, my stomach was churning with so much excitement that I could hardly sleep. This was definitely going to be the most fun this ten-year-old had ever experienced.

My mother got caught up in my excitement, and the next morning she helped me pick out my favorite blue and white dress. It had whispers of chiffon that rubbed against my arms and legs and made a soft, whistling sound with every step I took. The feminine sound added to the glamour and pleasure that I was feeling. As I stood and twirled in front of my mother's bedroom mirror, I saw how the baby-blue fabric made my blue eyes sparkle. It was the prettiest I had ever felt, and my cheeks were pink with anticipation.

"Mommy," I asked, "when will it be 11:00?" The clock was moving so slow; when would they get here? I went outside and stood on the gravel driveway, waiting for the big shiny Pontiac to come flying around the corner. I was careful not to let the rocks in the driveway scratch my shiny white shoes. I kept slipping as I ran up to the road, looking for the familiar car that would have friendly people with faces full of laughter sitting behind the sparkling windshield.

The clock kept ticking, but no car came. Minutes passed and they turned into hours. In my hand were three quarters that my parents had given me to spend at the fair. They were getting wet with perspiration and kept slipping through my sweaty, dirty fingers. I clutched them tightly, knowing that if I let them go it would mean the end of my dream.

I replayed the words of the invitation over and over in my mind. I had marked off the days on my calendar, so I knew that this was the right day. I had counted every hour until its arrival.

My three quarters finally slipped out of my hand. I had been forgotten. Had I done something wrong? Was I too little? Was I not pretty enough?

Finally, I allowed myself to cry. My shoes were scuffed, my dress was dirty and wrinkled, and my heart was broken. My mother's words, "*They probably just forgot,*" hurt even more: I was forgettable. I wanted to be remembered, adored, and swept away by my handsome cousins in their slick, red Pontiac. I let my scuffed white shoes drag on the ground as I went back into the house for supper. Everybody else acted as if this was just another normal day, as though my trying, personal ordeal didn't really matter. For me, it was the day I felt the searing disappointment of being forgotten, which made me feel insignificant.

This is not how the story was supposed to end. Every book that I had read in my ten years prepared me for a happy ending. Even at my young age, I had been absorbed in books of adventures in caves and on the high seas. I would fantasize about being one of those noble characters placed in tragic circumstances and romantic settings in these stories full of mystery and intrigue. By the time the story ended, everything worked out the way it was supposed to. There was always someone to rescue the beautiful maiden, and everyone was happy. Frequently, when I was in the midst of reading about an escapade, feeling as if I was walking a tightrope and thinking to myself that there might not be a happy ending, I would flip to the last page of the book to see if they would *live happily ever after.* Thankfully, they always did.

My framework for how life was supposed to unfold naturally became one of adventure and excitement. Even those rare moments of angst and disappointment would always work out in the end. There was always a rescuer, because that is how the script is written. Sadness and disappointment were foreign dramas that adults like my parents had to deal with, but not me. Needless to say, it was a crushing discovery that I made that day of the fair.

During my teen-age years, I tried to protect myself from being disappointed, but that unwelcome and increasingly familiar pain kept showing up. I kept hoping my parents would come to my school track meets, awards ceremonies, or sports events. I always looked for their faces in the crowd, but I never found them. As German immigrants, my parents found the English language laborious and awkward. I knew they were shy and couldn't find the courage to venture out into situations where they might have to speak in their broken English. Still, I always hoped I would see them but ended up always disappointed.

When I got married and had children of my own, I did everything I could to protect *them* from experiencing that horrific feeling of disappointment. My first-born child Michelle was only four when she experienced her first real disappointment at the hands of her mommy. How can a mother forget to pick up her child at pre-school? But that is what I did. The teacher called me to come and get her, and when I arrived, there was this adorable, blond, blue-eyed princess with sad, tear-stained eyes. Now, instead of protecting her from disappointment and rescuing her, I had become the *cause* of her pain. I did to her exactly what had been done to me, except worse; she experienced it at an even younger and more vulnerable age.

It is a harsh reality to learn that disappointments are part of life, and that they come in all shapes, forms, and degrees. Disappointments usually begin with some kind of expectation.

The Greek word for hope is *elpizo,* meaning to "to *expect* or confide, trust."[21] Every day of our lives, we hope that something exciting or profitable will happen. It may be as simple as hoping that the sun will shine so we can go golfing, or that a refund check will show up in the mail. It means that we have *expectations of something good.*

I love being involved in Bible studies where large groups of women gather to learn and nurture new friendships. Frequently, I have the privilege of leading these sessions in prayer. As I look up from the platform, I wonder what expectations are lurking behind those hundred pairs of closed eyes. I know that each woman came with anticipation—perhaps to form a new friendship, to share a time of talking with adults rather than pre-schoolers, to laugh, to swap stories, to learn about the Bible, to learn how to pray better, or to grow in their spiritual understanding. They all hope for something different. Some of those expectations will be fulfilled, while others will not. Yet, they will continue to hope. We all do.

EXPECTATIONS

From the time we were little children, we have learned to function by observing our families, neighbors, teachers, and other significant people. Through our life experiences, we expect people to act in a fashion that will please us. We become skilled at expecting good things to happen in a particular way, but there are serious flaws in our expectations of wanting something good to happen to us:

1. Assumed expectations
This is the most dangerous kind of expectation. We build an image in our heads of what something *should* look like, or how someone *should* act. The only problem is that the other people aren't privy to our mental images. We assume:

- That our best friend will always remember our birthday.
- That our husband will take out the garbage every Wednesday night.
- That when somebody says they are going to do something, they will actually do it.

- That people know how we feel.
- That our children will always call us on Mother's Day or Valentine's Day.
- That we will get a raise in pay at our annual review.
- That if I feel a certain way about an issue, my close friends and family will know that and work with me on it.
- That if it is important to me, it should be important to those who mean the most to me.

The list of *assumed expectations* is endless. We go through this life expecting things to happen the way we *think they should*. When they don't happen, we feel that people don't understand us or they have let us down; therefore, we become disappointed in them.

When I married Dick, I was one of those brides filled with expectations of being adored. Some of the things I *expected* to happen included that my new husband would be able to fix things around the house, he would affirm my beauty, and he would be the *rescuer* I had been looking for my entire life. I had grown up with a father who fixed absolutely everything. He wired our house with electricity; he built our fences, fixed leaks, planted gardens, and even baked bread on the weekends. I naturally *assumed* that my new husband would also be able to do all of those things. After all, I had seen one man perform those tasks, so I expected all men to share the same capabilities. Wrong! I discovered that my husband could not fix one thing. I was shocked, disillusioned, and angry. This was the first of many disappointments to go into my "Disappointment Box," a place where I mentally filed things away for a later date.

2. Everything will turn out if we plan carefully.
We have a vision in our heads about how we want something to look as it unfolds in our lives. Even though we plan very carefully to make that happen, we are disappointed when:

- We eventually spend too much money and too many hours flipping through wallpaper books to find the *perfect* pattern we had envisioned for the bedroom walls. When we put it up, it looks horrible.

- We plan a trip with a friend, and they back out at the last minute.
- Our teenager falls victim to substance abuse in spite of our prayers and parental love and guidance.
- We plan for our retirement, but our investments crash and we lose everything.
- We planned a family reunion, yet everyone is fighting.
- We put our child into every training camp imaginable, but he still doesn't make the team.

There are different degrees of expectations, and the disappointment may last anywhere from ten minutes to a lifetime. Some are minor setbacks, while others drive us to our knees with tears streaming down our faces.

As I am writing this, my daughter Michelle and her husband are in the process of adopting a second child. They planned very carefully and received many words of affirmation, hoping that they would get a baby. Twice in six months they came close to receiving their baby, but each time the birth mother decided at the last minute to keep the child. There is almost no category to describe this type of intense emotional pain. I will let Michelle tell you in her own words:

> "The hardest part for me when dealing with disappointment is at the peak of it feeling like God must have forgotten about me. When so many people tell you they are praying, and we're praying from the depth of our soul, does God not hear? It's hard to feel that God loves me right now. I poured out all my longings to Him and everything inside of me feels completely crushed, broken, and empty. God, where are You now? I want to know what happened to all the prayers. Were they not enough? Do you have to reach a certain number before they are answered? Why are some answered right away, and others never seem to be answered? I know the answer must be 'wait.' I've 'waited' beyond what I can humanly bear. Just how much perseverance do I need?"

Those are the words of someone in the depths of disappointment and grief. They did everything right and planned well. They are loving parents, and their arms are aching to hold another baby. Some disappointments leave us in such despair. We feel angry, crushed, and hopeless.

3. We expect others to follow through in matters of trust.

We realize that the people in this world are not perfect, and they will let us down. Although we make allowances for one's misinterpretation, we nevertheless expect others to uphold their end of verbal commitments, oaths, or contracts. There is a trail of destruction in broken marriages, friendships, and partnerships when this should not be the case.

If you are single, you have probably been disappointed in the romance department. You may have hoped that a friendship would become "more," but then it didn't. Words were spoken to you that implied there would be a wedding one day. Yet, it did not happen, and you are alone again.

Many of you have been that beautiful bride walking down the aisle in a cloud of organza, pearls, fresh flowers, and music. You see your new husband looking at you with love shining from his face. You look into each other's eyes and declare:

> *"I (bride) take you (groom), to have and to hold from this day forward, for better or for worse, for richer, for poorer, in sickness and in health, to love and to cherish; from this day forward until death do us part."*

When we say those words, we *expect* to be loved and cherished until the day we die. It is not long before we *expect* certain other things from each other. We hoped that our husbands would shop with us, listen to us, and help around the house and notice when we are tired. When they don't meet our expectations, our emotions swing anywhere from being mildly disappointed to feeling utterly crushed and angry. We hold expectations of other people as well:

- When we sign an employee contract, we expect the employer to follow through on all his commitments.
- When we sign a contract with a builder, we expect the job completed on the date agreed upon.
- When two parties sign an agreement of any kind, they are committing to something, and we *expect* them to comply.
- When we give our word to do something, we should be able to expect the other party to do likewise. After all, they said they would.

We can also become discouraged by observing broken trust in others' lives. I know a woman who at age forty was disappointed, not only in her unmarried status, but also in all the marriages she observed around her. She came to a defining point in her life where she thought, *What is the value of getting married, anyway? Everywhere I look, marriages are in trouble. Husbands are cheating on their wives, and marriages are filled with dishonesty and arguing. I am better off staying single.* Yet, she still had a longing to someday have a good marriage. Disillusioned that she would never see her dreams fulfilled, she ultimately experienced a nervous breakdown.

I am also aware that many young people today have opted out of marriage because of broken vows they have witnessed in their own families or with friends. For them, it appears easier to remain single to avoid the pain and disappointment of broken commitment. They realize once promises have been broken in relationships, it is almost impossible to restore them to their original state of intimacy, loyalty, and trust.

4. We fail to fulfill the expectations of others.

We have such a powerful drive within us to feel loved that we will do whatever it takes to fill that void. Carol Kent says, "All of us have an indescribable desire for love. We spend much of our lives trying to make relationships work so we can fill the vacuum inside our souls. Most of us would prefer to live with personal pain, emotional deprivation, and personal paralysis rather than risk the possibility of disappointing people who we think expect us to be models of Christian womanhood." [22]

We will do whatever people want us to do, in spite of the cost of our own time, emotions, personal plans, and energy. We wear ourselves out trying to please people around us to earn their loving approval. We also feel the need to work hard to earn God's love and approval. Rick Warren says, "Many people are driven by the need for approval. They allow the expectations of parents or spouses or children or teachers or friends to control their lives. Many adults are still trying to earn the approval of unpleasable parents. Others are driven by peer pressure, always worried by what others might think. Unfortunately, those who follow the crowd usually get lost in it." [23]

Of course, whenever we work hard to achieve something, there is always the possibility of failure. When failure comes, disappointment is right at its heels.

5. My life will be easier when I become a Christian.

Everyone has a different view of who God is and what we expect Him to do for us. I realize many people *expect* that when they become a Christ-follower, God will answer all their prayers, fulfill their purposes, give them joy, and even financial blessings. They hope that life will be a whole lot easier. When we find that life as a Christian is still full of struggles, we begin to wonder if God is real, if our convictions are faulty, or if He even cares about us. We pray, read the Bible and do all the right things, and yet our life still has its daily struggles, failures and disappointments. We *expected* more from God.

From Disappointment to Despair

Broken trust and unfulfilled expectations can leave us feeling anything from disappointment to despair, depending on the gravity of the situation. When I see the words "irreconcilable differences" on a Petition for Divorce, I believe there must have been a disappointment box in that home. Every time someone broke an expectation, another disappointment was placed in the box. One day someone got up and decided there were one too many disappointments; in fact, the box was spilling over. The pain of accumulated disappointment was too much, and there was no relief in sight. That person regressed from disappointment to despair to divorce.

Two nights before my wedding to my second husband Jack, our family got a call, telling us that my cousin Charles had committed suicide. The news made us all reel, but in the meantime, we had to prepare for a wedding feast. After the wedding celebrations were over, instead of taking our planned honeymoon, we drove up to northern British Columbia for the funeral. I was asked to do the eulogy, and I could not imagine a greater responsibility and honor than to say the final good-bye to my dear cousin Charles.

Charles was a bright, happy boy growing up; but between the bursts of laughter, he was in a lot of emotional pain. He learned to love photography, and through the lenses of his camera he discovered a world that was beautiful and perfect. His sensitive and loving nature yearned for a beauty that seemed to exist only in his photographs. To him, photographs were almost flawless, unmarred by the unfairness and disappointments of the world he lived in. One night, his disappointment box must have been full. Because he could not envision himself stuffing another disappointment in there, he took his own life. He wrote this poem before he died:

My Heart,
The loving gives life to my tired body,
    yet slowly kills my soul,
At first they blamed themselves,
    then they grew to understand it wasn't them,
It was others, people, life, and human nature.
    The world had tried too hard to condemn them,
but they would never forget her and how to care
    just for her in a special way.
His heart strained, twisted, and cracked,
    and that way, his heart said,
"Good-bye."

I tried to find words of comfort for the several hundred family members, friends, and co-workers gathered at the funeral. I remember saying, "Charles found it too difficult to live in a world without beauty. He had *expected* life to have less struggles and more laughter. I have learned from his death that I need to *love more, keep short account of my grudges, forgive quicker and make this world a better place to live.*"

What do we do with the disillusionment and pain brought on by those unfulfilled expectations that leave us gasping for air, questioning, and angry?

Six Keys to Finding Hope

1. Give yourself permission to hurt.

To the extent that there are varying degrees of disappointment, there also are different stages of pain. When we find that we can't get airline tickets during a required time period, we are disappointed, but we groan and sigh and come up with a different plan. This is not the case, however, when a husband packs his bags and moves out, or a teenager rebels against core family values. There are more intense disappointments such as illness, broken relationships, or lost dreams such as my daughter and her husband's attempt to adopt a baby. How do we deal with all these emotions and get rid of this horrible pain?

My heart aches for you if you are going through a painful time. You need to give yourself permission to suffer intensely. Be candid and allow yourself to be angry at the person, at the circumstance, even at God. God knows how you are feeling, so why not just be straightforward with Him and yourself?

Then, you need to allow yourself time to feel your sorrow. Every time we lose something valuable, we need to mourn the loss.

The Bible is very truthful about people mourning their losses. In the book of Job, there is a lot of disappointment and pain going on: "Then Job stood up and tore his robe in grief and fell down upon the ground...." He also "took a piece of pottery to scrape himself and sat among the ashes" (Job 1:20; 2:8 TLB). Job gave himself permission to feel his anguish and express it in the way that he could deal with his pain.

Didn't Jesus weep over the death of his friend Lazarus? Too often, our advice to our friends is to "get over it, feel better, and shake it off." But grief is a God-given emotion that helps us through the painful periods.

In Psalms, David's emotions are all over the place. One moment he is praising and glorifying God, and in the next breath, he is cursing his enemies. He often experienced a "King David meltdown." The book of Psalms is a wonderful reminder of the depth of our emotions and gives us permission to have our own meltdown.

Rick Warren writes:

> Pour your heart out to God. Unload every emotion that you are feeling. Job did this when he said, "I can't be quiet, I am angry and bitter and have to speak." God can handle your doubt, anger, fear, grief, confusion and questions.
>
> Did you know that admitting your hopelessness to God can be a statement of faith? Trusting God but feeling despair at the same time, David wrote, "I believed, so I said, I am completely ruined." This sounds like a contradiction: I trust God but I'm wiped out! David's frankness actually reveals deep faith: First, he believed God. Second, he believed God would listen to his prayer, Third, he believed God would let him say what he felt and still love him. [24]

A grieving period brings healing. These are the stages of grief that one may experience. They may all occur in this order or not, or you may only experience some of them. This will make you aware that if they do show up, they can be welcomed as ways to help you through your grief:

- denial (shock, disbelief, numbness)
- anger (resentment, blame)
- bargaining (negotiating with anyone—including God—who you think can change the situation to what you want it to be.
- guilt (If only I had done something...)
- depression (sadness as a result of admitting that it happened; can include anxiety, insomnia, loss of appetite, restlessness, hopelessness, apathy, irritability, and feelings of worthlessness)
- acceptance (the point where you accept the reality of what happened and know that regardless of the loss, life will go on and be good again).

Every grief situation is different and cannot be measured by a specific time. It can last anywhere from one day to a number of years. If we do not allow ourselves to acknowledge our pain, our grief may be with us for the rest of our lives.

In his book, *Shattered Dreams*, best-selling author and psychologist Dr. Larry Crabb encourages us to risk feeling the pain. He writes, "When you hurt, hurt. Hurt openly in the presence of God. Hurt openly in the presence of the few who provide you with safe community. Feel your pain. Regard brokenness as an opportunity, as the chance to discover a desire that no brokenness can eliminate but that only brokenness reveals." [25]

Sometimes we need help with our grieving process and pain. We must not be too afraid or proud to seek help from wise friends and trusted counselors. They can help get us back on our feet when we don't know what to do with the all-consuming pain. When I was going through an especially difficult time after the death of my husband and watching my father die of Lou Gehrig's disease, I got counseling for a period of time. It gave me an opportunity to be gut-level honest about my anger, fear, and disappointment.

I found out the hard way that if I don't accept my pain, no matter how ugly it is, I will become a victim of that pain. I know you and I don't want to carry that heavy burden of pain any longer than we have to.

2. Bring it into the light of God's promises.

In the same way that I was hanging onto my three quarters to give me hope while I was waiting for my cousins, we need to hang onto God's promises. When I let the quarters drop out of my hand, I acknowledged that I had been forgotten. Yet, God never forgets about us; instead, He promises that He will be with us *in* our pain.

"The Lord is close to the brokenhearted and saves those who are crushed in spirit" (Psalm 34:18 NIV).
- *God experienced pain as the Son of God, He knows Your pain, He can feel it, and He wants to heal you.*

"I will refresh the weary and satisfy the faint" (Jer. 31:25 NIV).
- *God wants to refresh you and give you new energy.*

"For I know the plans I have for you, declares the Lord, plans to prosper you and not to harm you, plans to give you hope and a future" (Jer. 29:11 NIV).
- *God has glorious plans for you and me. He wants to give us hope for our future.*

There will be times when we don't *feel* that God loves us, but rather feel disconnected and abandoned by Him. During those times, we need to *read* His promises. The Bible is the living Word that breathed new life at the beginning of creation, and it will bring new life into your spirit as well as rescuing you from your pain when you believe it.

Carol and Gene Kent experienced the anguish of loss when their only beloved son J.P. went to prison. In her award-winning book, *When I Lay My Isaac Down,* Carol shares what gave her hope:

"Hope becomes unsinkable when we realize our hope is not in having spouses or friends who will never disappoint us, or in enjoying financial security, or in achieving a certain level of success, or in having perfect health, or in watching children turn out exactly as we anticipated. Hope remains constant when we get to know the Source of all hope." [26]

Perhaps the psalmist said it best:

"But I stand silently before the Lord, waiting for him to rescue me. For salvation comes from him alone. Yes, he alone is my Rock, my rescuer, defense and fortress—why then should I be tense with fear when troubles come? (Psalm 62:5, 6 TLB).

When we bring our pain into the light of God's promises, we bring it out of the darkness of our pain to see it for what it is. Yes, it is painful, but we also begin to see that with God's help *we will make it.* We also realize that it was presumptuous of us to think that we could heal on our own and the brokenness would disappear quickly. By bringing our pain to God, we re-connect with Him, which allows Him to become the source of our new hope and healing. We will eventually be able to acknowledge what God has blessed us with rather than asking, "God, why have you not blessed me like I thought you would?" This will give us wisdom that will save us from the anguish of going around that same mountain the next time.

3. Let your friends help.

There is a reason that God has made us relational people. Let me encourage you to make time in your life to develop loving, intimate relationships with your close friends because they will be the ones you will need to call at 2 in the morning. We need a friend who can mourn *with* us.

Months after my husband died, my dad had to be put into the hospital. His body was getting weaker as he was going into the final stages of ALS, commonly known as Lou Gehrig's disease. This added trauma was starting to crush me because I was still grieving over the death of my husband. During one of my lunch hours, I ran up to the hospital to visit my dad, and when I found him I couldn't believe my eyes. There he was, lying in his bed unshaven and uncovered; he was cold and crying. He could no longer speak, so he wrote to us on a pad of lined paper. This is what he had written that day: "*Please help me and take me home. Please help me and take me home.*" He had written it over and over again until the page was filled. It felt like someone had stuck a cold knife into my heart.

During this time of angst and sorrow, I had a girlfriend staying with me in my home. When I walked through the door that night, she was waiting for me. A soon as I stepped into my kitchen, I let my emotions explode. I pounded the kitchen counters, sobbed, doubled over in anguish, and wailed in my pain. When I looked up, there was my friend sitting at the kitchen counter with tears streaming down her face. We sobbed and held each other until we were both exhausted. There is nothing like a loving friend who will cry with you, validate your emotions and give you permission to be angry in your pain. We need this kind of a friend who will *mourn with us*. These friends are the loving arms of Jesus that help the *brokenhearted*.

4. Refuse to grow bitter.

As I look at the faces of older people, I try to imagine how they have responded to life around them. Even though many of these faces are old and wrinkled, the ones who have been able to overcome disappointments possess a countenance that exudes joy. Then, there are others who have downcast, angry eyes: their mouths are sagging, their shoulders are squared defiantly, and their words shoot bullets of bitterness. I believe that they have been left with too much unresolved hurt and anger about the way their lives have turned out. They probably became a victim of their disappointments.

Disappointment shreds our life and faith and makes our faces look angry and old before their time. But the absence of hope is even worse because it makes our life intolerable. We must learn to overcome these disappointments by forgiving those people who have let us down. We *must* forgive those who have rejected us, betrayed us, ruined our lives, and left us bereft. We *absolutely must*; otherwise, we will become angry and then harsh. Unforgiveness will destroy our health, our friends, our relationships, and ultimately, our soul. It will harden our hearts and kill our hope.

5. Pray.

I believe prayer opens the throne room and ushers us into God's glory and power. The greatest assurance for receiving new hope will come while we are down on our knees. As we gaze up to heaven, we will gain a different perspective regarding our circumstances. Praying during this painful period can be very difficult. Our hearts can feel so empty and dry that we struggle to form words to express our emotions. God can hear the groaning of your soul, and He hears your cries. This is also the time to call upon everyone you know and ask them to pray for you. God promises that He will be near and that He will hear. Reading the Scriptures can also bring great comfort to you.

"Then you will call, and the Lord will answer, you will cry for help, and he will say: Here I am" (Isa. 58:9 NIV).
* *God knows we need help; He will hear us when we cry out.*

"The Lord is near to all who call on Him, to all who call on Him in truth. He fulfills the desires of those who fear him; he hears their cry and saves them, the Lord watches over all who love him" (Psalm 145:18-20 NIV).
* *God is always near to us even when it does not feel like it.*

"Do not be anxious about anything, but in everything by prayer and petition, with thanksgiving, present your requests to God" (Phil. 4:6 NIV).
* *God says to pray about everything. It will remove our anxious feelings and fear.*

My daughter Michelle writes:

"Throughout my eight years of infertility, it was so hard to carry on at times. The spirit feels crushed and broken after so many years of unfulfilled dreams. Eventually you either learn to live with the feelings of pain, or try to avoid situations that bring the pain, but it doesn't get easier. I often thought of Paul who lived with a thorn in the flesh. He was a great man of God, but he didn't live free from disappointment and pain. I guess the biggest lesson for me in all of this is that it doesn't pay to dwell on your pain. We can't expect a life that is free from suffering. After the initial pain subsides, we need to embrace the good things in life and dwell on them more than our pain. This does take a lot of discipline because it doesn't come naturally. It's a choice we have to make—to live life in spite of our pain. Instead of praying, 'God, take away my pain and disappointments,' perhaps we should be praying, 'God, help me to embrace life in spite of my pain and disappointments.' I pray that God is using these trials for something good. Right now, I don't know, but I hope I will someday."

Yes, right now we can't *feel* hope, but we have to believe that the pain will not be wasted— that there will be value in it someday.

6. Get an eternal perspective.

Most people understand things by seeing them. When we see something, it is proof that it exists, which, in turn, helps us to comprehend that it is true. We will lose hope, however, when we see life only as it is around us. God's Word tells us that since the life we see around us is temporary, we must set our hope on eternity:

> "Our light and momentary troubles are achieving for us an eternal glory that far outweighs them all. So we fix our eyes not on what is seen, but on what is unseen. For what is seen is temporary, but what is unseen is eternal" (2 Cor. 4:17, 18 NIV).

It is hard for us to imagine anything beyond what we see and experience right now, but God has a glorious hope for our future. We must believe this to be true if we ever hope to rise above our pain and disappointments.

Jesus lovingly tells us:

> "Do not let your hearts be troubled. Trust in God; trust also in me. In my Father's house are many rooms, if it were not so, I would have told you. I am going there to prepare a place for you. And if I go and prepare a place for you, I will come back and take you to be with me that you also may be where I am" (John 14:1-3 NIV).

So what does that place look like to you, and who is our rescuer?

At the beginning of this chapter, I recalled the times during my childhood when I read a story that was such a tangled web I was not sure of the outcome. I would flip to the back of the book to get reassurance that all the complex problems would somehow be resolved and someone would rescue me.

We also need hope beyond our daily disappointments and struggles.

Let's turn to the end of the Bible to understand the middle by seeing how the story ends. As our rescuer, God promises us, "He will wipe away every tear from their eyes. There will be no more death or mourning or crying or pain, for the old order of things has passed away" (Rev. 21:4 NIV).

On days that are difficult, we can say, "Thank goodness this life is not all there is." God has a beautiful new home prepared for us when we leave this earth. We will be living in a city that is "pure gold, as pure as glass," where the foundations of the city are "decorated with every kind of precious stone and where the gates are made of a single pearl." What a magnificent promise. We need to hang onto this so that we can live beyond our daily disappointments.

Unleashing the Beauty of Hope

If I could sit across from you right now, the first thing I would implore you to do is allow God to whisper words of hope and encouragement into your ear that this too shall pass. As we bring our disappointments into the light of God's promises and blessings, we will reconnect with God, and He will heal us a little more each day. There are always new seasons, and with every season, there is new hope. Just as the sun comes up every morning, each day will bring you a new ray of healing and renewed beauty. God's perspective of hope has the ability to take the furrows out of your brow, lift your head. and put new color into your cheeks.

Then, I would implore you to make it your goal to become a godly woman—not a woman who *desires for her life* to be godly. Let me explain the difference.

A woman who *desires for her life* to be godly wants everything and everyone in her life to be a part of her plans to achieve this goal. This is a wonderful desire, but who can sabotage that plan? Everyone! Every time someone or something does not live up to her *expectations,* she will experience disappointment and great pain, especially when this involves her dearest friend, husband, or children.

When a woman chooses to become a *godly woman,* her goal is to become Christ-like in every situation. She will not *expect* people to act a certain way, or to be a particular way for special circumstances; instead, she will allow the disappointments in her life to strengthen her and teach her to respond to life in a loving and forgiving manner. When she responds to life in this way, her beauty will radiate like a light in a dark place. Who can sabotage this woman's goal? No one except her, because this is between her and God.

The more we allow God to teach us how to love and forgive, the stronger we will become. Then, we can become that loving voice in difficult situations. We can determine things that are causing pain, not only to us, but to those around us and say with a strong voice, "I will no longer tolerate that kind of behavior."

To unleash our greatest beauty, we *must* let go of expectations. While we are on this side of heaven, people and life will inevitably disappoint us. Author Nancy Leigh DeMoss explains this very well:

> "The Truth is, every created thing is guaranteed to disappoint us. Things can burn or break or be stolen or get lost. People can move or change or fail or die. It took the loss of some of my dearest loved ones some years ago to awaken me to the Truth that I would always live in a state of disappointment if I was looking to people to satisfy me at the core of my being." [27]

While we desire the very best for people in our lives, we know we cannot change them or their circumstances. Our anger, unforgiveness, and unkind intolerance will not cause them to change but only cripple them and stop us from moving forward in our own lives. Our loving acceptance of who they are will cause them to respond to us differently and, in turn, teach us to love better.

We need to remember that we are also imperfect beings who will often disappoint people. We all struggle with sin and have the ability to hurt and disappoint each other.

Indeed, God will wipe away our tears when we go to heaven, but who will wipe away our tears now? Because of the triumph we've experienced during our own pain and struggles, we can now be the hands that wipe away others' tears in this lifetime. Strangely enough, because of our own pain, we can change the world by bringing the light of hope into the dark places of despair.

If we have children, we have an obligation to teach them about disappointment. We need to teach them that when disappointment comes, it is not because they did something wrong, but because disappointment is simply part of life.

If you are in a season of great pain right now, I want to encourage you to hang on. Just as a new day dawns every twenty-four hours, there is also an unshakable promise that your pain will turn into joy, and your ashes into beauty. Some pain is with us for only a season, and if we persevere through it, we will recognize that God does have something glorious waiting for us— even in this lifetime. Some seasons are meant for teaching us something new, some are for healing, some are for building our character, while others are simply painful. There is also the season of beauty and blessings. There is a season for everything: *"He has made everything beautiful in its time"* (Eccl. 3:11 NIV).

Your time of beauty will come: that is a promise. In the meantime, through our own disappointments, let's make this world a better place to live. Our God is a loving God through the good times as well as the bad ones. We have to believe this with all of our hearts.

We will become magnificent, godly women as we learn to praise God during our suffering, as well as praising Him with smiles of joy during times of great triumph. When we lay our pain under the light of God's blessings, we know that we are not alone.

Stop and ask God to Unleash Your Beauty

Begin by asking: God, what expectations and resulting disappointments are causing me unnecessary pain?

S—Scripture: "Be kind and compassionate to one another, forgiving each other, just as in Christ God forgave you" (Eph. 4: 32 NIV).

T—Thanksgiving: Thank You, God for all Your wonderful promises to give me hope for every single day of my life. Thank You for Your power of forgiveness, which brings the beauty of freedom into our lives. I also thank You that I can also pour that kind of forgiveness, compassion, and tenderness into people in my life.

O—Observation: I must let go of my *expectations* of people and the outcome of events such as experiencing the loss of a job, assuming my children and friends will act in a certain way, being selected for certain positions, or being recognized for an accomplishment. My job is to be kind and compassionate to everyone around me and to bring hope wherever I can.

P—Prayer: Heavenly Father, this whole topic of disappointment is so huge because there is so much pain and confusion all around us. As I watch the news on T.V. and see the hurt and disappointment in people's lives, it also causes me to be discouraged. I praise You and thank You that this life is not all there is, and that You have wonderful plans for my life—not just for the here and now, but in the glorious future that You have already prepared for me. I pray that I would see each incident in this life through the eternal perspective of Your promises.

Teach me to be a godly woman in all circumstances. Fill my heart so full of love and compassion for the people around me that my only desire will be to want the best for them—to love them and forgive them when they hurt me. Teach me to let go of *expectations* from this world. Teach me to expect only great and mighty things from you, oh God. Amen.

5

UNLEASHING THE BEAUTY
OF GODLY DESIRES
Me, Myself, and I

If I find in myself desires which nothing in this world can satisfy,
the only logical explanation is that I was made for another world.

—C. S. LEWIS

I CANNOT RESIST BEAUTIFUL, unusual things. It doesn't matter what it is—clothing, jewelry, artwork, glassware, china, or fabric—if it's beautiful and unique, I am compelled to explore it. I long to stroke it, smell it, hold it up to the light, or just stand there and dream about having it. It makes me feel good.

I had one of these moments in 1977 while on a corporate trip in Japan with my husband Dick. His company had paid for us to stay at a lavish hotel in Kyoto. Breathtaking beauty surrounded us; it was exquisite. Everywhere we looked there were unique artifacts, shimmering fabrics, and colorful gifts. Temptation was awakening my desires.

It started with a glance. She was lovely, and her dress was gorgeous. I couldn't take my eyes off her. The beautiful geisha doll in the glass case would be the perfect memento of my visit to Japan. I could already picture her sitting on the hearth of my living room fireplace in Canada. I had no idea how I would get her on the airplane, but that didn't matter. I desired her, so I bought her. But then I had to figure out how to get her through customs and onto the plane. What a hassle! Even though the case had a beautiful handle, it was a very awkward, extremely fragile 15-inch glass cube.

The flight from Japan to Alaska was the easiest part. The airline was very accommodating, allowing my beautiful glass case to have its very own seat. With her seat belt strapped on, she was safe and sound. The domestic connection flights from Alaska to Vancouver and Vancouver to Penticton, British Columbia, were more challenging. Fellow passengers shook their heads in bewilderment as they watched me attempt to keep the glass from shattering.

After twenty-three hours of airports, customs, flying, and hauling luggage, I walked through my front door and tenderly placed my treasure where I had envisioned it to be—on the hearth of my fireplace. It had cost a lot of money, come thousands of miles, caused a great deal of aggravation to airline personnel, security staff, and passengers, but oh, it was worth it. I had satisfied the desire of my heart.

Days passed, and dust collected on my new foreign object. Except for a glance now and then, the thrill of the purchase had worn off, and the doll was being ignored. One day, our big dog Brutus decided he wanted the doll. When no one was looking, he went into the living room, knocked over the case, broke the glass, pulled out the geisha doll, and ate her.

I was crushed…but only for a moment. The thrill of owning the doll had dissipated within a few hours of bringing her home. I hardly ever looked at her after that. The emotional process I went through with acquiring the doll involved feelings=selfish desire=impulse=temporary fulfillment=emptiness.

How often do we feel dissatisfied and crave *something, anything,* to make us feel better? When it is something that we really want, time and money seem to be no object. Many of my beautiful possessions have caused me more trouble than pleasure:

- There was the time I just had to get the copper-nickel, twelve-piece cutlery set in Singapore. I had to buy an extra suitcase and drag it through Thailand, Hong Kong, and China. My travel companions wished I would have left it behind in the hotel room.

- There was the diamond tennis bracelet I fell in love with on a Caribbean island. My sweet husband bought it for me as an anniversary present, and it was constantly on my wrist. One day I left it on my nightstand, and when I got home from work it was gone. I turned my house upside down looking for it and never found it.

- Then there was a rug factory in the marketplace in Marrakech, Africa. I can still hear the owner calling my name: "Miss Heidi, come over here, this is the most beautiful rug there is. We can make it for you personally and ship it to your home in Canada." He was right; it was beautiful. I did have it made and shipped to Canada. When I saw the air freight invoice, I almost fainted. That carpet still sits in my basement. I have tried several times to give it away, but no one wants it.

Frequently, we look for things that will *make us feel better.* Don't you find that eventually everything ends up becoming stained, broken, ripped, dented, or uninteresting? After the thrill of the purchase, the momentary pleasure is gone, and inevitably we are left feeling empty and looking for something new to fill us.

Being dissatisfied is not a terrible thing. God has placed a void in our soul that needs filling, and that void demands constant attention. It is only a terrible thing *when we fill it with the wrong things* that lead us away from Jesus Christ. When we find something else that is satisfying and gives us pleasure, we keep pursuing that thing instead of Christ.

Our Feelings

Women are exquisite creatures loaded with feelings. It is our *feelings* that start us down the path of needing things to make us feel better, look better, and give us delight. We anticipate the thrill of feasting our eyes on something beautiful or desirable and then actually touching it, owning it and taking it home. We also imagine looking at ourselves in the mirror and being younger or twenty pounds lighter, or having a different hair color, fewer wrinkles, or a different nose. The longings and desires we have are endless because we are never completely satisfied with the way we look and the world around us. When we fulfill one of our desires, we love that momentary rush of emotion and feeling of well-being; it is like a powerful drug. Unfortunately, it doesn't last.

God gave us our feelings: they are a marvelous gift from Him to be enjoyed. There is nothing wrong with them. They are that wonderfully complex part of the emotions that give us women such delight and laughter. We all long for the thrill of a good feeling.

Think about what you feel when you:

- Look at a newborn baby.
- Watch a bride walk down the aisle.
- See puppies or kittens playing.
- Observe hummingbirds zooming around a beautiful flower garden.
- View the sun setting in a blaze of color over the horizon.
- Behold moonbeams dancing on the water.
- Reach out to help a homeless person.
- Comfort a grieving friend.
- Discover new hope.
- Hear someone tell you that they love you.

All of these things elicit good feelings. It is almost as if someone hugged you, or put a warm blanket around your shoulders on a chilly, autumn day. They give us a sense of well-being, and they temporarily satisfy and comfort us.

But we also experience feelings that make us feel anxious, empty, and dissatisfied. They whisper to us that we need something we don't have, but if we get it, we'll feel better. These are the powerful urges of our *egos*. Our egos are huge and hungry monsters that pull us in the opposite direction of what God wants for our lives. They are urges that are never satisfied.

Recently, I participated in a Working Women's Golf Tournament. I was surrounded by beautiful, aggressive, and competitive women. At the awards banquet, a huge billboard with a picture of a stunningly, beautiful woman proclaimed these words: *"THE THREE MOST IMPORTANT PEOPLE IN MY LIFE: ME, MYSELF AND I."*

I stared at that billboard in disbelief. I looked around at all the women, and my heart ached for us. We were all trying desperately to compete in the world by feeling the need to focus on ourselves to find satisfaction. Believe me, that slippery slope never ends. These selfish, ego-driven feelings provide temporary relief but get us nowhere:

- The compulsion to purchase something—anything—just to make us feel better
- The need to manipulate a situation or person or to lie or steal in order to get what I want
- Pride
- A *hunger* for power to control people or circumstances
- A judgmental or contemptuous attitude towards other human beings
- The conviction that everything is about me and my happiness and that I deserve whatever I want
- The need to look beautiful at all costs

We live in a generation which tells us women we need to have *more and we must be beautiful.* We can hardly look at a TV, billboards, or magazines without having our senses assaulted and tempted in some way. The next time you stand in line at a grocery store, take a few minutes to read the magazine covers:

- "Strip Away Fat—and See Results in 9 Days"
- "Get Your Own Way Every Time"
- "Look Younger in 14 Days"
- "Power Makeover—What is the Price of Perfection?"

Everything is all about *feeling better.* The world not only entices us with many ways to feel better, but it also tells us we deserve it and we can do it. We are encouraged to fulfill our every desire through many easy avenues promoted in our society. After all, when we are hungry, we need to eat. If we want something, we should just go out and buy it. Never mind if we don't have the money, we can find ways to charge it on a credit card. If we are lonely, we look for companionship any way we can find it, even if it means pursuing the married man at work. If we don't like being married any more, we can just get a divorce. If we need a vacation, we'll go on a cruise even if we can't afford it.

In the last two days, I have opened my mail and have received pre-approved credit from three different credit card companies. At this very moment, I have access to over one hundred thousand dollars. I can fulfill all my desires in the next week.

I recently saw a documentary of a woman who had over thirty surgeries to give her the perfect body and beautiful face. She was only thirty years old, but her face looked like that of a perfect, plastic Barbie doll. It broke my heart to listen to her as she shared her desperate journey to find acceptance so that she could feel good about herself.

A very disturbing article in *Time Magazine* reveals that "A fast-growing industry called neuromarketing uses science to help markers understand how we respond to products….On a recent Wednesday night, Eleanor Phipp spent an hour watching commercial television. Nothing unusual about that—except that Phipp, 30, was in a dark room at a South London medical centre inside a loudly whirring functional magnetic resonance imaging (FMRI) scanner that mapped her brain as video images flickered before her eyes. Brain scanners, which use radio waves and a powerful magnetic field to trace oxygenated blood to areas of neural activity, are used mainly to study or diagnose brain diseases. But Phipp's brain was being scrutinized by researchers to see how it reacted to TV pictures—specifically, whether she responded to ads differently at night than in the morning…to better understand how our brain reacts to advertising, brands and products, reactions that for the most part occur subconsciously…this gives marketers a new tool to fine-tune ads and marketing campaigns, bolster and extend brands and design better products." [29] You and I are being manipulated by today's media to show us how to fulfill every desire of our hearts.

Our Feelings Lead to Desires

We are human beings who need to feel—good or bad; sometimes it does-n't even matter—just as long as we can feel something. Rarely are we so content with our lives that we do not desire something. Our need to feel pleasure and passion is so great that many times it will lead us down dangerous roads. Many women trade virginity or a marriage for the promise of a new relationship and better companionship. Others provoke people to anger, just so they can lash back in their own anger. Even though anger is a negative feeling, at least it is a feeling of some kind. People in our society are consumed with taking drugs: it is all about making them feel better.

As we grow in our Christian lives and try to become more like Christ, how do we handle these tumultuous feelings? How do we know if they are good for us or will just lead us down a road of devastation?

Let's see what the Bible has to say about our desires. In his letter to the church in Ephesus, the apostle Paul bluntly says, "All of us also lived among them at one time, gratifying the cravings of our sinful nature and following its desires and thoughts" (Eph. 2:3 NIV).

In Greek, the word for desire is *epithumia*. It is a noun which "describes the emotion of the soul, the *natural tendency* (italics mine) towards things evil. Such lusts are not necessarily base and immoral, they may be refined in character, but are evil if inconsistent with the will of God."[30] Thus, we see that the *natural tendency* of our emotions is to fulfill our desires with evil things.

While we are living in this world, we will constantly be bombarded and enticed by its ways of thinking and living. Those deceptive ways are meant to gratify our huge egos and that includes *Me, Myself and I.* "Whatever it takes to make me happy, beautiful, and feeling important" is what I'll do. That's the way of thinking that will take us down the slippery road to evil desires where we will not stop until we have gratified the cravings of our huge egos. We need something to make us feel better, so we *must* have it.

Godly Desires

We need to be aware that our natural inclination will always pull us away from God. Once we discover that *things* in this world are not fulfilling us, no matter how hard we try, where do we go from there?

Nancy Leigh DeMoss discusses this thorny issue: "First, we have to recognize that *we will always have unfulfilled longings this side of heaven* (Romans 8:23). In fact, if we could have all our longings fulfilled down here, we would easily be satisfied with staying here, and our hearts would never long for a better place." [31]

We can't just get up one morning and tell our feelings to stop tempting us. How, then, do we turn our *selfish, ego-driven desires* into *godly desires?*

God always has the answers in His wonderful instructional manual: the Bible. He tells us that we need to start by getting to know Him better. Psalm 37:4 says, "Delight yourself in the Lord, and he will give you the desires of your heart" (NIV).

Isn't that what we want—to have the desires of our hearts fulfilled? How do we make this happen?

First Delight—Then Desire

The word "delight" is set in the *present,* but the word "desires" is for the *future.* In order for something to unfold in the future, we need to plan for it today. To do this, we need to *intentionally* plan to change our habit of gaining instant gratification of a temporary pleasure to enjoying something more fulfilling. How can we change our habits to delight ourselves in the Lord in our daily lives so that our desires will lead to godly fulfillment in the future?

In Hebrew, the word for delight is *anag.* It means "to be soft, delicate, and dainty." [32] How do we find delight in God by being *soft and delicate?*

- We need to allow God to break down our preconceived beliefs that are preventing us from knowing Him intimately.
- Let's ask God to give us a soft heart.
- We need to be willing to allow God to change things in our lives that are not good for us.

- We need to intentionally learn about the wonderful character-istics of God so that we'll realize that He only wants good things for our lives.
- We need to stop being afraid of God and running away from Him, instead letting Him shower us with His amazing love.
- We need to deliberately slow down and take time to learn what the word "delight" means in our relationship with God.
- We need to know how to find Him so that we can learn to delight in Him.

Delights God Wants to Give Us

I believe there is nothing God wants to do more than to shower us with His love. He longs for us to delight in Him, so that we can be fulfilled. Just like a father who has his arms open wide and ready for his children to run into them, I believe God is just waiting for us to enter His presence. I believe God wants to share delightful, intimate experiences with us, and our greatest enjoyments are right at our fingertips. He tells us: "You will find me when you seek me, if you look for me in earnest" (Jer. 29:13 TLB).

There is one small word hidden in that sentence that will change every-thing about having the power to choose our desires. That word is *if*. God always gives us a choice about everything in our lives: He even lets us choose our desires. The more we seek God and get to know Him and all the won-derful things He wants for our lives, the more our desires will become godly.

Let's be honest with each other: no one can *seek* better than women. We will turn a city upside-down searching for things we want, such as a new pair of shoes or earrings to match a new outfit. Imagine what our lives would look like if we put that same kind of time and energy into earnestly *seeking* God and learning about His loving characteristics. What would our desires begin to look like if we understood that the essence of God is love and that He wants to fill our lives with His love and fulfill us with His good desires?

We can begin to delight in Him when we:

- Seek Him with all of our heart by reading the Bible, praying, doing a Bible study with a friend, and memorizing verses.

- See life through the eyes of little children. Children look at everything with awe and amazement. They jump in the mud puddles, smell flowers, sit and play, or read for hours. Children do not know how to hurry. Let's ask ourselves, "How did we get to be such smart adults that we have lost the wonderful simplicity of childhood?"
- Choose to be grateful instead of grumble.
- Realize that we are friends of God. Where else can we find a friend who loves us unconditionally, overlooks our faults, forgives us when we mess up, and prepares a place for us after we die?
- Notice miracles God places in our lives. They are there all around us: we just need to look for them.
- See everything that happens as gifts from God—whether good or bad, difficult or easy. These are all gifts meant to conform us more into the character of Christ and His love.
- Anticipate hearing from God. Slow down and listen!
- Surround ourselves with other people who also are on the journey to know God better.
- Recognize God in the beauty of nature.
- Become aware of His amazing love for us.

I have found that when I begin to earnestly seek God, I will find Him in ways, places, and voices I never would have imagined. The more I seek Him, the more I find Him. The more I love Him, the more I delight in my relationship with Him. The more I know myself, the more I am fulfilled.

When we delight ourselves in God daily (present), He will fulfill the desires of our hearts (future). As we begin to experience His kindness and gentleness, our only desire will be to walk in holiness.

We will want to become more like Him every day, bringing beauty to the world by reflecting His glory. Our desires will change from being ego-driven to God-driven. We will then be empowered by the loving promptings of the Holy Spirit rather than the wild, insatiable urges of the flesh.

Our Impulses Reveal Our Desires

How do we even begin to distinguish between our good desires and ego-driven desires? Our impulses will always reveal our feelings. Is God first in our lives? If we think He is but we're not sure, let's ask ourselves a few questions:

- What thoughts consume my mind?
- What is the first thing on my agenda when I get up in the morning?
- How much is God a part of my conversations with friends and family?
- When I make goals and plans, do they include God?
- If I had a day to do whatever I wanted, what would that be like?

It's easy for us to say, "God, you are the most important thing in my life." But if He's not, our actions will give that away.

Suppose I said to my daughter, "Honey, let's spend the day together doing things that you and I love to do." If I proceeded to do the laundry, water the plants, answer e-mails, talk on the phone, or read a book, the day would soon be over. I would not have done anything I said I would do. Obviously, doing all those things was more important to me than spending time with my daughter. The truth is that we will always have the money or make the time for those things that are most important to us. Even if we declare otherwise, our impulses will always give us away.

When we intentionally seek to delight ourselves in God, our natural impulse will more and more be to make Him the most important part of our agenda, goals, and dreams for the future. We will become godlier, responding to people around us with kindness and compassion and being content with what we have. We will be able to get beyond our own self-consumed world to see the pain and hunger in the desperate eyes of the needy orphans in Africa or the homeless man sleeping in the streets. Our hearts will become softer, and we'll find time to sit with someone who is lonely or sad. Instead of always being on a pursuit to satisfy our own egos, our joy in life will be to pour blessings out onto the rest of the world. Our desires will line up with God's desires, which is to love, forgive, and have compassion on the world around us. We will desire to care for others instead of focusing only on ourselves. When our will lines up with the will of God His desires will eventually become our desires.

In John Piper's book, *When I Don't Desire God*, he states, "But when you saturate your mind with the Christ-exalting Word of God and turn it into prayer, your desires and your prayers become spiritual." [33]

If we allow ourselves to be led by the Holy Spirit, listen to His voice, and obey His Word, we will begin to acquire good or godly desires. When we fill ourselves with God, His life-giving words from the Bible, and His love, we will be fulfilled. It will be just like we are coming off a long and miserable diet to finally be able to enjoy a fabulous meal, then pushing the chair back and saying, *"I'm finally full!"* We won't be hungry and tempted to want more.

Piper poses the question: "What is temptation? It is always, in one way or another, the deception that something is more to be desired than God and his ways. Therefore, the prayer for deliverance is that we would not fall for that deception but always taste and know that God and his ways are to be desired above all others." [34]

The apostle Paul knew the only thing that would fill us is God. Before he became a follower of Christ, he had everything. He had the right name and place in society, education, prestige, power, and a huge circle of influential friends. He gave all of these perks up after he had a life-changing encounter with God. God's desires became his desires, and he lived out the rest of his life pleading with people to follow God. He knew from experience that *nothing* in this life fulfills us like God's love. This is what he longs for you and me to experience:

"And I pray that Christ will be more and more at home in your hearts, living within you as you trust in Him. May your roots go down deep into the soil of God's marvelous love; and may you be able to feel and understand, as all God's children should, how long, how wide, how deep, and how high his love really is; and to experience this love for yourselves, though it is so great that you will never see the end of it or fully know or understand it. And so at last you will be *filled up* with God himself" (Eph. 3:17 TLB).

Wouldn't it be wonderful to live each day with a heart that is so full it has the capacity to pour out love to bless people around us, rather than one that is always trying to fill itself with material things? Wouldn't it be awesome to have a heart that is not always craving to satisfy its own selfish desires, but one that is content and at peace with the world around it?

UNLEASHING THE BEAUTY OF GODLY DESIRES

It breaks my heart when I see a physically beautiful, ego-driven, competitive, woman—one who thinks life is all about *Me, Myself and I.* The beauty of her face and body diminishes once the selfish motives of her ego are revealed. What kind of woman are you? If you are not sure, just look behind you. Are you walking away from bruised people and a trail of destruction, or do you leave people smiling and wanting to spend more time with you?

I find in my own life that I am learning to measure the fulfillment of my desires (in the present) against the consequences it brings (in the future). Here are some examples of how we can process this in our minds:

- The new promotion sounds wonderful, but how much will it take you away from your family and consume your mind?
- A divorce may seem like the answer, but what will it do to the rest of the family, the grandchildren, and your circle of friends? What will the consequences of this be fifty years down the road?
- Surfing the Internet looking for pornographic pictures may seem like fun and gives you a good feeling for a while, but what will it do to your children and your career when your secret is revealed?
- Craving for food tastes and feels so good. What will you do, though, with the extra pounds that get packed on so quickly?
- On any purchase that you make, balance the immediate desire with the consequences. Can you afford it? If you buy it, will you be short-changing your family in other ways?

- Those drugs are making you feel better, but are you getting addicted?
- Those outbursts of anger make you feel better for a while, but what is it doing to your children and friends?

True beauty comes when we realize that when our impulse longings finally become godly, they will not lead us into traps that cause us to manipulate others, experience angst, and toss and turn on sleepless nights. When our desires are pure, we will not have to guard any secrets and play mind games. Our conscience is always clear, so we can look everyone in the eyes with confidence.

Discovering our godly desires will be a lifelong journey for each one of us. It is never too late to start. If you are older and feel that you have wasted years on useless stuff and empty pursuits, don't despair. God is kind and gentle and will take each one of us where we are today and individually shape our souls for a glorious tomorrow. Godly beauty will be released in our lives when we begin to pour love out on others rather than giving in to all of our selfish desires. How do we do this in a practical way?

Beauty is unleashed more when:

- We are honest with ourselves and acknowledge the fact that our happiness and security are really our highest goals. Yes, we want to be godly and live a life of holiness, but it seems too hard and unachievable for us.
- We confess our failures and weaknesses in our day-to-day struggles with desires for "stuff" to make us feel better.
- We realize that God placed passions and desires in our hearts, and we are meant to feel them, enjoy them, and not feel guilty about them.
- We begin to delight in God and discover how He has uniquely designed us to live our lives; then. we will begin to find significance in the events of daily life.
- We realize that the more time we spend in the presence of God and *experience* His love for us, the more our desires will line up with His desires.

- We understand that there will be times we just won't feel like seeking God. During those times, we need to ask God to deal with our emptiness, our dryness, and our unbelief.
- We deliberately remind ourselves that everything—I do mean *everything*—we own in this life will be left behind someday.
- We surround ourselves *and connect* with godly women we admire. We need to let them help us and hold us accountable to our actions so that we can develop godly habits.
- We get involved in a Bible study that will require digging into the Word of God to get to know Him better.
- We realize that delighting in God comes first, and godly desires will follow. We must learn to live our lives realizing that instant gratification is not fulfilling.
- We find out what gives us this feeling of emptiness, by asking God to reveal any sins, hurts, disappointments or anger and then letting Him help us deal with it.
- We go through a healing process to get rid of our anger toward God. It is hard to delight in someone who we're angry with.
- We acknowledge that no created person or thing will ever completely fill us for any extended period of time.
- We go for a walk and ask God to give us a special surprise today.

There is no greater joy than joining with other women to seek God through a Bible study. By doing this, you will learn about our amazing God, build friendships, and find accountability partners to help you on this journey to pursue godly desires. You will have someone to laugh with when you mess up. There will be a shoulder to cry on when you despair, and there will be someone to pray with you when you feel like giving up.

Stop and ask God to Unleash Your Beauty

Begin by asking: God, what is a secret longing I have right now that has the potential to cause me heartache in the future?

S—Scripture: "Moreover, because of what Christ has done we have become gifts to God that he delights in" (Eph. 1:11 TLB).

T—Thanksgiving: Thank You for passions and desires that You have given me. Thank You that You consider me a gift to You. I praise You for feelings I have when I look at things that delight me.

O—Observation: I need to discern between good desires that will bring me fulfillment and ego-driven desires that will ultimately leave me feeling empty.

P—Prayer: God, I am in awe of the words in Ephesians 1:11, which says, "I am a gift that you delight in." My mind simply cannot comprehend that. I pray that You will help me to not only understand it, but to also begin living my life believing it with all my heart. To know that I am a treasure to You makes me want to spend time getting to know You better.

Thank You, God for giving me desires. I pray with all my heart that my desires would line up with Yours because then I know that joy and peace will be my greatest gifts. Thank You for helping me on this journey. As I begin to know you and *experience* you You more, I will know myself better. Search my heart and show me all those things in my life that are fleshly, ego-driven desires that will leave me feeling empty over and over again. God, fill me with Your Holy Spirit. Fill me with Your love and godly desires. Amen.

UNLEASHING THE BEAUTY OF MY NAME
Becoming Visible

One of the greatest diseases is to be nobody to anybody.

—MOTHER TERESA OF CALCUTTA

WALKED THROUGH the empty rooms, looking at framed photos of our family and choking back the pain of all the memories. It was suppertime on New Year's Day in 1995, and my family should have been around me, laughing and joking as we had always done. Instead, my daughter Michelle and I were the only ones left in our empty home that appeared to echo the hollow silence. My lonely thoughts were more oppressive than the dark evening sky closing in on us.

Only twenty-four short days ago, my husband had walked out of the house and said "Honey, I'll see you after the game." He was going off to play another game of basketball, the sport he had been passionate about his entire life. That night, he died on the court from a massive heart attack.

My husband Dick and I had overcome many obstacles in our twenty-eight year marriage. In our last few years together, we had finally reached a place where we communicated well enough to become best friends and teammates. It was a time that whenever I looked at him I thought to myself, *Life just doesn't get any better than this.*

During this time, everything else was going well in my life. I had a great career, my children loved me, we had many friends, and most important, I felt very close to God. I truly believed that all my significance and value came from knowing that I was loved by my heavenly Father; that He had a purpose in life for me and that when I died, I would go to a beautiful place called heaven. I was one of those bubbly, happy women bouncing through life day after day with a joyful energy that just would not quit. If anyone had asked me in those days where my personal identity came from, I would have smiled and confidently replied, "From God."

After a painful Christmas week, my daughter and I were beginning the New Year alone. We bundled up and ventured out into the cold night. I hoped my familiar neighborhood, along with the brisk night air, would awaken my senses and give me a feeling of reality and belonging. We walked side by side in silence, bracing ourselves against the biting wind. We had nothing to say: too many tears had already been shed, and we were both preoccupied with our own thoughts and memories.

As we walked along, I was drawn to the lights in our neighbors' homes that showed people moving around. I watched children playing and laughing, husbands and wives serving food, and friends mingling and chatting. "*That's what my family should be doing right now,*" I thought. I stopped dead in my tracks as I felt the empty longing and loneliness clutch my mind. All of a sudden, it felt as if time had stopped, and all the street noise was suspended in the air. I knew that I was still alive because I could hear my own breathing, but it felt as if someone had taken a big eraser and wiped away my future with all its hopes and dreams. Grief made my past a fog and my future undecipherable. In the present, I felt nothingness—faceless and nameless, as though I was invisible.

I had never experienced such crushing emptiness and loneliness. How could I feel this way when I had been so sure of who I was? I was the confident, joyful Heidi, not this person without an identity who felt as though the whole world was passing her by. Even though my daughter was standing right beside me, I felt bitterly alone.

When We Wish We Could Be Invisible

I smile when I remember as a small child pretending to be invisible. I recall sneaking into my grandma's kitchen, grabbing a piece of candy out of the bowl, and running out as fast as I could. I always hoped she had not seen me, but, of course, she had. As I got older, my wish to be invisible was even greater as my misdeeds increased:

- In grade seven, I stood around an old garage for hours with my friends for an entire year, smoking to my heart's content. At the end of that first year in high school, I looked around this garage and saw stacks of brown paper bags and cigarette butts. Throughout that entire year, my friends and I kept hoping and praying no one would see us.
- When I was fourteen, I took my dad's car for a little ride. My heart was pounding as I drove down the highway all by myself, hoping that no one would recognize me.
- Later on in my teens, I frequently sneaked back into our home past curfew thinking, *perhaps this time Dad won't see me.* He always did.
- Then, when I was married and had my own children, there were times when I wished I was invisible:
- Our family was fighting in the car on the way to church. This is not the way good Christian families act. I hoped nobody would see us.
- I was hiding fears and tears from my children.

We have all done things in our lives that made us wish we were invisible. We did not want anyone to see the bad thing that we had just done.

Being treated as invisible

It's one thing to want to be invisible, but it is totally another thing to be treated as if we were invisible. One of our greatest longings in life is to be a *somebody.* In his book, *Dare to Dream...Then Do It,* John Maxwell lists "Five Things I Know about People." The first item is, "Everybody wants to be a somebody." [35]

Throughout our whole lives, we will either consciously or subconsciously provoke others around us in order to get noticed. We need to know that we have significance—that we are *somebody.* We desperately need to know that we have worth. When people treat us as though we have no value, we feel as though we are a *nobody;* invisible. These feelings of worthlessness can result from either little day-to-day events or traumatic, defining events. You feel like a nobody when:

- You are being given an award at your school and your parents are too busy to come.
- You go to a school dance, but no one dances with you.
- You ask your husband to help around the house, but he continues watching TV.
- Someone else gets the raise when you *know* it is your turn.
- You have a great voice, but the choir director always asks someone else to sing.
- Friends are gathered in a tight circle, making you stand by yourself.
- Your name is not called out because it was not on the list. You are overlooked.

We really don't understand how much we depend upon the people in our lives and world around us to give us our identity and significance. We live out our identity through our accomplishments, hard work, and abilities. Until we experience a traumatic event or reach a crisis point in our lives, we never have to question who we are, where our identity comes from, or how our true self has been formed. I did not realize how much of my identity had been defined by my marriage to a successful husband, my role as a mother to two amazing children, my career, and my service to our local church.

WHO AM I?

On that brisk January night walking with Michelle, I felt lost and alone. As I stood looking up into the dark sky with its millions of stars, I felt as though the night had swallowed me up. My heart screamed for someone to see me—to notice my pain. The world moved all around me. Cars kept driving; people were walking and talking, dogs barking, and sirens screaming. For me, everything had stopped, and I stood still. I could not bear to feel so insignificant and *invisible*. Who was I right then? I had no idea.

I thought, *God, You're going to have to help me here. I've never felt this way before. You told me that You would never leave me or forsake me, and I need You right now.*

As I kept walking, comforting phrases and promises began to whisper through my mind— words here and there, enough to form Bible verses. My heavenly Father was reminding me of some things He had said to His children thousands of years ago. God knew we would all feel this way someday, so He gave us distinct reminders:

> "Lift your eyes and look to the heavens: Who created all these? He who brings out the starry host one by one, *and calls them each by their name.* Because of his great power and mighty strength, not one of them is missing" (Isaiah 40:26 NIV).

If God could call each of these millions of stars by its name, certainly He would know mine. He reminded me that I was Heidi: that He could see me, that He knew me, and that I was indeed a somebody. To Him, I was visible.

Until that calamity entered my life, I always assumed my identity came from knowing I was a child of God. When my whole life was turned upside-down, I realized I had never really been challenged on that issue before.

When everything is stripped away from us, we discover a lot of things, including questioning who we really are and what our purpose is in this life. As much as I hated to admit it, I was going full speed ahead on my own strength, confidence, and accomplishments and being the person the world expected me to be.

Never before had I been placed in such a vulnerable state. It was important for me to know that someone not only knew I existed, but also knew my name. Knowing that simple fact was enough to see me through the darkness of that New Year's night. I realized there is great empowerment from someone calling us by our name because it gives us a face and an identity.

The World's View on Names

Our self-worth changes from day to day when we depend on people around us to place value on our names. One minute we can be a hero, the next minute we can be dirt: it all depends on the situation. We love to be the hero and hear our names in front of these compliments:

- Hey, great job!
- Wow, are you ever creative!
- You have great kids.
- Did you really sew that outfit all by yourself?
- I love the way you decorate your home.
- You sure know how to teach a Bible study class.
- You are so good at your job.
- Congratulations on receiving your Ph.D.!

When these statements are exclaimed after our name, we feel a sense of accomplishment and pride. They shape us and give us our identity as a great mother, an excellent teacher, or an inspiring leader in our work-place.

It's different, however, when we hear our names in front of one of these lines:

- That's not the way we do it around here.
- You failed this course.
- Weren't you paying attention?
- You let too much pride get in the way.
- I'm so disappointed in you.

- You did not make the cut.
- The divorce papers are in the mail.
- You are stupid.
- Can't you do anything right?

Now we feel rejected, insignificant, and worthless—a *nobody*. It is horrible to feel that way. We will do almost anything for people to reassure ourselves that they value us—that our name means something positive to them.

We are so desperate to hear our names or see them in print that many of us will steal or lie just to see them there. We regularly read stories about sports heroes who take drugs to win an athletic event, marathon runners who take short cuts to be the first over the finish line, singers who lip-sync to other people's music, and. people who want to become famous by stealing secret formulas for cosmetics, drugs, or soft drinks. We thrill at being a *somebody*—to hear our names called out or see them in a newspaper or magazine. The desire for recognition is such a powerful urge within us.

God's View on My Name

We unleash our true beauty when we begin to comprehend how God views us. We love to hear the sound of our names. When they are mixed with a tone of intimacy and the rhythmic swing of laughter, our faces respond with instant smiles.

Our hearts quicken when we hear our names over the chatter and hum in a crowded room. Quickly, we turn our head and strain our ears to find out what is being said about us. We hope they are talking about something wonderful we said or did. When we hear someone calling our name and beckoning to us and hear the whispered, "*I have something to tell you,*" we feel chosen and special. There is a deep longing inside all of us for affirmation of our existence and the recognition of some extraordinary accomplishment.

What a thrill it is to run into an old friend or acquaintance who looks at us with fond remembrance, squeals with delight, and calls us by our name. It makes us feel like there is something worthwhile or unique about us that caused them to commit our names to their memory.

Whenever I teach a Bible study class or am involved in a mentoring situation, I always ask the women sitting in front of me to tell me not only their names, but who they are. I tell them: "I want you to tell me who you are. No, I don't mean what you do, your religion, what your abilities are, what you look like, or your role in society; I want to know who you are." They always look at me with a blank stare because they don't understand what I have just asked them. I help them to define themselves by the beautiful characteristics and qualities that God has placed in them. Some women find this an uncomfortable exercise. Until this point in their lives, they have functioned by living out their identity through the world's view, which always falls short of the beauty that God has placed within them. Many women, when they hear their name, feel unlovable, unintelligent, and worthless. This is the exact opposite of how God sees us when He hears our name.

THE WORD *name* in Hebrew is shem, meaning "through the idea of definite and conspicuous position. As a mark or memorial of individuality by implying honor, authority, character (italics mine)."[36] God is the only one who can give us that "definite and conspicuous position" in this life. After all, He is the one who created us. The psalmist David learned that God was His marvelous creator:

> "For you created my inmost being; you knit me together in my mother's womb. I praise you because I am fearfully and wonderfully made; your works are wonderful. I know that full well. My frame was not hidden from you when I was made in the secret place. When I was woven together in the depths of the earth, your eyes saw my unformed body. All the days ordained for me were written in your book before one of them came to be" (Psalm 139:13-16 NIV).

God knows when we will be born and when we will die. He knows how we are going to live out each day of our lives. Not only does God know the name of each of his stars, He knows my name, your name, and every little thing about you and me:

> "Can a mother forget her little child and not have love for her own son? Yet even if that should be, I will not forget you. See, I have tattooed *your name upon my palm* and ever before me is a picture of Jerusalem's walls in ruins" (Isaiah 49:15, 16 TLB).

God cannot forget about you and me, because He sent His Son to die for us. When the nails were pounded into Jesus' hands, those nail holes were for you and me. *They have our names on them:*

> "Long before he laid down earth's foundations, he had us in mind, had settled on us *as the focus of his love,* to be made whole and holy by his love. Long, long ago he decided to adopt us into his family through Jesus Christ (What pleasure he took in planning this!). He wanted us to enter into the celebration of his lavish gift-giving by the hand of his beloved son" (Ephesians 1:3-5 MSG).

You and I are the focus of God's love. Even before we were born, God knew that we would be His children and part of His loving family. Can we even imagine what it is like to be the *focus of someone's love?* That person watches our every move, cheers us on, wants to lavish us with gifts, and celebrate who we are, not what we *do.*

God's view of us is the same as when He first laid the foundations of the earth: chosen, blessed, beautiful and loved with a lavish love. That's the kind of identity I need: to know I am secure and safe in Him every single day, no matter what crisis comes along in my life.

UNLEASHING THE BEAUTY OF OUR NAMES

Every time we hear our names, our heads turn. Just to hear our names makes us feel like we have done or said something important. We also love it when someone has given us a nickname or term of endearment that sends a unique and special message.

I am absolutely crazy about all my grandchildren. I have endearing names for all of them, but the one that passes my lips the most is "*my precious.*" Every time I spoke to our grandson Matthew after he was born, I either started or ended the sentence with *my precious boy.* When he was learning to talk, one of the first sentences that crossed his baby lips was "I'm Nana's precious boy." He would not allow anyone else, including his mommy or daddy, to call him "precious." Even at that young age, he was identifying himself by the name I had been calling him from the day he was born. He knew that his Nana thought he was *precious.*

As I am writing this, Matthew is six. One day, I was sitting beside him in the car on the way to a wedding rehearsal. He leaned over, stroked my arm, and said, "You're *my precious* Nana." I absolutely melted. From the time we are born until the day we die, we need to know that we are someone's *precious.*

Can you imagine what it is like to be in the spotlight of someone's love and attention? To envision that every time they look at you, they are so overcome with passionate love that they call you "precious"?

I know that Someone. I found Him in the pages of the greatest love story ever told. The God who created our glorious heaven and earth tells me: "Fear not, for I have redeemed you; I have summoned you *by name; you are mine*" (Isaiah 43:1b NIV). *You are chosen and are being called by your name.*

When someone calls us by our name, beckons us to come over, and says to us, "*You are mine,*" we know we belong. Oh, how we need to belong to someone or something. We can belong to all kinds of families, churches, and organizations, but there is nothing that gives us more value than knowing we belong to God's family—that we are *precious.*

> "God will never walk away from his people, and never desert his *precious* people" (Ps. 94:12 MSG).

> "Others died that you might live; I traded their lives for yours because you are *precious* to me and honored, and I love you" (Isa. 43:4 TLB).

> "A good name is better than fine perfume" (Eccl. 7:1 NIV).

God is always beckoning us to come closer to Him so that we can tilt our ear and hear Him whisper our name. *He has something special that He wants to tell us.* Listen to His words of extravagant love and truth about how precious you are to Him. Let them penetrate your heart and remind you that you are more magnificent than fine linen or perfume.

We further unleash beauty in ourselves when we do the following:

- Receive all the world's applause and accolades with joy but not allow them to define who we are.
- Identify the lie that that we have to accomplish something to have a name.
- Search for God's truth about who we really are.
- Begin to identify ourselves as *God's precious ones.*
- Imagine what it feels like to know that we are "the focus of God's love."
- Try to define where we gather our identity from, being honest with ourselves, and lining the sources up against the truth of God's Word.
- Remind ourselves that if God knows the name of every star that He created, surely He knows our names.
- See God as an artist who created us. Just as an artist never forgets the name of his paintings, God, the artist who created You, cannot forget our names.
- We recognize that we really are beautiful.

Stop and ask God to Unleash Your Beauty

Begin by asking: God, show me what forms my identity.

S—Scripture: "The Lord your God is with you, he is mighty to save. He will take great delight in you, he will quiet you with his love, he will rejoice over you with singing" (Zeph. 3:17 NIV).

T—Thanksgiving: Thank You, God that You are always with me, that You have your eye on me and that You know my name. Thank You that You chose me, that I am the focus of Your love and that You rejoice over me. Thank You that my identity comes from the way You created me, not from my accomplishments or the world's applause.

O—Observation: Whenever I hear my name, I shall try to remember to filter it through God's powerful truth. I need to see myself as God's magnificent creation, rather than identify myself by the labels that the world has given me. Each time I hear the word *precious* I will remind myself that I am "God's precious child."

P—Prayer: My mind can hardly comprehend that You chose me before the foundations of the earth were formed and that You call me by my name. I need for You to know my name, God. I need to know that I am significant and that I have value. Help me to find my value through You as I begin to experience You more and more every day. Teach me to let go of the world's view of who I am and help me to stop looking for my value through accomplishments and accolades. Help me to focus instead on Your view of who You created me to be. Thank You that I am Your magnificent creation. Thank You that I have an identity in You and that I am *your precious one.* Amen.

7

UNLEASHING THE BEAUTY OF ADVENTURE
Could Be Trouble

Beauty...is the shadow of God on the Universe.
—Gabriela Mistral, Desolacion

HERE IS A HIDDEN JEWEL in the state of Montana: the magnificent Flathead Valley tucked away between Whitefish, Montana, and the Glacier National Park. In 1981, our family fell in love with the towering majestic Rocky Mountains, the roaring rivers, and blankets of velvety green valleys. Each year as we arrive for our vacation, my heart begins to pound as we come closer and closer to the mountains. Our eyes feast on the explosion of colors that are created by the crimson Indian paintbrushes, pink and white lady slippers, white daisies and the brilliant yellow buttercups. I am captivated by the rustic and peaceful countryside, which is like entering into another world. It is the secret, coveted escape from our cell phones, alarm clocks, and rigid routines.

One of our favorite activities is whitewater rafting on the Flathead River in June while the water level is still high from the snow run-off. On the morning of our adventure, we wake up with excitement and nervous chatter. As we drive down the highway that leads to our expedition, our vehicle is filled with the aroma of freshly brewed coffee. We cling to this warm, delicious comfort as long as we can.

Soon after we arrive at the rafting company, we squeeze into our wetsuits and unsightly water shoes. As we check out each other's attire and awkwardly grin at ourselves, we pile into the tour bus for the bumpy ride to the edge of the riverbank. I can see the gleam of adventure in the guides' eyes as they unload the rafts with a contagious energy as they shout familiar instructions to each other in preparation for the expedition. Then, we are guided to our raft and introduced to our other companions who will help us paddle and keep us afloat.

We are all very attentive when it is our turn to listen as the guides explain how to sit, paddle, and hang on during the rough spots. They take great care and extra time to explain that we will encounter many dangerous eddies.

The first time we went rafting, I had never heard of an eddy, so I listened intently as they explained what it is. I discovered that it is a current of water at variance with the main current of water that is so powerful it has the ability to take a raft and suck it into its vortex. "Beware," they warned us, "of a sucking, swirling mass of water that churns like a rotary beater." Now they had my attention, and I listened even more carefully as they gave instructions on how to paddle around them, and what to do in the event the raft overturned. Then they gave us the ratings of the rapids and their frightening names. An eddy which is rated zero means calm water; but when you enter rapids rated six, you'd better make sure your life insurance policy is up to date! We were going rafting into fours and fives. Just hearing the numbers made my heart pound.

Finally, we are ready to push the rafts into the river and start paddling. The sun is shining, the birds are chirping, and the mouth of the river is calm. I let the rays of the sun soak into my face as I paddle leisurely and chatter lightheartedly with our new companions. *There is nothing to this; it couldn't be easier,* I think to myself.

Soon, I can hear the roar of the rapids up ahead. We all crane our necks to the left and right, looking for the rocks jutting out of the river.

We have been warned about them, and they do indeed look dark and dangerous. Our guide tells us that the first rapid we will encounter is called "*Could be Trouble.*" I make sure my feet are tucked tightly underneath the ropes as we all begin to paddle furiously to guide the raft through the boiling water and away from the swirling eddies. With each desperate push on my oar, I am breathing and praying, "*Oh, God help us, help us, help us.*" I am terrified of the possibility of the raft overturning and one of us getting sucked into the dangerous eddies. Within seconds, we have made it through this first dangerous section of the river, and I can tell by the relief on all our faces that I was not the only one who had experienced fear. We look at each other and laugh nervously as we see our wet hair plastered against our faces. Our lips are blue, but we are exhilarated because we realize that we are *really* on an adventure. With newfound confidence and energy, we head into the next rapid.

I look further downstream, and my heart palpitates as I see jagged, monster-sized rocks jutting out of the river. The black, angry water is swirling and boiling, and the roar is deafening. The guide yells at us to paddle as hard as we can. "We are heading into the next rapid called "*Bone Crusher,*" our guide screams. "This is the most dangerous of all rapids, and the eddies are huge. Stay away from them. Paddle as hard as you can!" From the tone of his voice, we know this one is life-threatening. If the raft overturned here, we would be in big trouble.

We paddle furiously and struggle to stay away from the dark whirlpools of water just tempting and taunting us to fall into their trap. With every stroke of my oar and every breath, I exhale a prayer. We are all getting drenched in this ice-cold water, but we don't care. This is the peak of our great adventure!

We make it through the "Bone Crusher" rapid, and then "Jaws," and then "Screaming Right Hand." There is no time to catch our breath and relax. Finally, we see calmer waters up ahead. Now, we can feel the sun's rays hitting our ice-cold bodies and warming our hands. With shouts of victory, bursts of giggles, and high-fives all around, we pull onto the riverbanks. We made it! What an adventure! None of us would have missed it for the world.

COMFORT ZONE

Some of you who are reading this live for adventure. You can't wait for your next climbing expedition, skydiving experience, or kayaking trip down the Georgia Strait. But for the rest of us, we have found that we can't be living on the edge of an exciting activity all the time because it would eventually leave us emotionally and physically drained.

But there is something stunningly attractive about a woman who is willing to leave her normal comfort zone to step into new and unchartered territory. It may involve an element of risk in which she faces the possibility of failure and mistakes due to her inexperience, but she is not afraid to admit when she has never tried something before. Willing to laugh at her mistakes, she is also not afraid to look like a drowned rat with mascara running down her face and hair plastered against her head. This kind of a woman exudes a vibrant, contagious energy and attracts other people into her circle. She is fun to be around, and her laughter flows easily and without self-consciousness.

Let's face it: we all want our basic needs taken care of. We want food; a warm, soft bed; a hot shower in the morning; and a car sitting in our garage filled with gas. But some people orchestrate their lives so that they can always live in their own comfort zone. They do this either out of *fear* or *selfishness,* but the end result is always *comfort.*

We are also creatures of habit because habits bring us comfort. We love to sit in our normal church pews, visit with the same friends, wear the same clothes, dine at our usual favorite restaurants, follow the same routine, and travel the same route to work each morning. If we do our laundry on Monday and grocery shopping on Thursday, it all feels nice and safe because we know what to expect. We want to know our boundaries and keep everything within our safe, little box so that we will not make any mistakes. Our everyday habits are a security blanket that keeps us from worrying about failing or looking stupid.

Staying in our comfort zone may make us feel *comfortable,* but life can also become very predictable and boring. If we are never challenged with something new, we will become uninteresting. Some husbands and wives look at each other after their children leave home and wonder why they now have nothing to talk about. Their life together had probably been very conventional, with nothing to stimulate or challenge them individually. All of their energies, money, and time were probably spent on the children, and they just didn't take the time to expand their vision regarding their own talents and desires.

What is there to talk about unless we have read a new book, tried a new exercise, cooked an exotic recipe, used a different hairdresser, or taken an unusual vacation? We can only talk about the weather and "*what did you do today?*" for so long. Predictability can feel like someone has left you all alone in a room, and the walls are closing in. We may be living in our comfort zone, but we really are not *living at all.*

When we are not challenged, we don't grow, and we become humdrum and boring. We know how we will act and react, so we can predict how other people will react to us as well. We'll never experience the exhilaration of accomplishing something new or a victory over something that seemed impossible. I know someone very dear to me who heard these words: "*Why would you even want to try that? You'll look ridiculous when you fail.*" Those words crush my soul, yet I know that many of you have heard the same words in a different context.

As part of the unleashing of the beauty of our soul, we need to make time and give ourselves permission to live life as a great adventure. I agree with the words of David Foster:

"Today is God's gift to you. What you do with it is your gift to God and to the world around you. This very moment, as you read these words, as your heart beats, and as you contemplate why you live at this moment in history, don't forget to enjoy your own private miracle of life. Don't allow adversity to bankrupt your today by paying interest on the regrets of yesterday and borrowing in advance against the troubles of tomorrow. Plan on purpose to live fully and well now."[38]

That is what Jesus died for. He tells us: "The thief's purpose is to steal, kill and destroy. My purpose is to give life in all its fullness" (John 10:10 TLB).

When we dare to be women of adventure and risk living life in all of its fullness, we need to be aware that there will be eddies along the journey. An eddy in our daily sojourn can be described as *trouble that we encounter.* Some trouble that comes along can also leave us cold, with our hearts pounding, and praying with every breath. Just like the rapids that our guide warned us about called *"Could be Trouble,"* Jesus warns us about some trouble coming our way:

"In this world you will have trouble" (John 16:33b NIV).

What Kind of Trouble Is There?

This verse does not say *could* have; it says *will* have trouble. Whenever I came up with an outrageous idea at work or suggested something new and unusual, I had a boss who would say, *"Heidi, don't go looking for trouble; trouble has a way of finding us all on its own."*

His point was that trouble is a part of life, and it will happen whether we tempt it or not. I believe there are two categories of trouble in our life:

1. Trouble that you and I create.
When we are deliberately disobedient to God, we have to realize that there will always be consequences. That is the spiritual law of sowing and reaping. It is not necessarily God's punishment upon us; it is merely the consequences of our actions. For every action, there is a reaction. It is both a physical and spiritual law.

When we deliberately hurt people, we will end up being hurt. When we betray a trust or lie, it will destroy relationships. If we steal or commit a murder, we will probably go to jail. If we have an affair outside of our marriage; it will likely end up in divorce. If we are emotionally distant from our children when they are little, they probably won't desire to have much to do with us when they get older. Causing trouble at work, lying, cheating, or stealing are some destructive actions that will only bring pain into our lives.

We also run into trouble when we are deceitful or manipulate people and situations to bring about our vision of life as we think it should be. Eventually, this will backfire on us, and we'll wonder where the trouble came from. We created it.

When we drop a rock into a clear pool of water, we see the ripple effects of that rock for a long time. It is the same way with decisions that *you* and I make. If they involve bad choices, the effects will be felt for some time afterwards.

Mankind has been making bad choices since the beginning of creation. Deliberate disobedience started in the Garden of Eden, and we are still reaping the consequences of that act, which is called sin.

Stories of trouble caused by bad choices

A. Eve deliberately disobeyed God and ate from the tree of life. God warned her, but because of her bad choice, we are still reaping the consequences of her sin (Gen.3).

- CAUTION: *Deliberate disobedience ends up hurting a lot of people.*

B. Sarah, the wife of Abraham, couldn't wait for God to fulfill His promise to them. God had promised them a son, but dear Sarah was getting old and past her child-bearing years. She decided to help God out by taking matters into her own hands. She told Abraham to sleep with her maidservant Hagar so that they could have the son God had promised. When tension brews because of this poor decision, Sarah blames Abraham for all their trouble (Gen. 20-21).

- CAUTION: *Helping God run this world will always cause trouble.*

C. Rebekah had two sons, Esau the eldest, and Jacob, her darling favorite. She set up an elaborate scheme to ensure that the family blessing went to her special Jacob instead of the rightful heir, Esau. Even though her manipulation and deceit succeeded, Jacob was forced to run for his life (Gen. 27).

- CAUTION: *Playing favorites with our children will only cause trouble and heartache.*

D. Miriam became increasingly jealous of her brother Moses' position and influence. Since she could not find any fault with the way Moses was leading the Israelites through the desert, she started attacking his Cushite wife. God was angry at her for this and struck her with leprosy (Num.12).

- CAUTION: Pride and jealousy will always cause pain and trouble.

The Bible is full of stories of people who ran into trouble. Likewise, every time we are blatantly disobedient to God, sooner or later trouble will stare us right in the face, and we will wonder how it got there.

2. Trouble as part of life

Jesus said, "There *will* be trouble" in this world. Just as there were rocks jutting out of the water and eddies trying to suck us into their orbit during our whitewater rafting trip, the journey of life has its own mysterious and challenging eddies which threaten us:

- You are in the doctor's office and hear the word "cancer." You can't believe that they are actually talking about you.
- You find out that one of your children is hopelessly addicted to drugs.
- Your husband comes home and tells you that he no longer loves you.
- Your home is destroyed by a hurricane or fire.
- Your loved ones are killed in a tragic accident.
- The baby you have been waiting for with anticipation and delight turns out to have a severe deformity or illness.
- One of your children disappears.
- Your husband dies at an early age.
- You were sure you heard God about following your hopes and dreams, but the school to which you paid your full tuition to get your new degree closed its doors.

Even when you are living life to the fullest in obedience to God, the events of life can swallow you. You seem to be doing everything right, yet you feel as though you are being sucked under by an eddy. Nothing is turning out the way you thought it would. In fact, everything is falling apart after your hopes and dreams get smashed into a million pieces.

Trouble just comes along and sideswipes you when you least expect it. You can't see any of the fullness of life that Jesus was talking about.

The apostle Paul's life was marked by obedience to God, but he provided great examples of one who encountered many eddies on his journey. He writes:

> "I have worked harder, been in prison more frequently, been flogged more severely and been exposed to death again and again. Five times I received from the Jews the forty lashes minus one. Three times I was beaten with rods, once I was stoned, three times I was shipwrecked, I spent a night and a day in the open sea, and I have been constantly on the move. I have been in danger from rivers, in danger from bandits, in danger from my own countrymen, in danger from Gentiles; in danger in the city, in danger in the country, in danger at sea; and in danger from false brothers. I have labored and toiled and have often gone without sleep; I have known hunger and thirst and have often gone without food; I have been cold and naked. Besides everything else, I face daily the pressure of my concern for all the churches" (2 Cor. 11:23-28 NIV).

Paul ran into a few eddies, didn't he? Was it because he was disobedient? I don't think so. He was not concerned about his comfort zone because he knew without a shadow of a doubt where he was going. He knew what his calling in life was, so he would not let hunger, cold showers, hard beds, and shipwrecks cloud his vision. He knew his *fullness* in this life was living for Jesus, and all the *trouble* along the way was just part of the surprising adventures in the journey.

Stories of trouble—then triumph

A. *Trouble:* Twenty-five centuries ago, Daniel could have despaired when he was deported to a foreign country. Not only was he placed in surroundings where nothing was familiar, he found himself facing an egocentric king who wanted him to worship idols made of gold. Daniel, in obedience to God, stood firm, refusing to bow down and worship the golden idols. For his disobedience to the king, he was thrown into a lions' den.

- *Triumph:* When Daniel was thrown into the lions' den, the lions never touched him. He was then appointed ruler over the entire province of Babylon and placed in charge of all its wise men.

B. *Trouble:* There were three other courageous men in Daniel's time who would not give into a decree to bow down to an image of gold and deny their true God. Shadrach, Meshach, and Abednego were thrown into a fiery furnace for their obedience to God (Dan. 3:16-27).

- *Triumph:* When the king looked into the furnace, he saw a fourth person with them to save them from the flames. The king saw that the fire had not harmed their bodies, nor was a hair on their heads singed, their robes were not scorched and there was no smell of fire on them (Dan. 3:25).

C. *Trouble:* The apostle John, the beloved disciple of Jesus Christ, because of his obedience to God, was exiled to the island of Patmos (Rev. 1:10).

- *Triumph:* He was personally taken up to heaven by Jesus to receive a vision of what was to come.

D. *Trouble:* Hebrews 11, the "Hall of Faith," is full of names of people who were obedient to God. Yet, many were flogged, chained, imprisoned, stoned, sawed in two, and put to death by a sword, as well as enduring ridicule and wandering in deserts and caves. None of them received what had been promised.

- *Triumph:* God had planned something better for them in eternity.

All of these people finished well. They lived their lives to the fullest because they knew where they were going. They *were not afraid* to follow what they believed to be true in their hearts.

Motivational expert John Maxwell tells a story about a man who finished well:

"Bob Ireland crossed the finish line on Thursday, November 6, 1986, as the New York City Marathon's 19,413th and final finisher—the first person to run a marathon with his arms instead of his legs. Bob was a forty-year-old Californian whose legs were blown off in Vietnam seventeen years before. In 1986, he recorded the slowest time in the Marathon's history: four days, two hours, forty-eight minutes, seventeen seconds. When asked why he ran the race, he gave these three reasons:

1) to show he was a born-again Christian,
2) to test his conditioning, and
3) to promote physical fitness for others

'Success is not based on where you start,' said Ireland. 'It's where you finish—and I finished.'" [39]

Part of living the great adventure of life is *finishing well.* Many of us will experience so many failures, tears, and disappointments that we will want to quit along the way. But don't give up! Keep trying over and over again because our finish line of victory is in the glories of heaven. Say with David Foster: "Like Caleb, I want to be a life-changing, soul-feeding, spirit-lifting force. During my brief time here, I want to shape my world, not merely be shaped by it. Daily, I pray, 'Lord wake me up before I die,' not 'If I should die before I wake…'"[40]

Unleashing the Beauty of Adventure

There is such beauty in a woman who knows that *in this life there will be trouble.* A woman who knows her purpose in life is willing to risk adventure and embraces trouble as part of the journey. She unleashes the beauty of her soul by the way she handles difficulties when they appear. There is nothing beautiful about a woman who pouts when life doesn't go her way. None of us like to be around people who always want to be in their comfort zone, are boring, or get moody, angry, or whiny.

My husband Jack and I love to go golfing on the beautiful courses here in the Okanagan Valley in British Columbia. There are a lot of ways to get into difficulty on the courses with its sand traps, ravines, lakes, and tall grass. When the golf ball lands in a horrible spot and is difficult to hit out, we tell each other: *"Play the ball where it lies."* This sentence applies to every area in our lives as well. What it says is this: *"OK, this is not the way I anticipated that this would look like. It's ugly, but this is how it has turned out so now we must deal with it. Let's work with what we have and make the best of it."*

A woman of beauty does not look at trouble as a personal affront to her; instead, she realizes that this is part of life and does not blame God and others for her difficulty. My dear beloved friends, let's allow God to unleash beauty in our souls *during* times of trouble. These are times when we can let the rest of the world see the radiant beauty within us.

A woman of beauty:

A. Knows that the power of prayer will carry her through these swirling eddies of life;

B. Is not afraid to cry or be seen with mascara running down her face;

C. Surrounds herself with her friends, and lets them help her through this treacherous part of the journey;

D. Allows herself a time to be angry or disappointed;

E. Feels free to tell God about the depth of her pain;

F. Stands firm in her belief and love for God;

G. Will not let her heart grow bitter;

H. Understands the seasons of her life. She believes that her spiritual journey is very much like the four seasons on this planet. After autumn, there comes the promise of winter; but there will be another spring, and then a summer;

I. Understands that "trouble" will eventually make her even more beautiful.

When a woman pursuing beauty seeks God during her troubles, He may answer her like He did the writer of Psalms:

"I sought the Lord, and he answered me; he delivered me from all my fears. Those who look to him are radiant; their faces are never covered with shame. This poor man called, and the Lord heard him; he saved him out of all his *troubles.* The angel of the Lord encamps around those who fear him, and he delivers them" (Psalm 34:4-7 NIV).

Oh, that we would not miss the great adventure of living life extravagantly in every way imaginable. It may be in our day-to-day activities of doing laundry, walking the dog, or shopping for groceries. Adventures may occur whether we are hiking up a mountain in the springtime or riding the rivers in a raft. They may happen when we are learning to play a piano, trying a new gourmet recipe, or dancing in our living room in our bare feet. We may be singing a new song, snorkeling, snowboarding, writing an article, loading a new computer program, wearing orange shoes, or running on the beach. Oh, let's you and I let our hair fly in the wind and the rain fall on our faces, get our shoes muddy, and laugh until the tears stream down our cheeks. Let's not think that every time someone scowls that they are scowling at us. If the rest of the world wants stomp on our adventure, let them, but they cannot rob us of our joy. Trouble will come to us, no matter what—if we are at home safely tucked away in front of our TV or watching whales in the ocean. Which one would you rather be doing? I pray that we will let the wind blow through our hair, slide on the marble floor in our socks, wear our laciest underwear, and laugh until we are doubled over.

Stop and ask God to Unleash Your Beauty

Begin by asking: God, how can I handle trouble better?

S—Scripture: "I want you to trust me in your times of trouble, so I can rescue you and you can give me glory" (Ps. 50:15 TLB).

T- Thanksgiving: Thank You, God, that no matter what difficulty I am in, I can call on You twenty-four hours a day. Your hotline is always open. I praise You that You are my rescuer in times of trouble. Oh, how fortunate I am that You died so that I could live an abundant life— a life of adventure.

O- **Observation:** Whatever trouble I am in right at this moment, I choose to *STOP,* take a deep breath, and pass it from my hand to God's. I will trust God to work it out in light of eternity rather than worry about what it looks like right now.

P- **Prayer:** Oh, heavenly Father, I thank You for Your great kindness to me. I thank You for sending Your Son Jesus Christ to come into the world so that I can life live to the fullest. I ask that You teach me how to do that more and more, day after day. I do not want to live a frantic life that has no value or meaning or a boring existence that has no fulfillment. I want to live a life of new experiences, fresh adventure, and joys that I have not encountered before. I ask that You teach me to embrace trouble in a way that it will make me more radiant each time that I encounter it. Thank You for the gifts, fun, and creativity that You have put into my soul. I ask that You release them in me more and more every day. Amen.

UNLEASHING THE
BEAUTY OF MY HOME
Stress, Impress, or Bless

Spread love wherever you go: First of all in your own house...let
no one ever come to you without leaving better and happier. Be
the living expression of God's kindness: kindness in your face,
kindness in your eyes, kindness in your smile.

—MOTHER TERESA OF CALCUTTA

OUR HOMES ARE BOTH reflections
and extensions of our personalities. When you step into my home, I
unveil mysteries about me in a way that you can see and touch. In a society where we have become so dependent on restaurants and fast food
spots, an invitation to come into each other's homes has become a special rarity. I believe hospitality, however, is still one of the most generous,
loving, and intimate gestures we can extend to others. Our family has always
loved inviting people into our home. The invitations have been either very
spur-of-the moment, "let's see what's in the fridge" get-togethers or finely
crafted events that have culminated in five-course meals. The following

statement has dramatically changed my perspective about inviting people into my home:

Treat your company like family, and your family like company.

Do you remember your mother saying to you: "Don't touch that cake; it's for company?" I can still hear those words echoing in my ears; they made me realize that company was more important than me. I cringe when I recall saying those same words to my own children. Certainly, there are times when you simply cannot cut into a special cake, nibble on an exotic appetizer, or mess up a perfectly formed dessert plate; but our message to our family members must always be that they are the most important ones of all. Mother Teresa said, "*Love begins by taking care of the closest ones—the ones in your home.*"

Once I grasped the concept of "treating company like family and family like company," my entire way of "doing hospitality" shifted. On one memorable weekend, I prepared a five- course meal for my family. We got all dressed up, lit candles, put on music, spread linen napkins onto our laps, and treated each other as though we were royalty. To this day, that meal has become a model for hospitality in our home.

WOMEN SET THE TONE

Stress

Like it or not, we women set the tone in our homes. When we get up with a smile on our faces and laughter in our voices, our families begin their day feeling encouraged, joyful, and energized to tackle the day with a positive attitude. Think about those mornings when we hit the snooze button too many times and end up running late. Somehow on those mornings we burn the toast, our hair just won't look the way we want it to, the children fight, and we snap at everyone because of our frustrations. Those are the mornings when people slam doors and mutter under their breath. The chances are that it started with us women. We stand there looking bewildered, wondering how it happened.

Life is not that much easier for those who start the morning without children. You pull a suit out of the closet, and it has a huge stain on the sleeve. As you're putting on your pantyhose, you stick your fingers right through the mesh. You spill coffee on your skirt. The dog's food dish gets knocked over. Just as you are running out the door, you hear the phone ringing. Then, you remember that you forgot to fill the car with gas. By the time you come into contact with other people, your attitude exudes those frustrations, and fairly soon they are snapping back at you. We have to realize that people respond to us on the basis of the words and energy flowing out of our hearts.

Impress

People can sense when we invite them into our homes simply to impress them. With forced smiles, we are tensely waiting for something to go wrong. When we try to make an impression on people, we are on constantly on our guard, more worried about failing or looking inadequate than having fun. We don't take joy in preparing and serving the meal because everything is about perfection. Perfectionism is a *joy-stealer* that will make us tense. Our guests feel our forced gestures of hospitality, and even though the evening may go perfectly, there is an undefined tension in the air. Guests will often feel obligated to make token comments of approval because they sense our need for affirmation. After our company leaves, we replay the evening over and over in our mind. We look for flaws and score how well we did. This leaves us drained, rather than energized to do it again.

Bless

When we sincerely desire to bless the people who come into our home, they feel it the minute they walk through our door. The beautiful, godly energy that flows out of our spirits permeates the air and is not something that we can fake or craft like a soufflé. This kind of genuine energy only comes out of a deep desire to bless people. When this heartfelt motivation is evident, guests relax, laugh, and feel like part of the family. We can make them feel this way by saying things such as:

- "Don't worry about your shoes. Take them off or keep them on—whatever is most comfortable for you."
- "There is more ice in the ice maker. Help yourself."
- "Come and sit by the kitchen as I finish preparing the meal."
- "Tablecloths can be washed. Those stains will come out in the washing machine. See all these other stains: they are memories of all our other meals."
- "Those footstools are for feet, not just for looks."

The point is: people matter more than things. It is as though we open our arms wide and welcome them into our family. Guests feel free to be who they are when they laugh, tell stories, and mingle around the house. Everyone can feel the beauty of spirits flowing freely. Let's face it: people are not coming into our homes for us to exercise our perfectionism; they are coming for fun, love, and intimacy.

Mother Teresa, the Albanian-born Indian missionary and founder of the Order of the Missionaries of Charity, knew how to express love, often by feeding people. She reminded us that *"the hunger for love is more difficult to remove than the hunger for bread."* By inviting people into our homes, we can feed them *and* give them love. Treating company like family lets us relax. There is no need to be afraid of overcooking the vegetables, removing a spill on the white carpet, or forgetting to put out the cream for the coffee. Our intention should be not merely to succeed, but to *bless*. We can't bless others with material things and perfectionism: the blessings will rather come from the love and generosity that we extend to people who come into our homes.

By inviting people into our homes, we not only can feed them *and* give them love, but sometimes we can even save their lives. Corrie Ten Boom experienced this over and over during World War II:

"Corrie Ten Boom's family was torn apart by the Nazis, with most of her immediate relatives perishing in concentration camps due to their harboring of Jews in their home. It was a sacrifice they were willing to make, for God had given them a heart for hospitality. In her book *In My Father's House*, Corrie writes about her family's penchant for taking in guests as she remembered it from childhood: 'Many lonesome people found a place with us; there was music, humor, interesting conversation and always room for one more at the oval dinner table. Oh, it's true, the soup may have been a bit watery when too many unexpected guests came, but it didn't matter. Years afterward on my trips around the world, when I have been dependent on the hospitality of others, I believe that I have enjoyed the reward for the open doors and hearts of our home.'" [41]

After our guests leave, we will, of course, be tired, but we will feel blessed because we gave our best in cooking and preparing our home. We gave God's best in us: *love.*

Our Homes, Our Havens

Our home needs to be a haven—a safe place where we long to go at the end of the day. It needs to be a place where we can walk around in bare feet, leave books beside the couch, take off our makeup, and play with each other affectionately. Even though it may be a humble, small place, it can be a sanctuary where we can find peace, rest, and joy. We need to make our home a place of beauty, and one way to do that is by eating meals together.

While my children were growing up, I was employed as a legal administrator in a law firm. Between working all day and driving children around to baseball, soccer, basketball, gymnastics, piano lessons, and church activities, there were not many hours left in the day. One place where we always met and reconnected was at our evening meal around 6 p.m. To this day, my children rib me about "having to be home for dinner at 6:15." We felt it was important for the family to come together to talk about our day, air grievances, and laugh about funny incidents. The evening meal was the designated time for this.

After half a century of families grabbing quick meals on their way out to the car and passing each other in the hallways and in the garage, people are beginning to realize the importance of actually sitting down and being together. I believe the best place and time for that is the family mealtime.

Time Magazine published an article on the "Magic of the Family Meal." It said:

> "Studies show that the more often families eat together, the less likely kids are to smoke, drink, do drugs, get depressed, develop eating disorders and consider suicide, and the more likely they are to do well in school, delay having sex, eat their vegetables, learn big words and know which fork to use... A meal is about civilizing children. It's about teaching them to be a member of their culture." [42]

A regular meal together seems like such a simple solution to some of our family difficulties, but we realize that with all the demands on our families these days, it is not that easy to arrange.

Creating Beauty in Our Havens

My children call me "the ambience queen." They knew from the time they were little that we only went into restaurants that had "ambience." We select restaurants by their mood, décor, style, and feel. My children can walk into a restaurant, stand there for a moment, look around, and say, "Forget it, Mom, this place has no ambience." Or, they look around, sniff the air, and exclaim that, "Yes, this place has the coveted ambience. It's safe to go in and share a wonderful meal together." Ambience involves the evocation of senses that draw us into a place where we feel that we can find solace, beauty, or comfort. We can create this kind of atmosphere with décor, pleasant music, lights, and smells. For our family, the sounds and smell of garlic sizzling in butter draw us into the kitchen to explore its source. How can you and I create ambience?

It can start right on your front steps at the door. A doormat that says "Welcome" or a flowerpot that has twinkling lights on it says, "We've prepared our place because we have been looking forward to your visit." You can fill your home with the soft lighting of candles or you may wish to put out fresh flowers in a vase. Hospitality is not about buying more fancy objects, however; it is about the little details of expressing love and welcome to our guests.

God has created natural gifts at our fingertips in our gardens or nature around us. They provide us with all we need to create a place of warmth and beauty. If you gathered sea shells during your ocean trips and lugged them home because you thought you might use them some-day...*someday* is here. Place some candles around them so they can be a conversation piece about your holidays last summer. The next time you have family or friends visit you from the prairies, ask them to bring back some wheat stems for your Thanksgiving decorations. Around Christmas, I keep bags of fresh cranberries and holly in my fridge during the season. With fresh greenery, cranberries, candles, and a hot, simmering beverage, our homes can smell wonderful and say "welcome" to everyone who walks through the door.

Hospitality is also about getting everyone involved. When our families come home for Thanksgiving, I love to go on nature walks with my grandchildren. We head out for the woods and vineyards to collect pinecones, berries, old twigs, and even beautiful rocks. Then, we bring them back and use them to create a centerpiece for our Thanksgiving meal. This not only adds ambience to our event, but it also gives us something to talk about, as well as create memories of our time together.

God has created a world for us that is so big and beautiful that we will never fully comprehend it or see the end of it in our lifetime. What fun we can have by creating beauty right out of God's creation. It is all about spending time together and creating beauty and memories versus spending money and creating false impressions.

Entertainment or Hospitality?

Let's be very clear about the difference between impressing and blessing. Impressing is e*ntertaining,* and blessing is *hospitality.* Author Robert J. Morgan vividly describes these distinctions:

- "The model for entertaining is the slick women's magazines with the alluring pictures of food and rooms. The model for hospitality is the Word of God. Christ sanctifies our simple fare and makes it holy and useful.

- Entertainment looks for a payment—the words, 'My, isn't she a remarkable hostess…'
- With no thought of reward, hospitality takes pleasure in giving doing, loving, and serving.
- Entertaining says, 'I want to impress you with my home, my clever decorating, and my gourmet cooking.' Hospitality, seeking to minister, says, 'This home is a gift from my Master. I use it as He desires….' Hospitality aims to serve."[43]
- *Entertaining* involves flaunting what we have and impressing people. It is about working hard to make everything look perfect and wearing ourselves out to astonish people with our skills, rather than with who we are. The slick magazines can still be fun and worth looking at because they give us creative ideas and inspire us, but the difference is our intention. If we scour the magazines to find new ways to impress people, it will ultimately only cause us more stress. *Hospitality* is about sharing our homes and serving people with love, not things, allowing us the freedom to bless and be a blessing.

EATING TOGETHER IS A SPIRITUAL EXPERIENCE

What is it about eating food together that creates such a sociable atmosphere? We all long to be a part of some community, finding some of this in our favorite coffee shop where we stop to chat with a friend. We love to gather on a hot evening at the ice cream shop for an ice cream cone, or sit on the patio of an outdoor restaurant for hours swapping stories. I feel that eating together is almost a spiritual experience—a building of community. The Word of God contains many references to the intimate connection between food and fellowship. First Peter 4:9 exhorts us: "Cheerfully share your home with those who need a meal or a place to stay for the night" (NIV).

Our motive for sharing our homes should include doing it *cheerfully*. As Jesus traveled from village to village, he was often fed and cared for by friends and strangers who welcomed Him into their homes. Acts 2:46 and

47, one of my favorite Scripture passages, is engraved on a painting in our dining room: "*They broke bread in their homes and ate together with glad and sincere hearts, praising God and enjoying the favor of all the people*" (NIV).

Let's share our homes with pure, joyful motives. In His final hours on earth, with the shadow of the cross hanging over Him, Jesus spent His last evening sharing dinner with His disciples. He chose to share life-changing information with them that night around a table. It was a place of intimacy created by mouths enjoying the same food, bodies reclining around the table, and eyes meeting across the plates. Here, they enjoyed intimate community.

A table should be a place to share what is meaningful with each other. After all, this was the place Jesus commanded us to remember Him by the breaking of bread and wine.

UNLEASHING BEAUTY IN OUR HOME

Hospitality is a beautiful and creative gift from God—one that we can enjoy and explore for the rest of our lives. God created us for relationship and community, and one of the best places to express this natural instinct can be in our homes. Let's not forget to "treat our family like company." Our children, family members, and close friends need to know that aside from God, they are the most important people in our lives. There is something very powerful about sharing love in our homes. The *Time Magazine* article about family meals continues:

> "...there is something about a shared meal—not some holiday blowout, not once in a while but regularly, reliably—that anchors a family even on nights when the food is fast and the talk cheap and everyone has someplace they would rather be. And on those nights when the mood is right and the family lingers, caught up in an idea or an argument explored in a shared safe place where no one is stupid or shy or ashamed, you get a glimpse of the power of this habit and why social scientists say such communion acts as a kind of vaccine, protecting kids from all manner of harm." [44]

I am sure that we have never thought of meal times as *life-changing*. Yet, when we do something as intimate as eating together and sharing concerns and ideas on our minds in a safe and loving environment, it will change our behavior.

Now that my children are older and married, they have become very comfortable entertaining people in their homes. From the time they were young, I would seat them on the kitchen counter right beside me as I worked in the kitchen. They were allowed to stir, taste, sprinkle, and help wherever their little hands could reach. To this very day, we love to be together in the kitchen—creating, laughing, and nibbling. When my son Donovan came home for Christmas a few years ago, I asked him if there was anything special he wanted to do during the holiday season. His familiar response was, *"Mom, I just want to hang out with you in the kitchen, creating new recipes."*

My daughter is an amazing cook who has learned to prepare meals for large groups of people without getting stressed out about what things look and taste like. During the harvest season on the huge farm where she lives, she has to prepare big meals and take them out to the men in the fields where they are working. Donovan has also become a gourmet cook, and he is passionate about creating exquisite dishes that are fun to prepare and delightful to present. Some of our most memorable, fun times are in the kitchen and around the dinner table.

I believe this all started as a result of our regular mealtime ritual. Because I was adamant about doing this, I believe our family has reaped great rewards. We must intentionally develop this ritual, despite the challenges of everyday life.

In the summer of 2006, our children Ken and Janice, along with their three sons, came to spend time with us during their vacation. When our oldest grandson, Brendon, who turned fourteen that year, showed up at our door, he waved a mousse recipe at me the minute he walked into the kitchen. He also brought with him blackberries that he hand-picked for the sauce and garnish. This time, I got to sit at the kitchen counter and watch as he and his mom spent hours preparing the layers of white and chocolate mousse. When it came time to serve dessert that evening, he proudly carried his masterpiece to the dinner table, and we all *oohed* and *aahed* over his magnificent creation. We took pictures and then put our spoons into this much-anticipated delight. What a wonderful moment for all of us to experience! This was just another family bonding time that would create delicious memories for a very long time. It also carved a very special spot for Brendon in our kitchen that has kept him close to us and away from all the dangerous temptations teenagers are faced with every day.

UNLEASHING THE BEAUTY OF HOSPITALITY

When our motives for entertaining guests are focused on impressing instead of blessing, it can be stressful and exhausting to share our food, our guest rooms, our resources, and our valuable time. To unleash the true beauty of a hospitable heart, we need to start by checking our motives for inviting people into our homes. Hospitality is not just about having a meal together. It is an event that:

- fosters interaction;
- nourishes relationships;
- breaks down walls;
- encourages laughter;
- connects people and allows intimacy to return;
- gives time to honor and worship God; and
- expresses our love to other people.

Imagine the impact we can have on people when we share what we have in our homes. We can't measure the results of hospitality, but God tells us that we never know who and what we are affecting: "*Do not forget to entertain strangers, for by so doing some people have entertained angels without knowing it*" (Heb. 13:2 NIV).

Beauty is unleashed when we treat everyone who comes into our lives as part of our family. After all, we never know when one might be an angel. Someday, we will all be a large family sharing intimately in heaven for the rest of our lives. Let's practice now; the rewards are heavenly.

Blessed to be a blessing

Everything in our home can be perfect when people walk through the door, but if our motives are not right, and if the presence of God is not in our midst, entertaining is just a formality and too much hard work. In Exodus 39:43, God asked Moses to bless the tabernacle after it was built. I believe that God meant the place to be a blessing to all who entered there. Likewise, when our home was finished in 1995, my husband Jack and I asked God to bless our home so that all the people who passed through it would receive a blessing. That is still the intent and motive of our hearts: to bless everyone who passes through our doors. After all, there is no place like home to share food, blessings, and the "good news of Christ" hand-in-hand.

Stop and ask God to Unleash Your Beauty

Begin by asking: God, how can I bring regular mealtime and intimacy back into our home?

S—Scripture: The apostle Paul made the following request of Philemon: "And one more thing: Prepare a guest room for me, because I hope to be restored to you in answer to your prayers" (Philemon 2:22 NIV).

T—Thanksgiving: Thank You, God for a place to lay my head, have a meal, and share my home with other people. Thank You that we live in a land of abundance so that we have enough to share with the world around us. Thank You for all the people who share their homes as an expression of their generosity and love.

O- Observation: Our house is not just a home, but a place where people's lives can be transformed.

P- Prayer: Thank You, God for our homes. Whether we live in a house, condominium, apartment, basement suite, or travel trailer, it is the place You have given us that can become our haven. Thank You for making us relational people, so that when we share a meal together, deep intimacy can take place. Help us not to be afraid to have people into our home who are either unlovable or may seem like strangers. You did many miracles in people's homes, and we know that You still do miracles today. Help us to love those who we thought we could not love. May we realize what a blessed people we are so that we can bless all those whom You have placed in our lives, along with those who walk through our doors. Amen.

9

UNLEASHING THE BEAUTY
OF GOD'S GLORY
Double Rainbows

Man is the individualized expression or reflection of God imaged forth and made manifest in bodily form. How is it then, I hear it asked, that man has the limitations that he has, that he is subject to fears and forebodings, that he is liable to sin and error, and that he is the victim of disease and suffering? There is but one reason. He is not living, except in rare cases here and there, in the conscious realization of his own true Being, and hence of his own true Self.

—RALPH WALDO TRINE,

"THE GREATEST THING EVER KNOWN"

SEVERAL YEARS AGO, I began the practice of asking God for a specific word, phrase, or picture that could be the focus of my studies for that coming year. Since January of 2005 was almost over and I still had not received any direction for the coming year, I knew it was time for a long walk. My feet venturing out and connecting with God's creation always gave me clarity.

On a cold and dark January evening, I bundled up and started walking through the vineyards, then up and down the hills of our beautiful neighborhood. I knew that I would hear from God if I would just quiet my heart and take some time to listen. Each time I put one footstep in front of the other, I repeated this prayer: "God, do you have a word, a phrase, a verse, or something that will give me focus for the coming year?" I walked, waited, and listened. Even though my mind wanted to wander by taking in the beauty of the city lights and freshly fallen snow, I caught the word, *glory.* "*Glory,* Lord? What do you mean by *glory?*" I kept asking. Then I knew I heard it as clear as though someone was speaking directly to me: "*Heidi, be a reflection of My glory.*"

THE DIRECTION was very clear and more than I had ever bargained for. What did that mean, and how could anyone do that? Who can fathom and understand God's glory? How could I, a sinful human being, be a reflection of His glory? I felt sure those words had been impressed upon me by God, so I began researching the subject as soon as I returned home. My Bible, commentaries and research books started flying out of their shelves.

WE ARE ALL A REFLECTION
OF GOD'S GLORY

My friends chuckle when they see me inspired because they know that a new study always "gets my jets going." This was particularly true of the subject of g*lory* because it was so indefinable. It was magnificent, but yet so unreachable and hard to comprehend. I found that God's glory is greater than anything we can define or grasp in human terms. In the days to come, the pages of the Bible and other research books soaked up every moment of my thoughts and time. Many verses that had been passed over now began to jump off the pages of my Bible. The first verse that brought some clarity and got my heart pounding was, "And we, who with unveiled faces *all* reflect the Lord's glory...." (2 Cor. 3:18 NIV).

The realization came to me that God's Word on that cold January night was not just for me, but for *all* of us who have received Jesus Christ as our personal Savior. We all reflect God's glory while we are living out our lives on His earth. I could not represent the whole world, but I needed to know that it was meant for me: Heidi. How could I reflect God's glory in my day-to-day life, in my area of influence in my home, and as a wife, mother, and grandmother? How could I do this at my gymnasium, the grocery store, my church, my neighborhood, and especially, in my workplace?

This realization soon expanded beyond just a nice, Christian thing for me to do: it was something that God has commanded all of us to do in *every* area of our lives. He reminds us:

"Everyone who is called by my name, whom I created for my glory, whom I formed and made…" (Isa. 43:7 NIV).
• *Everyone*

"So whether you eat or drink or whatever you do, do it all for the glory of God" (1 Cor. 10:31 NIV).
• *Everything*

"And all of them, since they are mine, belong to you; and you have given them back to me with everything else of yours, and so they are my glory." (John 17:10 TLB).
• *Embodiment*

Those words encompassed every single area of my life. There was no getting away from any of it. It was an overwhelming responsibility, so I needed to know how to get started.

When Jesus was walking on this earth, He was representing the glory of His Father. When we eavesdrop on His personal conversation that He had with His heavenly Father before He went to the cross, we find out many things that He desired for us after he left this earth: *"I have brought you glory on earth by completing the work you game me to do"* (John 17:4 NIV). He then goes on to say that He was handing this glory over to us: *"I have given them the glory that you gave me"* (John 17:22 NIV). This verse tells me that when we receive Jesus Christ as our personal Savior, we become the visible hands, feet, and voice of an invisible God for the rest of the world to see and hear. We reflect His glory. That is very clear, and it is a huge responsibility.

I realized that I could not just get up one day and decide that I was going to be a reflection of God's glory. I knew that this glory would only come from God's holiness in me. I also knew that I could not make myself holy, but I had to seek God to help me with this process. As human beings, we are very visual, so I needed to know what this would look like.

"Show Me Your Glory, Lord"

As I continued to study the word *glory*, I became fascinated with the relationship that Moses had with God, recorded in the book of Exodus. One of these dialogues caught my breath: "Then Moses said, "Now show me your glory" (Exod.33:18 NIV). Now, that is bold!

One day with reverent awe and boldness, I also asked God, "*God, will You show me what it means to be a reflection of Your glory?*" I knew that He would show me in His time and in His way, so I waited with great anticipation.

I believe God loves to delight us. He must have taken great pleasure in creating the earth and showing off His great sunsets, dolphins, redwood trees, and the stars in all their splendor. When God was creating the world, this is how He felt at the end of each day: "And God was pleased with what he had done" (Gen. 1:25b TLB). I believed that the insights God would show me would also please me immensely. I simply could not wait.

Weeks and months passed, but I never gave up on my hope that God would show me in a tangible way what it meant to reflect His glory. I knew that it had to be fashioned uniquely for me, so that it would clear for me to understand it in such a way that would affect me forever. When I studied the Hebrew meaning of glory, I knew that it would be magnificent. *Kabod* meant "weight [in a good sense]; splendor or copiousness; glorious; glory; and honor."[45] While I was waiting for God to show me His glory, I went on a quest to discover what His *splendor* looked like. "Splendor" meant magnificence, brilliance, finery, majestic, or grandeur.

It was now the month of June in 2005. One Saturday morning, my husband Jack and I decided to go for a long walk through the rolling hills and vineyards where we live. Even though it had been raining all morning, we grabbed our umbrellas and bravely ventured out into the wet summer air. It was a warm rain that made the air smell fresh and sweet. On this splendid morning, the summer flowers and foliage had just been washed by the rain and were bursting with fresh, brilliant colors. We could see the grapes taking shape on their vines in their different hues of green. God was really showing off His beauty to us that day. Close to the end of our walk, the sun broke through the clouds, and we saw the most splendid rainbow. It was so close that it touched our side of the mountain. We felt that if we could reach just a little bit higher, we would be able to touch it. The colors were so crisp and dazzling that we could make out every individual shade: violet, indigo, blue, green, yellow, orange, and red. If that wasn't enough, what I saw next literally made me stop and took my breath away.

Above the first rainbow was another rainbow. Yes, of course, I had seen a second rainbow before, but never like this one. I knew without a doubt that what I saw next was God's delight to show me. It was His way of revealing to me what it meant to be a *reflection of His glory*. The second rainbow was a *reflection* of the first, a fact which I had not known about double rainbows. The colors I saw now were backwards, starting with red and ending in violet— the reverse of the colors of the first rainbow. This was God's way of showing me that I am *reflecting the beauty* of Him as I walk this earth. God's glory to mankind is shown in a visible way through splendor and beauty.

As I observed the magnificence of God in the rainbow, I just stood there in awe wanting to fall on my knees and worship. When we encounter such a dazzling revelation, the beauty and glory of God can be so overpowering that we don't what else to do but worship Him. Now I know that when we encounter the magnificent beauty of God we will never be the same again. Stormie Omartian says, "The more we worship God, the more we see that His holiness, wholeness, purity, and goodness make us holy, pure, and good."[46] William Temple declares, "To worship is to quicken the conscience by the holiness of God, to purge the imagination by the beauty of God, to open the heart to the love of God, and to devote the will to the purpose of God." [47]

The more we encounter the beauty of His presence, the more His glory will be manifested in our hearts. I knew I needed to more about the characteristics of God so that His beauty in me could be nurtured and then unleashed.

Pursuing God's Beauty

To understand God's glory, we need to try to understand His beauty. We are human beings who are visual creatures: we need pictures and colors. We need a framework of something that we can see or imagine. Here are some images of that beauty:

- *God is dazzling like a flame and has a halo like a rainbow.*
"From his waist up, he seemed to be all glowing bronze, dazzling like fire; and from his waist down he seemed to be entirely flame and there was a glowing halo like a rainbow all around him. That was the way the glory of the Lord appeared to me" (Ezek. 1:28 TLB).

- *God is revealed through a cloud.*
"And at that moment the glory of the Lord, coming as a bright cloud, filled the temple so that the priests could not continue their work" (2 Chron. 5:14 TLB).

- *God is strong and invincible.*
"Open up, O ancient gates and let the King of Glory in. Who is this King of Glory? The Lord, strong and mighty, invincible in battle. Yes, open wide the gates and let the King of Glory in. Who is this King of Glory? The commander of all of heaven's armies!" (Psalm 24:7-10 TLB).

- *God is surrounded by beauty, as brilliant as sapphire stones.*
"And they saw the God of Israel; under his feet there seemed to be a pavement of brilliant sapphire stones, as clear as the heavens" (Exod. 24:10 TLB).

- *God is as beautiful as precious jewels.*

"It shone with the glory of God, and its brilliance was like that of a very precious jewel, like a jasper, clear as crystal" (Rev. 21:11 NIV).

GOD'S GLORY is so powerful and so beautiful that no human can survive while being in that presence. He tells us in His encounter with Moses that He would reveal His glory to Moses, but He had to put Moses in the crevice of a rock to protect him. He said, "*You cannot see my face, for no one may see me and live*" (Exod. 33:20 NIV).

The King of Glory is revealed through you and me. This is such an awesome responsibility that it makes some of us run away from God. How can we possibly live up to that kind of holy standard?

OUR DISTORTED REFLECTION

Before we can even begin to see ourselves as a reflection of God's beauty, we need to see the truth of our own beauty. How can we reflect something that we feel we are not? The word "reflect" means that we are to *give back or show an image of.* From the time we are born, our beauty and worth is shaped through the words, people, and circumstances which have transpired in our lives. If harsh words have been directed at us or if we have lived through difficult, painful, and unfortunate circumstances, we will not be able to see much *splendor* in ourselves. Some of us have heard words like: "Why bother trying, you will never succeed anyway," or "Why should we pay for more education for you? You'll never really get anywhere." Those words have crippled us and locked us up from knowing and reaching our full potential.

It is as though we are looking at our reflection in a murky mud puddle. We just can't get a clear picture of who we are, and we certainly cannot see our beauty. To begin to see ourselves clearly through the eyes of the One who created us, we need for Him to expose the lies of our human understanding of the way the world has shaped us.

The Greek word for glory is *doxa,* which signifies "an *opinion, estimate* (italics mine), and hence, the honor resulting from a good opinion. It is used (1) of the nature and acts of God in self-manifestation, i.e. what He essentially is and does..."[48]

We need God's *opinion* of our beauty because our own opinion is distorted. As our creator, He is the one who knows us. We cannot listen to people's judgments about who we are. Whether it is a good opinion or distorted, bad opinion, either one will fall short of who we truly are.

I believe it is God's greatest desire for us to see ourselves as beautiful. He wants to remove every obstacle that is holding us back from seeing ourselves that way. Isaiah 61:3 tells us how God wants to treat us: "...to bestow on them a crown of beauty instead of ashes, the oil of gladness instead of mourning, and a garment of praise instead of a spirit of despair" (Isa. 61:3 NIV). God desires to put a glorious crown on our heads so that we can see ourselves as beautiful. What are some of the obstacles distorting your own image?

- Your physical appearance?
- Your filthy language?
- Your lack of education?
- The place where you live?
- Unresolved hurt and anger from your past?
- Destructive addictive habits?
- Harsh words that have been spoken against you and that you have believed?
- Lack of money?

GOD'S SPIRIT IS OUR GLORY

We have to determine right here and now if the world has placed our distorted values on us. The King of kings and Lord of lords of the universe wants to crown us with beauty. I believe once we grasp that concept, our thought life will change, the filthy language will begin to clean itself up, and the bad habits will begin to disappear. This is a daily process of growth if we choose to spend time with the One who is waiting to bestow that crown on us.

Stormie Omartian says, "When you spend time in the Lord's presence in worship and praise, when you worship the Lord in the beauty of holiness, your countenance will be changed too. The change that happens in your soul will be seen in your face. When you bask in the beauty of His holiness, it will exude a compelling radiance through you more profoundly than anything else can. And it will be magnetically attractive to the world that longs for what you have, even though they can't identify what it is."[49] I say that this quality is the beauty of God's glory revealed through you.

But before we put ourselves on a guilt trip by telling ourselves that we can never live up to those expectations, we need to remind ourselves that we can never attain perfect glory. While we are residing on this earth, we will be imprisoned by our sinful bodies and distorted thinking. The complete expression of the glory of God is a journey that begins in this life and is only completed in eternity. "For all have sinned and fall short of the glory of God" (Rom. 3:23 NIV).

- But, the more we bask in God's presence, the more His beauty will rub off on us.

"….are being transformed into his likeness with ever-increasing glory, which comes from the Lord, who is the spirit" (2 Cor. 3:18b NIV).

- This is a moment-by-moment, day-by-day process.

So, we can't get up one morning and decide that we are going to have it. It cannot be faked, nor can it be accomplished by just trying harder. The glory that pours out of us from the Holy Spirit abides in us. The more we allow God to work in our lives, the more His splendor will be revealed. We have absolutely no hope of the beauty of Christ radiating from us if the Holy Spirit is not dwelling in us.

God Will Not Share His Glory

A word of caution is in order here. As we begin to allow God's glory to be revealed through us, we must overcome the temptation to claim it as our own. The enticement to promote our own glory is a very powerful temptation. We are constantly tempted to let the rest of the world know we have value and fame. Once we begin to hear accolades about our greatness, pride creeps in, and we want to hoard that applause because it just feels so deliciously good. We must recognize this as self-promotion; instead of reflecting God's glory, we will be stealing it from Him. God will not share His glory with anyone: "I am the Lord; that is my name! I will not give my glory to another" (Isa. 42:8 NIV).

Unleashing the Beauty of God's Glory

A woman who *chooses* to make God recognizable in her life has embarked upon an ideal maturity process to reveal God's beauty. There are many ways to reflect beauty. Some are general things we all can do, but there will also be many that will be uniquely designed for each one of us.

Things that all of us can do:

- *Seek God with all of our hearts in everything we do.* We need to learn to worship Him. What does that mean? Stormie Omartian says that "worship is... coming in contact with the holiness of God by the power of the Holy Spirit, and letting the beauty of His holiness rub off on you and make you beautifully holy and wonderfully whole." [50]
- *We are meant to glorify God through every area of our lives, including our body.* We can glorify Him in the way we dress. Let's dress tastefully, with cleanliness and beauty. That does not mean we have to spend a great deal of money. We can wear simple, clean, beautiful clothes that don't reveal our bellies, thighs, and bras straps. Let's be aware of what kind of messages we are sending to the world about our bodies.

- *We can especially glorify God with our words.* Our words have the power to speak life or death, so let's speak with kindness and compassion. Mother Teresa says, "Kind words are short and easy to speak, but their echoes are truly endless" and "True holiness consists in doing God's will with a smile."
- *We can glorify God with our actions.* Our generosity with time, money, and kind words to people when they are in a time of need are the most beautiful things we can give them.

Reflecting God's beauty through your uniqueness:

What are you contributing and displaying to the world with the talents that God has given you?

- If you love working with flowers, do you plant a beautiful flower garden? Do you randomly give flowers to people just to cheer them up?
- If you love writing, do you write notes of encouragement? Do you write e-mails and send them to uplift people in times of despair?
- If you love sewing, you can help out with sewing projects for organizations overseas.
- If you are a speaker, do you speak words of love, beauty, and encouragement?
- If you love creating and are an interior designer, do you pray for people in their homes? Are you easy to get along with while you are working with them?

Whatever career or place of opportunity God has placed you in, can you honestly say that when you leave the building, people are happier and kinder because they have been in your presence? God has called all of us to live a life of holiness: "For God has not called us to be dirty-minded and full of lust, but to be holy and clean" (1 Thess 4:7 TLB).

As soon as our feet hit the floor in the mornings, this thought should be uppermost in our minds. It will be a constant struggle, because our natural inclination is to bring glory to ourselves. Let me encourage you not to get weary or discouraged. Some days will be good, but on other days we will feel like a complete failure. Let's just remember that it is God doing the work in us…not *us*.

Since that rainy morning on the walk with my husband through the vineyards when God showed me His double rainbow, I have seen myself in a completely different light. I realize that whatever I do and say reflects the person whom I am representing. If I say I am a Christian, then I am representing my heavenly Father and my creator—the one who made heaven and earth. With all the ugliness, anger, and pain in our world today, people hunger for beauty of any kind. If I am not adding beauty to this world, then I am robbing it of what God has asked me to do.

I love to wear a perfume that defines who I am. When I have been in a room, I love it when someone says to me, "Heidi, I can tell that you were in here because I can still smell your perfume." My perfume reflects my personality and leaves a scent that characterizes who I am. My friends can tell who I am by the fragrance I leave behind.

What kind of fragrance am I leaving behind as I represent God on this earth? When I leave a room, can people also say, "There go the hands, feet, and love of God?" Will the world know who God is by how I represent Him on this earth? Do my words of love and kindness reflect His characteristics?

These are hard questions I have to ask myself every day, especially when I don't feel like being nice. During those tough days, I just have to remind myself that my human striving and phoniness cannot reflect true beauty. I need to constantly soak in the presence of the one who will give me the fragrance that will let the world know whom I represent.

Other ways to unleash and recognize God's beauty:
1. Look around you. God's beauty is everywhere.
2. Ask God to show you His beauty. Anticipate His answer.
3. Every time you see a rainbow; be reminded that you reflect that kind of beauty of God.
4. Listen to the way you describe yourself. If it is not in line with the way God created you, then it is a lie that you need to disregard.

5. Reflect God's beauty in your workplace or grocery store. Say something kind to someone who is unkind to you.
6. Bring a flower into your home in the coming week. Intend to declare beauty.
7. The glory of God *is* beauty. Try to understand it every time you see a jewel, a sunset, a flower, a new baby, a bride, a snowflake, or a baby bird.
8. God's rainbow is a promise that He will never again flood the entire earth. It is also a promise that as long as the earth is here, the seasons will always come in their regular cycles. Be aware of these seasons and the wonderful promises that God gives us.
9. Watch a bird and the way it soars.
10. Look for pictures of jasper and sapphire.
11. Read Psalm 33.

Stop and ask God to Unleash Your Beauty

Begin by asking: God, does the world see Your beauty in me?

S—Scripture: "For all have sinned and fall short of the glory of God" (Rom. 3:23 NIV).

T—Thanksgiving: Thank You, God, that I don't have to work harder or fake Your glory. Thank You that Your glory is revealed through the Holy Spirit living in me.

O—Observation: I have no hope whatsoever of the presence of God being recognized in me if it was not for the Holy Spirit dwelling in me. I need to realize that God's glory is "ever-increasing" in me as I mature in my spiritual walk with Him.

P—Prayer: Thank You, God, for the brilliance and beauty of the rainbow. Thank You for delighting us by displaying Your beauty everywhere. God, help me to understand what it means to be a reflection of Your glory while I am walking on this earth. Help me to know how to do that in this fast-paced, hurry-up world in which I live today. Teach me day by day how to see Your beauty and how I can reflect this beauty wherever my feet take me. Teach me how to do that with my words and actions. Thank You for being so patient and kind to me while I am learning and growing. Amen.

10

UNLEASHING THE BEAUTY OF PURE MOTIVES
The Stinky Heart

The best and most beautiful things in the world cannot be seen or even touched. They must be felt with the heart.

—HELEN KELLER

"WHERE IS THAT SMELL coming from?" I was blissfully pecking away on my laptop in my office which I had named "Angels Corner." This nickname naturally came about as I kept adding to my collection of angels given to me by women whom I adored. There are angels looking at me through eyes sculptured out of copper, ceramic angels holding hands, wooden angels staring at me with their painted eyes, and beautiful fabric angels that appear to have just arrived from heaven. Working in this serene environment inspired me as I prepared for a seminar called "Taking Care of Your Heart." But as much as I was enjoying what I was doing, I could no longer ignore the stench growing stronger by the minute from somewhere in the room. My eyes darted around the room as though I was actually trying to see the source of the smell. Then I spotted my partially unpacked suitcase sitting in the corner.

My husband Jack and I had just returned from visiting with our children and grandchildren on their oceanfront property on Vancouver Island. The back patio of their west coast home overlooks the majestic Georgia Strait, where we often sit and watch cruise ships, sea birds, and mammals such as sea lions. Visiting them is like inhabiting a piece of heaven.

As soon as I got out of our car, I rounded up my three grandchildren and laid out my plans. I told them, "Nana is preparing to talk to some people about hearts. It would give me so much joy and make me so proud of you if you would help me make a heart from the sea shells in the ocean." They politely looked at me with eyes that were slightly glazed over, forced some smiles at me, turned around, and went back outside to play. It was obvious that they had no desire to dig around the sands and rocks of the ocean with their Nana.

I was not about to give up my dream because I could already visualize displaying a beautifully crafted heart to the women at the seminar. They would be so impressed that my grandchildren loved me enough to do this for me. Within a few hours, I noticed the tide had finally gone out. Of the three grandchildren, I called out to the youngest, "Ryan, would you like to come to the ocean with Nana to collect beautiful seashells so that we can make a heart?" Up bobbed his little blond head, and with a grin on his face and a sparkle in his bright blue eyes, he followed me out the door.

Excitement like that is contagious. When I looked behind me, there was a trail of two other boys following us out to the ocean, just like the pied piper. Then the fun began. We started digging around in the murky ocean water, pulling out sea shells of all shapes and sizes. "Look over here, Nana. Isn't this one beautiful? Nana, come and see this one. Oh, come and see what I found."

I too got caught up in their enthusiasm and started searching in the warm, velvety water and slipping over the slimy, ocean rocks. My eyes caught a glimpse of a beautiful, perfectly formed shell that I thought would look great on my sea shell heart. Ryan saw me picking it up and quickly grabbed my hand. He informed me, "No, Nana, you can't take that one; there is something alive in there." I peered inside the shell but could see nothing, so I ignored his warning. In addition to taking just that one, I took another three. The shells were too perfect to pass up, and besides, Ryan was just a child. What did he know about sea shells? I shrugged off the feeling that I had deliberately ignored his warning. I was blatantly disobedient, thinking that I knew better.

Soon our hands and pockets were bulging with shells, so we were ready to start the construction of the heart. From the little crawl space under the staircases, we pulled out Bristol board, glue, and construction paper. Eagerly, we cut out a heart on brown paper about twelve inches high and took turns pasting beautifully colored shells all over it. I was overjoyed when I saw the final result: an array of shells in the shape of a heart. How unique! What a great tool it would be for me to use as an illustration for my speaking engagements on matters of the heart. I thanked them and proudly tucked it inside one of the pockets of my suitcase.

Several days had passed, and the living thing Ryan had warned me about had indeed died inside the shell. Now the heart smelled so bad that I could hardly hold it without it burning my eyes. I pulled this treasured artwork out of the suitcase and left it outside on the patio. Little Ryan had been right. Because he had grown up by the ocean, he knew the names of most of the sea shells and species which lived there. Ryan knew more than I did about sea shells, after all, he had grown up living near the ocean. He had warned me that there was something alive inside my beautiful shell that would end up rotting and smelling but I did not listen. I thought I knew better and could get away with ignoring Ryan's warning.

The sea shell heart sat on the patio for several days, but as soon as I brought it back into the house, the pungent, sour, sewer-type smell permeated every room. Eventually, I sealed it in a plastic bag and put it in the basement. I was not able to use it for my seminar, all because I chose not to listen to the wise words of a six-year-old who knew the names of all the shells.

BEAUTIFUL HEARTS

There was nothing wrong with me wanting to have a beautiful sea shell heart. Likewise, God wants us to have beautiful hearts. He sent His Son

Jesus Christ to die for you and me, so that we could be liberated from the ugliness of our sin to enjoy the beauty and radiance of being a child of God. He knows that when we receive forgiveness from our shame, guilt, jealousy, anger and other sinful stinkiness, our hearts will exude Christ's beauty wherever we go. Yet, God cautions us about what we put into our hearts, because that is what will pour out of us.

In the same way that Ryan warned me about putting that particular shell into my sea shell heart, God warns us: "Above all else, guard your heart, for it is the wellspring of life" (Prov. 4:23 NIV).

Sounds wonderful, doesn't it? Who doesn't want a beautiful heart that has springs of life flowing from it? Why is it so hard for us to have this kind of joy bubbling from our hearts every single day?

What Causes Stinkiness

In order for me to create that beautiful sea shell heart, I should have listened to little Ryan. He said, "No, Nana," but because of my deliberate disobedience, I ended up with a stinky heart that I was unable to use. Again, I was struck by the unique way that God continues to teach me His life-changing truths. An afternoon on the ocean with a six-year-old boy taught me that *disobedience always causes stinkiness.*

In order to have the joyful "springs of life," we need to look at the first word in that verse.

The word "keep" in the original Hebrew language is *natsar*, which means "to guard (in a good sense), to protect, maintain, or *obey* (italics mine)."[51] It is that one word tucked away in there that determines the outcome of either beauty or stinkiness in my life: *obey.*

OH, HOW MANY TIMES do we just want to have our own way and simply close our minds to the warnings around us! We also close our eyes to God's Word, thinking, "Maybe this time I can get away with it and do it my way." Disobedience is the road to stinkiness, which will rob us of our joy.

We are disobedient every time we think we can do anything in our lives our way—without Christ—like Frank Sinatra who crooned these words in his 1968 signature song, "My Way":

"And now as tears subside, I find it all amusing
To think I did all that, and may I say, not in a shy way,
Oh no, oh no, not me, I did it my way."

One area in my life I chose to do "my way" was perfectionism. This was already a deadly disease in my life *before* I became a Christian, but unfortunately, it became even worse *after* I received Christ as my personal Savior. I thought, *"If I'm good enough, work hard enough, and do all the right things, God will love me and approve of me."* But rarely did I ever feel it was enough, so I just kept trying harder and harder, doing it "my way." As a Christian, I wanted to look good for God, after all look how He pulled me out of a pit of sin and ugliness. I also worked very hard so that people would accept me and approve of me. I actually thought all this striving and hard work was the "right" way.

I sought happiness and peace by keeping my house in perfect order and making sure my lists were completed perfectly. My perfectionistic thinking confused hospitality with entertainment, which meant that my dinner parties were supposed to go on without a hitch. My pantries were going to be filled with peaches and cherries, and the children would be well- grounded and obedient. Like many perfectionists, I sought to stand out from the crowd. This is what a perfectionist needs: to be better than the rest or fulfill some unreasonable, abstract standard, all for the stamp of approval from people around her, and, of course, God.

Perfectionism

Perfectionism may seem like a virtue in some people's eyes, but in reality, perfectionists are ugly to live with. They are difficult to please because they are always striving, as well as dragging everyone else along with them. Perfectionists are also difficult to have as friends: it's not a matter of "if" things go wrong, but "when", because you can never meet a perfectionist's expectations. Actually, they are merely women who are desperately looking for love using the only avenue they have been taught. Their slavish way of thinking tells them that if they are perfect, they will:

- Be loved.
- Have God's approval.
- Finally receive their parents' approval.
- Feel safe.
- Feel fully alive, believing that they have earned their worth.
- Feel connected to other people by earning their approval.
- Finally be able to relax when everything is in its rightful place.

Carol Kent tells us that, "If I please all of the people in my life with flawless behavior and control everything and everyone around me, I won't have to admit my deep insecurities and fears." [52]

It is impossible to control the people or circumstances around us to help us attain that perfect view of ourselves and life. Sometimes the pressure to be perfect is almost too much to handle, and we end up feeling incompetent and worthless. Hopelessness sets in, with depression right on its heels.

MANIPULATION

Manipulation hooks up with perfectionism as another disobedient behavior and is not just stinky, but has such a pungent odor that it drives people away in disgust. Manipulation fits together with perfectionism because it gives us control so that we can create the perfect environment around us and in us. In order to do this, we have to manipulate people and circumstances to fit our time, our agenda, and our way. We need to be made aware, however, that whenever we take over God's job of running the universe, sooner or later we will run into obstacles.

Manipulating people and events to get what we want is not part of God's plan for our lives. When we manipulate victories, we may find enjoyment, but it is very brief and rarely ours to keep. We will never truly experience God's joy for our lives, or fully understand God's purpose for us, because we are too busy creating our own individual life plans.

We will soon discover that we cannot manipulate people and circumstances in our lives without leaving a trail of destruction. People will eventually get tired of our game and leave us behind. Instead of taking the time to enjoy true loving relationships, we fill our lives with activities that temporarily make us feel better but have no eternal value. We value the perfect completion of tasks rather than spending time with people during the process.

Manipulating for love

Most often, we instinctively manipulate people *for love* because it is what we need the most to survive emotionally. As human beings, we are so desperate to know that we are loved that we will do whatever it takes to have it. Our lack of security makes us do ugly, stinky things. Let's face it: as women, we are great manipulators, using cunning along with all our female charms and subtle words to get our way. From the beginning of creation until this very moment, looking for love has been one of our greatest struggles. Let's look at two stories in the Bible that give us a very clear picture of the ways women have manipulated people and circumstances to give them what they thought they wanted.

1. The Story of Rachel and Leah (Gen. 29:31-30:24)

Here is the story of two women locked in a cruel contest for their husband's affections. Rachel was loved by her husband but could not conceive. Leah could conceive, but didn't have her husband's love. They both manipulated love by having more and more children. The plot thickens as Rachel lets her husband sleep with her sister in exchange for a mandrake plant (a love plant to help barren women conceive). Rachel and Leah both ended up giving their maidservants to their husband to sleep with him. They learned that there is no happy ending to manipulation.

2. The Story of Delilah (Judg. 16)

Delilah was a calculating woman who was aware of her sensual powers and frequently used them to manipulate men for her own personal gain.

She feigned affection for Samson so that she could find out where his power came from. By pretending to love him and allowing him to use her body, she manipulated Samson to get rich; then she betrayed him so that she would become rich.

As women, we can use our sexual powers, beauty, and sweet words to easily obtain things or manipulate love. Remember, though, that what we manipulate to possess is rarely ours to keep. When our carefully orchestrated manipulations fall apart, it will eventually break our hearts.

Getting Rid of Stinkiness

So what are we to do with this stinkiness that causes us to allow circumstances to escalate way beyond our control? Oh, I know that you and I both want hearts that are so filled with beautiful things that the radiance will exude from us wherever we go. In order to have it, we must remember that the word *obey* is the ticket to our life of *joy*. Nobody likes the word *obey;* it insinuates that we have to do something we really don't want to do. But God has put that command in His Word because He knows that this is the only way we will find peace in our lives, which will ultimately lead to lasting joy.

As perfectionists, we are rarely at peace because we are always striving to put something in order or achieve an ultimate vision. Our mind is always working, measuring results, double-checking on all the details, filling in all the blanks, and checking items off our "to do" list. Jesus tells us: "When you obey me you are living in my love, just as I obey my Father and live in his love. I have told you this so that you will be filled with my joy. Yes, your cup of joy will overflow" (John 15:10, 11 TLB).

Just how is obedience going to give me more joy?

- God tells us not to worry; He will take care of our needs (Matt. 6:25).
- He tells us not be afraid (Matt. 14:17).
- He says that He will help us carry our burdens (Matt. 11:28).
- He promises that we will have an eternal home after we die (John 14:2).

- He will remove all our sins (1 John 1:9).
- He will give us wisdom (James 1:5).
- We are exhorted to pray so that our prayers will heal us (James 5:13).

This *cup of joy that will overflow* is what you and I want. God intends for us to experience authentic joy, free from the need to be perfect and manipulate circumstances and people. Strange as it seems, the way to discover this joy is through simple obedience. In order to do this, we have to give up control of doing it our way, and begin to do it God's way.

Perfect in Him

The world around us holds up the ideal of perfection as a laudable goal. We hear about perfectionism in many areas of our lives—in our workplaces and, unfortunately, in our churches. We are advised to do things with excellence to honor and glorify God, but to us that implies perfection. At my job, I work with numbers all day. All of those figures need to be put into their perfect spots in order for the financial statement to be correct at the end of the month. Frankly, we are often dissatisfied with a project unless we hear that it was done perfectly.

The Scriptures encourage us to aim high: "Be perfect, therefore, as your heavenly Father is perfect" (Matt. 5:48 NIV). When Jesus tells us to be perfect, we have to understand that God's idea of perfection is radically different from that of the world's. The world's concept of perfection is:

- A perfect, svelte body;
- A perfect, happy, happy family;
- An influential career;
- Influential friends.

Perfectionism involves doing our best for all the wrong reasons. It is all about you and me, not about God. Here is the shocking part: the end result of our efforts can look exactly the same, but the difference lies in the *motive* of the heart.

We become *perfect in Him* as we become more like Him. The longer we spend time with people, the more we take on their qualities and characteristics. Likewise, the more time we spend with Jesus, the more we will be perfect, like Him. We need to find out what Jesus is like by reading the Bible, talking to Him in prayer, and discovering His beauty through creation and His promises of hope. Unfortunately for us perfectionistic women, spending time with Jesus has absolutely nothing to do with "doing", but it has everything to do with "being with Him." The more we get to know Jesus, the more we will trust and obey Him. It is hard for a perfectionist to let go of the doing, but that is what must happen if we want to find complete joy.

Throughout the Bible, people tried to fix their relationship with God with animal sacrifices, the firstfruits of their crops, or gifts of money. But God took care of all our sin by sending His Son to die on the cross for you and me as the final sacrifice so we could experience His wonderful grace. Grace simply means a free gift of new life.

In order for us to experience joy in our lives, one crucial point of *obedience* is accepting God's gift of grace in our lives. Grace and joy go together.

The Greek word for grace is *charis*: "that which bestows or occasions pleasure, delight, or causes favorable regard."[53] It applies to beauty or the gracefulness of person. The Greek word for "joy" is *chara*, which means joy or delight. They are connected: both come from the same root word. When you begin to receive and understand grace, you will experience joy. *Perfectionism* steals joy, but *perfect in Him* creates joy.

Paul gave this word of encouragement to the early church in Corinth: "But he said to me, 'My grace is sufficient for you, for my power is made perfect in weakness'" (2 Cor. 12:9 NIV). It is hard to comprehend this, but God's power is really demonstrated through our weakness, a principle that should give us courage and hope. We need to learn to rely on God for our effectiveness, rather than on our own strength and energy.

If we are perfectionists, we'll find it hard to accept that concept. It is difficult to let go of a lifetime of pushing ourselves to be strong and relying solely on ourselves to make everything perfect. It will not be easy to accept when God says, "It's OK, you can stop now; all you need is My grace."

We are supposed to do our best only as a *natural response* to God's love in our lives. The more we learn to love God with all of our hearts in everything we do, the more we will begin to experience His grace and quit working so hard to earn His love. Let's face it: we can never work hard enough to be perfect in this life, so let's quit trying. Let's just take a deep breath, obey God, and let Him run the universe.

Unleashing our Beauty Through Pure Motives

I am constantly in the process of learning how to apply God's grace in my life. The more I comprehend the word "grace" and let it travel from my head into my heart, the more I am released from my own prison of perfectionism. I don't believe I have fully begun to comprehend this little word that grants me freedom from my daily striving. Nevertheless, I am so grateful that God continues to teach me with such kindness through humorous and life-changing stories with objects as simple as a sea shell. If I would have obeyed little Ryan, today I would be the proud owner of a beautiful sea shell heart sitting in my Angels Corner office. Sadly, I thought I knew better. Each day I am trying to obey God in every area of my life, so that I will radiate the delightful aroma of a beautiful heart wherever I go. I am so tired of stinkiness! Every day, God is trying to teach me about grace because He has a more glorious life for me than I could ever imagine. He is telling me to "loosen up" and let Him run this universe.

In order for me to give up my ways of perfectionistic thinking, I had to realize first of all that I had this stinky disease and understand how it affected my life and the lives of people around me. Until I acknowledged that I had these stinky traits, I was not able to let go of them. God can only unleash our beauty when we are finally willing to hand over our stinkiness to Him. In order to release our perfectionism and manipulation, we have to acknowledge that we have these stinky traits.

Do you:

- Get irritated when things don't go according to your plan?
- Lay awake at night agonizing over a project that you are not satisfied with?

- Find yourself playing with words just to get your way?
- Go back and "fix" things other people have done?
- Believe that if you never did another "perfect thing" in your life, your parents/children/husband/friends would still love you anyway?
- Believe that God loves you just for who you are, not for what you do?
- Check your response when someone is displeased with something you have done?
- Let other people help you finish your projects?

Sometimes the results of excellence and perfectionism can look the same because the motive is hidden deep within our hearts. We always have to ask ourselves if we are obeying God *along the way*, or choosing to do it *our way?*

We unleash beauty in our hearts when we grasp the concept that we cannot earn God's love. As the essence of love, God does not know how to do anything but love you and me. The more that you and I trust Him and *obey* the words that He has laid out for us so clearly in the Bible, the more that we will progress in our spiritual growth by reflecting Christ's characteristics. We need to relax and laugh more. There is something very liberating about being around a woman who does not have an agenda for everyone and everything in her life. She is fun, joyful, and her flexible and relaxed attitude is contagious.

Every time we do it "our way" and not "God's way," we will end up with stinkiness in our lives. Thus, in order to unleash our glorious beauty of pure motives, we need to:

- Begin to understand the word "grace"
- Accept the help God sends us
- Comprehend that we do not have to be perfect in order for God to love us, or to earn God's love
- Obey God's Word
- Have pure motives to bring glory to God in everything that we do
- Refrain from doing everything to bring attention to ourselves
- Stop rating all our achievements

- Be able to let someone else finish our task or project
- Walk away from something that we know is not the way we envisioned it to be
- Welcome anybody into our home even though it is messy that day
- Do everything, not to complete an agenda, but with the motive of love

In *The Pursuit of God*, A. W. Tozer says, "Now over against this set almost any Bible character who honestly tried to glorify God in his earthly walk. See how God winked at weakness and overlooked failures as He poured upon His servants grace and blessing untold.... The man of God set his heart to exalt God above all; God accepted his intention as fact and acted accordingly. Not perfection, but holy intention made the difference." [54]

Can you see God's grace in that statement? Not *perfection*, but *holy intention*. When our pure motives involve obeying God and trusting Him for what He wants to work out in our lives, the result does not have to be perfect. Can we accept that as fact and learn to live that way?

When we have lived a life of perfectionism, it will not be easy to adopt a new way of thinking and acting. To this very day, I still question what I do by holding it up against the light of eternity. I ask myself, "Will anybody care about this next week, or five years from now? Is anybody going to lose sleep over this besides me? Will anybody notice or even care if all the napkins and candles don't match?" At the end of the day, it's all just "stuff." The only question that is my measuring tape these days is, "Did I love people during the process?" If I am not sure that I loved well, then I know there is some perfectionism in me that still needs to die. It tells me that I paid more attention to the details of the "stuff" than the people involved.

We must come to the point of abandoning everything that causes stinkiness in our lives. Until we get disgusted with the way we are trudging through life trying to earn love through perfectionism, there will always be a struggle to obey God by accepting His marvelous gift of grace.

Taking a sea shell that little Ryan told me not to take was a small act of disobedience. The stinkiness resulting from that act was not life-shattering; all it did was pinch my pride and cause me some embarrassment.

But disobedience to God has a greater impact on our lives. When we try to live "our way" we will be robbed of all the joy and freedom that He intended for our lives.

Stop and ask God to Unleash Your Beauty

Begin by asking: God, what disobedience or wrong motive in my life is causing stinkiness?

S—Scripture: "For God is at work within you, helping you want to obey him, and then helping you do what he wants" (Phil. 2:13 TLB).

T—Thanksgiving: Thank You, God, that I do not have to work hard to earn Your love. Thank You that it is not about perfection, but holy intention.

O—Observation: Obedience is so important to God that He wants to help me obey Him. He loves me so much that He wants me to enjoy what I am doing. How glorious is that?

P—Prayer: Father, I simply fall on my knees when I hear the word "grace". Teach me to not only comprehend that word in my head, but allow its meaning to flow into my heart as well. I ask that You would soak my heart in grace so that all the stinkiness will be washed away. I ask You, God that you show me any perfectionism in my life. Make it very clear to me when I am trying to run this universe instead of letting You do it. Forgive me for those times that I have manipulated others and situations to accomplish things "my way," even when I knew that it was not part of Your plan for me. I ask that You would quicken my heart when I am disobeying You. Show me the plans that You have for my life so that You can mold me into the person You created me to be. Forgive me for creating my own life plans. Show me more and more every day to stop trying to earn Your love, but rather to allow Your love to flow through every fiber of my being. I ask that in Jesus' name. Amen.

11

UNLEASHING THE
BEAUTY OF PRAYER
Prayer Is a Melting

Our hands soil, it seems, whatever they caress,
but they too have their beauty when they are joined in prayer.
Young hands were made for caresses and the sheathing of love.
It is a pity to make them join too soon.

—ANDRE GIDE, FRENCH AUTHOR (1869–1951)

HE RICH COLORS of Africa were my inspiration. Its rustic red soil, golden ripe mangoes, and yellow-wood and baobab trees warmly invited my mind to use some of those very colors in my keynote address and presentation for "The World Day of Prayer 2006." Some women from Africa had written an inspiring and prayerful program called the *Sign of the Times,* and I was honored to be speaking on behalf of the city of Kelowna. To complement the rich, visual colors of Africa, I decided to incorporate colorful fabrics as part of my illustrations.

On the day of the event as I was speaking from this large platform, my eyes connected with the faces that were gazing up at me. As I made eye contact with members of the audience, they smiled or nodded in agreement with what I was saying. I always find these nonverbal gestures so encouraging because they give me more energy and spur me on. Throughout my message, a friend behind me displayed the rich, vibrant fabrics which brought life and meaning to what I was saying. Halfway through my message, my lapel mike sputtered and went dead, and then the entire auditorium went black. I had no idea what happened, but my instincts told me to keep speaking. Unaware that there was an electrical black-out in this part of our city, I kept waiting for the sound and lights to come back on any minute. From every part of the audience, people jumped up to open doors and bring in flashlights and candles so that there would be some light in the auditorium. I tried to ignore all the distractions by concentrating on notes that I could barely see. Feeling confused and helpless, I kept speaking. I could no longer see any of the faces in the audience, so it felt like I was speaking into a big, dark hole. People tried to put candles in front of the fabrics to display the colors, but it was a futile effort. The electricity did not come back on, so the colorful, vivacious images for the message had been lost, leaving the remainder of my message lifeless and without resolution.

The strangest part for me on that stage was speaking to an audience with whom I could no longer make eye contact or assess their receptivity and energy. Whenever I speak, I feel like I am *communicating* with my audience rather than just *talking* to them. That day I found out how unresponsive and empty it feels to be talking to someone when I am not sure, first of all, if they are even there, and second, if they are listening. It just feels all meaningless and useless.

This unusual occurrence helped me to understand the frustrations people experience in their prayer lives, as well as the importance of knowing that we are *communicating* with God rather than just *talking* to Him.

We have all experienced *talking* to someone when it feels like we are speaking to a concrete wall. Even though they are standing or sitting right in front of us, their eyes are vacant, so we know their thoughts are not focused on us. As little children, we remember asking our parents for something but finding them unresponsive because they were either too busy or distracted to answer us. Many people feel the same way about prayer, believing that God is not interested or too busy to answer our feeble prayers. It feels like we are talking into a big, black hole, and we're not sure that anyone is even there and listening.

Prayer is *communicating* with the Most High God. He longs for us to be in such a close relationship with Him that when we are talking to Him, we will know that He is there listening, nodding, and smiling as our most eager supporter or best friend. He also wants us to stop and be quiet long enough to hear Him talking to us with a still, small voice in our soul.

From the soft voice of a child's first prayer to the raspy, whispered one uttered with an aged Christian's last breath, prayer is the greatest power and privilege on this side of heaven. Prayer is a gift from God that gives us an opportunity to talk with Him anytime, anywhere. To be able to communicate with Him, we don't need special equipment or technology. We can do it any time, day or night—sitting, laying down, standing up, or walking. We can do it with our eyes closed or wide open. There is no special formula or format. If we can think or talk, we can also pray.

Whenever I am involved in a conversation or teaching about prayer, I notice that people often get quiet and their eyes shift downward. I can palpably feel their guilt and awkwardness. As Christians, most of us realize that there is great power in prayer. We know that we should pray, and we want to, but we make these excuses:

- We don't know how.
- We feel intimidated by the way other people pray.
- We don't feel like it.
- We're not convinced that it makes any difference.
- We're too busy or tired, and we don't have any extra time.
- Why would God want to answer my prayer?

And so, we heap even more guilt on our shoulders.

Many people make a determined resolution that says: From this day forward I am going to have a prayer life. I'm going to do it because I know it is good for me, and I know I should. It's like making an appointment with the dentist to get one's teeth cleaned, or starting on a dreaded vitamin and exercise program.

So, we establish mind-numbing rituals such as these:

- "I'll pray every time I stop at a red traffic light."
- "I'll fill in one name I'm praying for on each calendar square."
- "I'll set an alarm on my phone or computer and every time I hear it I'll pray."
- "I'll pray while I am jogging or riding an exercise bike."
- "I'll get up at 5:00 each morning to pray."

When we use these gimmicks to satisfy our New Year's resolutions, they will probably fail dismally because they sound like drudgery and hard work. Over time, however, these rituals can become powerful, life-changing disciplines *if* there is *passion and relationship* drawing us to the designated place and time.

Prayer is not something that comes naturally to us. As women, many of us have earned the right to be independent. We have learned that if we want things done, we must attend to them ourselves. Many of us never ask for help from anybody; we'd rather do it ourselves.

Prayer is not a rigid set of rules but a passionate relationship to be experienced with our heavenly Father. It does not involve *talking* to Someone through humanly generated formula prayers, but it is rather about *communicating* with Someone who is listening, loves us back, and is zealous about us living a fulfilled life. We need to feel as if Christ is sitting in a chair in front of us, leaning forward eagerly to catch every one of our words. In order for us to pray willingly and favorably, we need to understand it and become enthusiastic about it.

PASSION

If we are not passionately in love with God and captivated by Him, prayer feels more like just another obligation to fulfill, such as writing "thank you" notes, or punishment, such as working at a hard marriage. Life already has too many responsibilities without adding one more thing to our "to do" and "guilt" list.

1. We become passionate when we learn about the power of prayer.

We know that we are instructed to pray; the Bible is very clear about that: "Always keep on praying" (1 Thess. 5:17 TLB). How do we do this?

My own passion for prayer started in the early eighties when my pastor's wife, Helen Block, taught a Sunday evening series on prayer. During those years, going to church on Sunday evenings was "the right thing to do," so I attended more out of duty than a willing spirit. Yet, these lessons surprised me because I learned principles of prayer that I had never known before. It was also the first time I understood the concept of the power of prayer in our lives.

Helen taught this series from her own intimate passion with a loving God, and I was able to catch her energy and transparent desire for God. Her personal life was a living testimony about the peace she experienced through the power of prayer during her ongoing battle with cancer. I watched her as her body was ravaged throughout the different stages of cancer, but I also witnessed God restoring her body time after time. She believed in prayer with every breath of her being, and her passion spurred me on to explore it further.

This teaching was my first step toward understanding that a loving, powerful God wanted to have an intimate relationship with me through one-on-one communication. With concentrated discipline, I established a special time to meet with God on a regular basis. Now that I had the knowledge about prayer, I longed to start on my path of putting it into practice. I got up at six each morning to spend time with God in worshipping Him, reading the Bible, and praying. The more I prayed, the more I learned about God's great love for me. The more I fell in love with Him, the more I became passionate about prayer.

2. We become passionate when we realize how much we are loved.

Love has the greatest power to motivate us. In my earthly relationships, I need to know that the person I am talking to loves me enough that I can trust them with my feelings, my hurts, my anger, and my future. Yet, each of us has a different vision of who God is. What does your God look like?

- Is He an angry God looking down at you and pointing a finger at you because you are always doing something wrong?
- Is He unreachable, uninvolved, and emotionally absent?
- Is He a God whom you believe that you can only talk to when you get to heaven?
- Is He there for other people who have more education and study the Bible more?
- Is He a God who cares about the pain in this world?

Our view of God is often formed by experiences we encountered as little children. If we were raised in a loving home that was full of laughter and acceptance, we will see Him as a loving, gentle, and attentive God. On the other hand, if we were raised in an atmosphere of anger and harsh words or had an emotionally distant father, we will see God as an irritated, impatient, and unkind tyrant whom we can never please.

Whenever I teach a Bible study, I always tell my participants that I will pray regularly for them. In one of my studies, there was a delightful, energetic woman named Beth. She was unfamiliar with the concept of speaking to a holy God who would listen to her hurts and desires and care about the everyday challenges in her life. When I asked her if she had any request for her life that I could pray for, she looked at me puzzled and replied, *"What channel is God on, exactly?"*[55] I grinned at her unusual response. Later, she explained to me that she thought God was someone you talk to when you get to heaven. This notion of a God who hears us while we are still on earth was a difficult one for her to grasp. As we talked more about our loving God's desire for us to communicate with Him through prayer because He wanted to have an intimate, passionate relationship with us, it gave her a whole new picture of who God really was. Just as Helen inspired me to explore prayer in the eighties, I also hoped to give Beth boldness and insight to begin approaching heaven's door with her own prayers.

The entire Bible is a book of God's love letters to us:

"This is how God showed his love among us: He sent his one and only Son into the world that we might live through him. This is love: Not that we loved God, but that he loved us and sent his Son as an atoning sacrifice for our sins" (1 John 4:9, 10 NIV).

In *The Life-Changing Power of Prayer,* T.W. Hunt describes the nature of our God who cares:

"Prayer can have no meaning unless it takes into account God's total nature. He is holy; we come to Him on those grounds. He is love: we pray knowing that He is concerned about our needs. Because He is merciful, God understands and cares about our needs." [56]

Although I have read many books on prayer, it was only when I actually began to pray that my passion was fueled. In the secret place of prayer, I discovered the tenderness of a holy God who cares for me and only wants the very best for my life.

3. We feel our passion rising when we know someone is listening.

The word "communicate" means, "to share in or partake of; to give or interchange thoughts, information, or the like." [57] Prayer is not a *transaction* between God and man; it is an *interaction or interchange of thoughts.* Communication builds a relationship through dialogue. God tells Isaiah: "Come now, let us reason *together"* (Isa.1:18 NIV).

One of our greatest satisfactions in life is knowing that someone is listening to us. Many of you may feel like Beth when she asked what frequency God was on. How do we dial into Him and know that He is actually listening? God encourages us to call on Him because He is available twenty-four hours a day, 365 days of the year. In essence, we have a hot-line to God. Even though we may not always sense His presence, He promises that He is always there:

- "...the Lord will hear when I call to him" (Psalm 4:3b NIV).
- "Hear my prayer, O Lord; listen to my cry for mercy. In the day of my trouble I will call to you, for you will answer me" (Psalm 86:6, 7 NIV).
- "Call to me and I will answer you and tell you great and unsearchable things you do not know" (Jer. 33:3 NIV).
- "Before they call I will answer; while they are still speaking I will hear" (Isa. 65:24 NIV).

In the midst of all the heartache and worry that we deal with in our everyday existence, we need to know that there is a greater power that we can turn to. We need to know that someone is listening who cares enough to hear our pain and our angry and confused hearts. Gordon MacDonald shares this very thought in his book *The Resilient Life:*

"Lord, do you mind if I shout at you out of my heart? I recently prayed. I found myself angry, boiling at the news that streams from Africa of dying and orphaned children, raped women, homeless refugees, millions of women with AIDS, villages with poisoned water...There are prayers for my family, my friends, for the church around the world....There is the genuine ache in my heart to be a deeper person, one who reflects more of the character of Christ. It doesn't come fast enough and that demands prayer." [58]

If I don't believe that God is listening to me, it will feel like I am speaking into a big, black, empty hole where nobody cares. It is exciting when we begin to experience answers to our prayers, because then we know for certain that God is very close to us, listening intently.

Patricia Raybon, author of *Mountain Mover,* shares how her prayer life started:

"So Patricia began to pray to know God. Every morning, she started praising God's names, names she'd heard all her life but never stopped to think about: '*Jehovah Jireh,* my Provider! *Jehovah Rapha,* my Healer! *Jehova Nissi,* my Banner in times of war!' Then something happened. For the first time in my life I felt God listening. Suddenly, I realized *this* is prayer." [59]

When I started to pray for Beth and she began to see visible results to answered prayer, her excitement was unquenchable. She stated, "*The idea that God is on some sort of 'frequency' like your favorite radio station is exciting, daunting, exhilarating, scary, and frustrating—to name a few things. This is something one might experience when we are 'still and hear.'*" Beth grasped the concept that when we are quiet before God, we discover that He is listening, loving, and just waiting to hear from us. Through this experience God not only changed Beth's circumstances, but He also did something even more miraculous: He changed Beth's heart.

DOES GOD ANSWER PRAYER?

This is the big question everyone asks. Absolutely, yes; God does answer prayer. But I believe that we are really looking for the formula that will make God answer our prayers in the way we want. If we were able to find it, we would be able to say that we have unraveled the mysteries of God. The God we pray to is the God who created the majestic Rocky Mountains, placed each star in the heavens, designed each flower, and told the oceans where to stop. He designed the fingerprint of each newborn baby and gave the fish their various colors. He knows everything in His creation intimately, from the tiniest ladybug to the elephants roaming the African plains. How can we challenge and question the mind of someone who did all this? We have to realize that this God still knows more about our future than you and I.

We want God to be a "go to" person who will give us what we want, when we want it. We hurriedly mumble a prayer and then expect to turn around and find the answer immediately. God is interested in every detail of our lives, but His utmost intention for our lives is that we grow in character and faith, while He shows us His love and prepares us for our eternal future. God also works on a different timetable than we do: He does not work on a twenty-four-hour clock. For Him, one day is as a thousand years, and a thousand years is like one day. It is difficult to create a method, ten-step program, or formula for a God whose ways and thoughts are much higher than ours. He reminds us: "As the heavens are higher than the earth, so are my ways higher than your ways, and my thoughts than your thoughts" (Isa. 55:9 NIV).

God is our heavenly Father; He created us and we are His children. Let's put that into the context of our earthly family. When we were children and asked our fathers for things, did they always give us what we wanted? Because of the love my earthly father had for me, I know he would not have given me the keys to his car when I was thirteen, or allow me to climb a step- ladder and paint the ceiling when I was five.

As little children, we loved to run to our parents when we had a broken toy or needed help with something. It would have been so easy for them to fix everything for us right then and there. We would have been able to grab that toy and run and play again. When our parents took the time to show us how to fix something, we got to build a relationship with them by spending time together, learning to talk to each other, and thus getting to know each other better.

Our earthly fathers do whatever it takes to protect us, prepare us for the time we leave home, and build our character. I believe that God is no different. He is like our earthly father, desiring us to come to Him with our broken toys, our broken dreams, and our hurting bodies. This is not just so He can fix them, but so He can also build our character and create a loving relationship with us while doing it. In the process, He can change us into the people He created us to be.

We have to trust Him with His answers of Yes, No, and Wait. In Hebrews 11, we read two different answers to faithful prayers:

1. *Yes*
   "…who through faith conquered kingdoms, administered justice, gained what was promised, shut the mouths of lions, quenched the fury of the flames, and escaped the edge of the sword; whose weakness was turned into strength; and who became powerful in battle and routed foreign enemies, women received back their dead, raised to life again" (Heb. 11:33-35 NIV).

I love the "yes" answers in my life. Yes, Heidi, you can accept that speaking engagement. Yes, I will heal your ankle. Yes, I will help you with that complex financial situation at work. Yes, I will give you a heart-connection friend. Yes, I will give you that time of rest. Yes, I will help you work out your holiday plans with your children.

I must confess that all the "yes" answers to my prayers over the years have motivated me to pray more. They have also convinced me that there is a God who listens. He is not distant, but so close that He can hear my words and listen to the whispers of my heart.

2. No

"Some faced jeers and flogging, while still others were chained and put in prison. They were stoned; they were sawed in two; they were put to death by the sword. They went about in sheepskins and goatskins, destitute, persecuted and mistreated....They were all commended for their faith, yet none of them received what had been promised" (Heb. 11:36-39 NIV).

None of us like the "no" answer because we are like little children who want what we want when we want it. We think that when we get what we want, it will make us feel better, and we will be happier.

My husband Jack's former wife Donna was actually my employer for a short period of time. When she was going through the final stages of cancer, I watched and listened as people prayed for her. I have never heard such powerful, genuine, and confident prayers from those believing that God would heal her. For over a year, people met in her home and prayed with fervency that I have never experienced before. But God said "no," so she died. On this side of eternity, we will probably never understand the "no" answers of God. We must believe that God only answers "no" when He has something better waiting for us.

3. Wait.

"I will wait for the Lord, who is hiding his face from the house of Jacob. I will put my trust in him" (Isa. 8:17 NIV).

Waiting for somebody to do something is very frustrating because we need to see results right away. While we are in a *waiting mode,* we feel aimless and without resolution. As I am writing this, I have a friend who is waiting for an answer from God about a new career. She was so sure that she heard from God about the new direction in her life. He answered all her other prayers with a very definitive "yes." Now all of a sudden, every door has closed. She is now hearing *wait*, and it is so very difficult. When we hear "wait," it feels like we are sitting in the middle of an intersection and don't know which way to turn.

Even though God asks us to pray, our earnest prayers cannot convince or persuade Him to answer in the way we want Him to. Gordon MacDonald says:

> "Many times I have gone to prayer with results in mind. I wanted to gain control over the people and events I was praying about by dictating to the Father my views on how things should come out. When I do this, I am looking at people and events through an earthly lens and not a heavenly one. I am praying as though I know better than God what is best for the outcome." [60]

When talking to people who are concerned that God is not answering their prayers, Bill Hybels uses an outline that he borrowed from a pastor friend:

"If the request is wrong, God says, 'No.'"

"If the timing is wrong, God says, 'Slow.'"

"If you are wrong, God says, 'Grow.'"

"But if the request is right, the timing is right, and you are right, God says, 'Go!'" [61]

God is only on one frequency: the *love channel*. Because He passionately loves us, every answer that He gives us will help us become more joyful people, develop stronger character, make us wiser, and prepare us for eternity.

STARTING TO PRAY

I personally believe that worldly distractions are some of our greatest obstacles in beginning a vital prayer life. We live in a noisy, high-stimulation generation that offers so many other exciting activities to entertain us. On most days, everything looks much more appealing than spending quiet time with a God whom we can't see. Here are some ways to overcome distractions:

1. Go away and shut the door.

The first thing we need to do is find a quiet place where we can be alone. We need to turn off the phone, stop checking our e-mail, and close the door in our room. This is how we will begin to know who God is. Psalm 46:10 says, "Be still, and know that I am God" (NIV). When Jesus taught His disciples to pray, He said to them:

> "Here's what I want you to do: Find a quiet, secluded place so you won't be tempted to role-play before God. Just be there as simply and honestly as you can manage. The focus will shift from you to God, and you will begin to sense his grace" (Matt. 6:6 MSG).

Jesus knew that He needed to be alone with God in a quiet place. When we get away from the noise and interruptions of the world around us, we can be open and honest before God. We can say what we want and don't have to be ashamed about it. This needs to be a safe place where we can begin to talk and listen to God so that we can build a relationship of authenticity and trust with Him.

2. Pray the Scriptures.

God speaks to us through His Scriptures. One of my favorite places to read God's words is in the Psalms because they are filled with emotions of praise, worship, honesty, and anguish. Their vivid language rescues us from boring repetition in our prayers. In fact, the words in the Psalms are as relevant today as they were in King David's time. As we begin to read them, they can become the launching pad for taking us beyond our usual, general prayer: "Lord, we pray for Aunt Lila, and bless the new neighbors." We can either read the Psalms silently or make them into a prayer spoken aloud. This exercise not only gives us spiritual nourishment, but it also keeps our mind focused. Before we begin reading, we should always ask God to speak to us through the Holy Spirit so that our hearts will respond in prayer to what He is showing us. By the time you have read all 150 chapters, you will be propelled into an exciting prayer pattern that you will be eager to use regularly.

Praying Scriptures out loud will also allow you to hear what your voice sounds like. Sooner or later, a time will come when someone will ask you to pray for someone or in front of a group. Your heart may begin to pound so hard that it feels like it is coming out of your chest. Praying Scriptures out loud not only brings you great joy and keeps you focused, but it also prepares you for the inevitable...praying out loud.

3. Find the best time of the day.

Each of us will be less vulnerable to distractions when we are praying at the time of day that we are the most alert. This will be different for everyone. Gordon MacDonald says,

> "All of us will find different parts of the day best for our spiritual disciplines. I am a morning person; but one of my closest friends tells me that he finds the evening hours best. Whereas I begin the day in prayer, he ends it that way. Neither of us has airtight arguments for his choice; I think it is a matter of individual rhythms. Daniel of Babylon solved the problem by being a morning and evening person—and a noontime person too." [62]

There is no "right" or "wrong" time for prayer. Our different personalities will determine which time of the day will work best for us.

4. Write in a journal.

This is a wonderful exercise that can keep us focused by its tangible results. Journaling not only eliminates distractions, but it also allows us to pour our hearts out to God on paper. There is something very healing and therapeutic about writing out our prayers. I personally find that when I write my prayers, it feels like I have recorded my struggles before God in a very honest and concrete way. This brings me great peace and leaves me with a sense that I have accomplished something.

Journaling is not for everyone, however. When I first heard about journaling, it intimidated me because all I could picture in my mind was someone hunched over their desk, writing spiritually inspired chronicles. Now I know that journaling is just a form of writing out our most intimate thoughts and feelings. It can be just one more avenue to explore in order to overcome distractions when beginning our prayer time.

5. Follow a prayer pattern.

For those of you just starting your prayer life, it is good to have a template of some kind to help you to know what to pray and how to keep focused. There are also many wonderful books available that have prayers written by other people which can enrich our lives and keep us devoted in our prayer life.

Another method that is easy to understand and use is called **ACTS.** This is what it means:

A *Adoration:* Take time to acknowledge who our great God is, praise Him for His loving attributes of power, goodness, and love, and thank Him for being the source of all our blessings. By worshipping and praising God, we allow our hearts to open up in our relationship with Him. Just because He is in heaven does not mean that He is distant from us. He is different from the world because He is an invisible spirit, but He still hears us. We can start our time with God simply by saying as I often do, "I praise You for the beautiful world that You created for us, and I am thrilled to be alive today."

C *Confession:* God is holy. When we are confronted by His holiness, we recognize the sin in our lives. By confessing our sins, we are acknowledging that we are sinners. God will not hear our prayers when we *deliberately harbor* sin in our hearts: "…but your iniquities have separated you from your God; your sins have hidden his face from you, so that he will not hear" (Isa. 59:2 NIV).

When we confess our sin, it will bring us back into beautiful harmony with God. "If we confess our sins, he is faithful and just and will forgive us our sins and purify us from all unrighteousness" (1 John 1:9 NIV).

We need to come clean before God because nothing is hidden from Him anyway. When our guilt and shame is out in the open, we always feel better. God also knows that when we confess our sins, their power and bondage over us is broken. We may say something like, "I confess that I was jealous of the other women across from me in the room. I know that jealousy is a hurtful and destructive emotion. I am sorry and I ask that You forgive me. Thank You that You forgive us of our sins." It is so comforting to know that God *always* forgives us: that is what He died for.

T *Thanksgiving:* When we thank God for everything in our lives, we acknowledge that He is the provider of everything. We are told in the Scriptures to pray with thanksgiving:

- "Devote yourselves to prayer, being watchful and thankful" (Col. 4:2 NIV).
- "...always giving thanks to God the Father for everything" (Eph. 5:20 NIV).

When we look around and begin to thank God for things in our lives, it will open up a floodgate of realization about how much He blesses us. We all know how much we love it when someone remembers to say "thank you" to us. God is no different. In fact, we enter God's heart through thanksgiving. Thank God for everything you can, and see how it blesses both you and Him.

S *Supplication:* The word simply means to "petition humbly." This is the part in our prayer time when we can place all our burdens and requests into God's hands. We are told to ask freely and boldly:

- "You do not have because you do not ask God" (James 4:2 NIV).
- "If you remain in me and my words remain in you, ask whatever you wish, and it will be given you" (John 15:7 NIV).

- "Ask and it will be given you; seek and you will find; knock and the door will be opened to you. For everyone who asks receives; he who seeks finds; and to him who knocks, the door will be opened" (Matt. 7:7-8 NIV).

Before I even considered approaching anyone with such boldness, I would have to feel confident that this person loves me and has only my best interests at heart. We need to know that when we pray the way we have been commanded to—*in the name of Jesus*—He will be a friend who will love us through anything.

He needs to be the kind of friend you can go to at 3 in the morning. He needs to be the kind of friend that we can bang on His door until He comes to help. We need to know that He loves us enough not to get annoyed with us, to gladly help us in our need, and to love us through our struggles. This is the kind of confidence and boldness we need to have when praying to our God. He loves us so much that He tells us to come and *knock on His door.* He wants us to come to Him with all our burdens, bruises, and anxiety. He doesn't mind us knocking until He comes and gives us what we need, but we need to do it believing and expecting that He will answer.

SIMPLE PRAYERS

Many women come to me and say they would like to pray more but don't think they can "do it right." After assuring them that there is no "right" or "wrong" way, I always tell them that if they can talk, they can pray. I think many people get very intimidated by listening to people who pray eloquent, long, and academic prayers filled with "thees" and "thous."

One of the experiences I treasure greatly is hearing a brand-new Christian pray. Their simple, childlike, honest sentences make my heart leap with new hope. It is almost the same feeling I had after hearing my own children say, "Mommy" for the first time. It didn't matter that it was the only word they said, or that they spoke it with the awkwardness of a baby, but that they *spoke my name.* I truly believe God longs to hear our authentic, unrehearsed, stumbling prayers. These are the unedited and unfiltered prayers that come right out of our hearts and reach the very throne room of God.

Another simple prayer which we can use is the most famous of all prayers: *The Lord's Prayer.* Jesus Himself taught His disciples:

> "Our Father in heaven, hallowed be your name, your kingdom come, your will be done on earth as it is in heaven. Give us today our daily bread. Forgive us our debts, as we also have forgiven our debtors. And lead us not into temptation, but deliver us from the evil one" (Matt. 6:9-13 NIV).

People hear our words, but God hears the true motives of our hearts. Let's make our words few, but with honesty and consistency.

Prayer Is a Melting

One of the most compelling authors on prayer is Mme. Guyon, who wrote *Experiencing the Depths of Jesus Christ* in 1685. This inspiring book has not only been a disciplined study course for me: it contains words that have entered my soul as pure joy:

> "What is prayer? Prayer is a certain warmth of love. Ah, but more! *Prayer is a melting!* (italics mine) Prayer is a dissolving and an uplifting of the soul. This warmth of love, this melting, this dissolving and uplifting causes the soul to ascend to God. As the soul is melted sweet fragrances pour forth from a consuming fire of love…and that love is in you. It is a consuming fire of love in your inmost being, a fire of love for God." [63]

Any of these steps that I have listed will help you to begin your prayer life. Yet, remember that active steps and determined discipline will only last until something easier or more exciting comes along. The passion for a consistent prayer life will not happen until the little pilot light turns into an all-consuming flame that will melt the coldest heart.

Unleashing the Beauty of Prayer

I believe our beauty is unleashed when we realize that we are not responsible for the welfare and harmony of the entire universe. It is true, however, that at the time of creation, God gave us dominion over all the earth:

> "So God created man in his own image, in the image of God he created him; male and female he created them. God blessed them and said to them, 'Be fruitful and increase in number; fill the earth and subdue it. Rule over the fish of the sea and the birds of the air and over every living creature that moves on the ground'" (Gen 1:27-28 NIV).

In a sense, we are God's managers while we live on the planet earth, but I think that many of us think we could—or need to—run this world single-handedly. Satan will try to make us believe that we can do it all in our own power and in our own wisdom. He will do everything to make us live independently of God. This is Satan's way of making sure we live a life of defeat that will diminish our self-worth and eventually crush us. We have to realize that we need the direction, guidance, and support of the one who has put us in charge of this life: God.

In my workplace, for example, I have received my vision and company's mission statement from our dealer because he owns the business and knows which direction he wants to take it. As the controller, I go to him time and again to ask him for guidance so that I know what results he is looking for. Then, I need to bring him the desired results. Likewise, in our prayer life, we are too often so close to a situation that we don't have the insight or wisdom to see the bigger picture. To gain the bigger picture, we need to pray to our God, who knows the beginning from the end, and can see around the next bend in our journey.

Our days are packed with so many responsibilities that we need someone to give us insight and supply us with good judgment. Many of us women, however, are too proud or uncomfortable to ask for help. We need to be bold to pray, not only for ourselves, but also for each other. A friend once told me, "I have difficulty wrapping my brain around the fact that I can ask God for something I need. I was only taught to do grati-tude prayers as a child and not *asking* prayers. I think this is tough for women. I know many women who are superb in giving; they give, give and give until they cannot give anymore. While they may cry out 'Please give me strength, Lord' in desperation when they are at the end of their rope, most women would *never ask* for another to pray for them. The idea of others being a vessel to God speaking on your behalf is very pow-erful." [64]

A woman becomes more beautiful when the stress and burdens of the day are lifted from her shoulders. The Word tells us that is what God is there for: "Cast all your anxiety on him because he cares for you" (1 Pet. 5:7 NIV). We need to run to Him and shout, "Help me make wise deci-sions!" He wants to take our load of sorrows, guilt, anger, irritation, weariness, rejection, and unworthiness off our shoulders because He knows they can be too much for us at times.

IN OUR FAMILY, we have five children, eight grandchildren, sons-in-laws and daughter-in-laws, and they all live far away from us. We wish we could live closer so that we could interact in their lives, spurring them on and guiding them through some of their struggles. But we can encourage them—in a different way.

In 1998, my husband Jack and I decided to start meeting early each morning in our *prayer chairs*, two wing chairs that sit near our fireplace. We are surrounded by windows that overlook the vineyards, the moun-tains, and our glistening Okanagan Lake. The view is pure splendor. Each morning in this glorious setting, we pray for our families. We praise God for their victories, and we pray and cry about their disappointments and pain. Through prayer, we have discovered that we can be a vital part of their lives.

When our grandchildren were very little, they would climb up the stairs early in the morning and crawl up on my lap and snuggle in my arms while we prayed. They are getting older now, but this last sum-mer, Matthew, who is already six, came up the stairs and headed right for my lap. They all know they need to sit quietly until we are finished, but there is a peaceful, spiritual presence during that time that envelops all of us and allows us to enjoy the sweetness of that moment.

Once we are comfortable with our simple prayers, we discover that we can shoot up prayers to God all day long to give us strength as well as encouragement and assistance for the people around us. Throughout the day when we get frustrated or irritated, we can shout a prayer of HELP! God hears those direct and honest prayers. Instead of getting aggravated with an unruly and screaming child in a grocery store, for example, we can look over and shoot up a prayer for the harassed mother. When we hear the sound of an ambulance siren behind us, instead of feeling annoyed that we have to pull over with a mess of scrambled cars on the side of the highway, we can choose to stop and pray for the person whose life is in danger. I know that my God answers all our desperate and candid cries for help, both for ourselves and others around us.

I began this chapter by telling you how the lights went out when I was speaking at the World Day of Prayer. While I was speaking into the darkness, people came up on the stage and tried to illuminate the colors of the brilliant fabrics by putting candles in front of them. It was impossible, however, to grasp the beauty of the combination of the different colors with the little flickers of feeble candlelight. The whole intent of using the colorful fabric as an illustration was lost because of the darkness.

Try to imagine the discovery of your emerging prayer life in the same way as if you were viewing the beautiful colors of the fabrics for the first time. The more you allow the light of God's presence into your life by actually praying, the more you will believe in the beauty and power of prayer. The magnificence of prayer will become as captivating as the radiance of those fabrics. The most amazing discovery will be that we will see ourselves dramatically transformed by His power. Instead of praying for God to change other people or circumstances, we need to start by asking God to change us. We will then be victors in all areas of our lives.

Stop and ask God to Unleash Your Beauty

Begin by asking: God, give me wisdom to know how and when to pray to You.

S—Scripture: "If you want to know what God wants you to do, ask him, and he will gladly tell you, for he is always ready to give a bountiful supply of wisdom to all who will ask him. He will not resent it. But when you ask him, be sure that you really expect him to tell you, for a doubtful mind will be as unsettled as a wave of the sea that is driven and tossed by the wind" (James 1:5, 6 TLB).

T—Thanksgiving: I thank You, God, that we can approach You any time of the day or night. It says here that You are always ready and will gladly give us wisdom. God, You are awesome and I thank You for caring about every area of my life. Thank You for the hot-line to heaven.

O—Observation: I need God to help me with my unbelief regarding prayer. It is hard to imagine that someone who is invisible would have an interest in my life and want to give me wisdom to live it. God can empower and release me from my doubtful mind and help me to believe in the power of prayer. I need to learn to trust Him with whatever answers He gives, whether it is "yes," "no," or "wait."

P—Prayer: God, I thank You for giving me the avenue of prayer. It is wonderful to know that I have access to Your wisdom and power any time of the day or night. It seems almost too good to be true but I thank You for Your great love that expresses itself to me in so many ways. I confess that I need Your help in every area of my life. This world can be a complicated and confusing place to live, and there are so many decisions to make every day. I ask You for a big dose of wisdom for every one of those decisions. God, help me to find a quiet place each day so that I can communicate with You at a time when I am alert and fresh. I realize that prayer is the greatest power we will have access to in this life. Lord, teach me to pray. Amen.

12

UNLEASHING THE BEAUTY OF VICTORY
The Phantom of Shame

Our broken lives are not lost or useless. God's love is still working.
He comes in and takes the calamity and uses it victoriously,
working out His wonderful plan of love.

—ERIC LIDDELL

E HAS EXILED himself to the labyrinth of the catacombs underneath the Paris Opera House. It is his freakish face that has kept him imprisoned in these hidden chambers. Even though his mask conceals his face, his soul still cannot hide his mysterious powers and the brilliance of his opera music. He is the Phantom of the Opera, pursuing the beautiful, young Christine.

Christine's late father has promised her a music tutor, so the Phantom comes to be her *Angel of Music* and her teacher. She cannot see him, but his is the voice that speaks to her behind the mirror in the dressing room while he is teaching her to sing his beloved music. One night in her dressing room, the huge mirror slides open, and the Phantom draws Christine into his world underneath the Opera House. There in his chambers, he reveals his love for her, as well as the philosophy and essence of music.

While visiting his residence, Christine falls into a trance and awakens the next morning to find the Phantom sitting at his organ, absorbed in his compositions. Her curiosity compels her to approach him from behind and remove his mask. As he turns toward her, she sees his face and is horrified. He watches in horror as his beautiful Christine recoils from him in disgust. In a state of anger, he grabs her by the hair, and she falls to the floor. Once his anger has diminished, Christine feels safe enough to return his mask, and the Phantom once more becomes tender towards her, agreeing to return her to the outside world.

Toward the end of the final act, the Phantom sadly realizes that all his influence, manipulation, and trickery will not get him what he wants. Even though he has captured Christine and held her hostage in his chambers, he cannot make her love him. At the end of the story, Christine confronts him with the words that encapsulate this sad and desperate love story: *Your true disfigurement lies not in your face, but in your soul.*

Likewise, the deformity that defiles our souls and makes us hide our true selves from the world is *shame.* The Phantom is so ashamed of his grotesque features that he not only covers his face with a mask, but also has to learn to be content hiding in the cellar. He has been banished from a world that has inflicted pain upon him because of his outward deformity, and is therefore unable to release the hidden beauty of his mastery of music.

Shame is an excruciating and punishing awareness of our human inadequacy. Believing that we are too flawed to be worthy of acceptance into society, we hide. I believe shame is one of the most debilitating and painful emotions that we can ever experience. Although rarely talked about, I believe that by unveiling and exploring its ugly tentacles, we will be able to unleash our greatest power: self-worth.

"*Shame on you!*" I believe we have all either heard those words or said them. We need to come to the realization of how damaging those words are to our soul. They make us recoil and long to withdraw from this hurtful world. We need to be aware, however, that there is power available to overcome these debilitating emotions.

Mankind did not always feel shame. When Adam and Eve walked in the garden with God, they were completely naked: "The man and wife were both naked, and they felt *no shame*" (Gen. 2:25 NIV). How wonderful it must have been to feel so safe and free. Yet, as soon as they dis-obeyed God and sinned, they started to feel shame: "....I heard you in the garden, and I was afraid because I was naked; so I hid" (Gen. 3:10 NIV).

Indeed, because our *sin causes us to feel shameful,* our instinct is to hide it from everyone around us. Shame began with our original ancestors and followed us down through the generations. How do we get rid of it?

WHY DO WE FEEL ASHAMED?

From our early childhood, we have developed our own belief system of how adequate, smart, or pretty we are. This is further shaped by our responses to our environment, both inside and outside the home, as well as the culture we have been brought up in and the rules we have had to follow.

When children are mistreated, criticized, abandoned, humiliated, or too harshly disciplined, they get the message that they are "bad" because they have done something wrong. They feel unworthy and unwanted: they don't fit in. This feeling of *shame* morphs into inferiority, which gives them low self-esteem.

With today's media, we are always comparing ourselves to the air-brushed models on the magazine covers, the rich and famous, the CEO's, and athletes. Major causes of shame in women include the failure to live up to society's standard of attractiveness and competence.

The motherhood years are especially difficult ones for us as young mothers competing against the endless, rigid expectations for raising children in this generation. Exhausted, we find it difficult to keep up with the status quo and often fear that we will never measure up. In addi-tion, we feel even more shame when we are afraid to speak up for ourselves.

Then, there are the years when we establish our careers. We compete against salaries, personalities, degrees, and the struggle between our career and family responsibilities. When we don't succeed in our pursuit of an esteemed career, we feel inferior, believing that we are not smart enough to make it. As we get older, we struggle with our appearance, regrets, and feelings of inadequacy about the seemingly few contributions we have made to our homes and society.

We may also be ashamed of a crime we have committed, an addiction, or an abortion, all the while fearing that we will be found out. The *guilt* from wrongdoing that has not been dealt with will cause this horrible, destructive *feeling of shame.*

One of the most damaging causes of shame is keeping secrets. We may be protecting someone who has done something shameful to us, or our own shameful sins and secrets. The secrets of shame will not only destroy our self-worth, but it will also affect our health. The degree of our secret-keeping will determine the degree of our spiritual and physical well being.

We can never hope to meet the expectations of the world around us, which makes us feel inadequate, stupid, flawed, and *ashamed.* We feel alone on this. Not wanting to add to our shame, we hide our inadequacies, fears, and vulnerabilities behind a mask of respectability.

What Does Shame Feel Like?

Unlike *guilt,* which tells us that we have *done something wrong, shame* is the feeling of *being wrong.* Shame is like you or I being trapped in a slow-moving nightmare. It may look and feel something like this:

In my dream I am in a lavish and beautiful ballroom, surrounded by men and women dressed in elegant tuxedoes and exquisite gowns and wearing extravagant jewelry. I look down at my dirty, torn clothes reeking with a horrible smell. Everyone is staring at me with disgusted repugnance and disdain. Alone and bewildered, I try to run away, but it feels as though my feet are stuck to the ground, so I am helpless in my attempt to run away and hide. I stand there, cowering in humiliation. I feel guilty but don't know why. Although I'm opening my mouth to explain my horrible appearance, I cannot form any words. I desperately want to belong, but I know everyone just wants me to leave.

This is the same way I felt when I was in the fifth grade and our family was going through a difficult financial period. At the beginning of the school year, I did not have any shoes that fit because my parents did not have enough money to buy me a new pair. My mother gave me her shoes to wear, but they were ladies' shoes with wedge heels. I remember that other students stared at my feet and laughed at me when I was wearing them. Even though I tried to be confident, I cowered under their verbal abuse. I felt like I did not belong—ugly and unloved. *I felt ashamed.*

Recently, I watched the movie, *The Greatest Game Ever Played.* In one scene, there is a social gathering at a very prestigious country club in which one of the club members says to a guest, "You may be invited, but you don't belong."

We all have stories of feeling alone, different, ugly, and unwanted. That feeling of shame follows us through every passage of our lives, and we feel as though we will never be rid of it.

What happens inside my head when I feel shame?

Our feelings that come from this burden of shame show up negatively in many areas of our lives. We are often unaware of the ways this feeling causes us to be people who need to compensate for our feelings of imperfection, isolation, being trapped, and powerlessness:

- We feel unimportant, so we try to become perfect. After all, if we never make a mistake, we will never have to feel ashamed.
- If we criticize others, we will feel better about ourselves.
- We feel embarrassed and regretful for not being able to fix life to make it better.
- We become oversensitive when others insinuate that we have done something wrong.
- We are indecisive, out of our fear that we will make a wrong decision and look foolish or stupid.
- We do everything to control our outer physical image because it is the only thing we have control over. We don't really want people to know how ugly we are inside.
- We feel that we have to please everyone around us so that they will like us and make us feel better about ourselves.
- We feel rejected.

- We can become depressed, have an eating disorder, and turn to self-mutilation or other serious physical and emotional disorders.
- We feel helpless to change.

Now that we know how crippling shame is, let's not despair because there is good news: we don't have to live with shame anymore. By allowing God to help us dismantle it and identify it, He can bring healing into our soul.

Two Types of Shame

In order for us to deal with shame, we have to be able to identify it. There are two types of shame:

1. Circumstantial shame

This is a type of shame that accepts blame for inappropriate things. Often sensitive to their environment, women feel vulnerable and responsible when things go wrong. I believe that we feel if we could have gotten the opportunity, we probably would have fixed it:

- "I was responsible for the bad things that happened to me in my childhood."
- "If we were not so poor, we would not have had to live on food stamps."
- "I am responsible for keeping the secret about my husband's addiction to pornography."
- "I am responsible for the missed opportunities of getting a better education, raising perfect children, enjoying better health, developing more friendships, and marrying a different man."
- "It is my fault that we got a divorce."
- "If only I had been stronger, I could have stopped the abuse."
- "My son is taking drugs, so I feel like a terrible mother."

When we take on the burden of other people's responsibilities and choices and things go wrong, we feel the *shame* of that failure. Jesus does not condemn us, so why do we condemn ourselves? The apostle Paul reassures us: "Therefore, there is now no condemnation for those who are in Christ Jesus" (Rom. 8:1 NIV). He also kindly tells the Corinthian church: "I am not writing this to shame you, but to warn you, as my dear children" (1 Cor. 4:14 NIV).

If we have no part in decisions that other people make or what they do to us, we have to release ourselves from the guilt caused by shame. This *shame* that we keep locked away in our secret box keeps defiling and crippling us, but it is not ours. We have permission to get rid of it.

2. Sinful shame

This kind of shame results from the *guilt of wrongdoing* that has not been dealt with. It is intended to motivate us to do the will of God and learn to live in purity, honesty, and freedom. When the people at the bottom of Mount Sinai danced naked before the golden calf, they had cast off this type of shame that would have prevented them from engaging in this lewd behavior.

Real shame is always meant to draw us into the loving arms of our heavenly Father through sorrowful repentance.

JESUS HAS COMPASSION FOR SHAME

Throughout the Gospels, we see Jesus displaying loving tenderness and kindness toward women who covered their shame.

1. Jesus overlooks our status in life.

There is the story of a woman who lived a sinful life that came uninvited into a Pharisee's house. When she found out that Jesus was there, she brought in an alabaster jar of perfume and knelt before Him: "As she stood behind him at his feet weeping, she began to wet his feet with her tears. Then she wiped them with her hair, kissed them and poured perfume on them" (Luke 7:38 NIV).

Jesus did not remind her of her sin and shame, nor did He rebuke her or tell her to leave. Because of her demonstration of faith, Jesus said, "Therefore, I tell you, her many sins have been forgiven, for she loved much" (Luke 7:47 NIV).

Let us put ourselves into this woman's shoes. *Would we have believed the accusing condemnation of the Pharisees and the guests, or would we have believed the kind and reassuring words of Jesus that she was forgiven?* Just as Jesus covered her shame with His love and forgiveness, He will also cover yours and mine.

2. Jesus overlooks the boundaries of social, economical, and cultural barriers.

The Jews despised and looked down on the Samaritans because they were a mixed race. Jesus radically loved people, no matter what their race, color, religion, or social status was. One day as Jesus was walking through Samaria, He was tired and thirsty from His journey. While He was resting by a well, a Samaritan woman came to draw some water. She had gone through five husbands and was now working on getting her sixth. Jesus asked her for a drink of water. By doing this, He crossed the social and cultural barriers of that time. After He offered her the gift of spiritual living water, she did not walk away from the well ashamed with her eyes downcast, but instead went back into town rejoicing and claiming that she had encountered the living Christ.

I believe that Jesus lived out these examples for us because He realized the shame that mankind lives with. By His open display of that kind of love, we can rest assured that He will forgive us and cover our shame with His warm blanket of love and kindness.

JESUS COVERS SHAME

God sent His Son Jesus Christ into our world to teach us how to live without shame. Jesus Himself was also familiar with shame. He was abandoned by His friends, falsely accused of blasphemy, beaten with a whip, ridiculed, taunted, stripped of His clothes and forced to walk down a street carrying His own cross. He had to endure the shame and pain of wearing a crown of thorns that pierced His skin and watching as men threw dice for his clothes. One of the criminals who hung on the other cross hurled insults at Him and mockingly said, "Aren't you the Christ? Save yourself and us!" (Luke 23:39 NIV). What did Jesus do with all that haunting, debilitating shame?

He *scorned shame.* How does that help you and me?

The writer of Hebrews tells us: "Let us fix our eyes on Jesus, the author and perfecter of our faith, who for the joy set before him endured the cross, *scorning its shame,* and sat down at the right hand of the throne of God" (Heb. 12:2 NIV).

This meant that when shame began to attack Him and threaten His spirit, He said, "I will not yield to you." He did not run a poll on public opinion about what happened or put together a committee or focus group to find out how this all weighed out in society. He did not care what people thought because, first of all, He knew they were wrong, and second, He understood His purpose for coming to earth. He knew that his mission was to bring glory to his heavenly Father, along with freedom and peace to all mankind. For all of these reasons, He looked *shame* right in the eye and *scorned it.* I believe that Jesus died disgracefully to teach us that we not need to worry about what others think.

There is always some past shame that will try to undermine or threaten our faith and our self-worth; however, we can say with confidence: "I will not yield to you because Jesus died to free me from that shame."

REMOVING THE SHAME

1. Reveal unresolved guilt.

Shame is the debilitating emotion that piggybacks on unresolved guilt. In order to allow God to remove our shame, we have to take an inventory of our guilt. We need to able to discern between *false* and *real guilt.* *False guilt* is guilt that we have taken upon ourselves which is not really our responsibility. This includes wrongdoing that has been done to us at a time when we were either too young or too helpless to protect ourselves. It also involves circumstantial situations either in our home or in society when we took ownership for other people's sinful and hurtful actions. This is guilt that does not belong to us, so we need to let it go.

In order to bring complete freedom and healing to our soul from shame, we need to resolve *real guilt*. Real guilt results from sins that we have committed for which we have never repented. It also comes from anger and unforgiveness that we are deliberately harboring against people who have hurt us or committed wrongdoing against us. To remove all shame from our lives, we need to address all the areas of unresolved hurt stemming from guilt through forgiveness in these three areas:

a. We need to forgive those people who have sinned against us and hurt us deeply.

b. We need to repent for our wrongdoing to others.

c. We need to forgive ourselves.

When we begin to deal with all the guilt in our lives from *doing wrong*, we will then be able to remove our feeling of shame *of being wrong*.

2. Remove guilt through forgiveness.

In their book *When You Can't Say "I Forgive You,"* Grace Ketterman and David Hazard tell us how difficult and painful forgiveness really is:

> "If you are like many people we know, you may want to be free of past offenses, but you still carry bitter memories of, or hard feelings toward, those who have wronged you. No one seems immune from this urge to carry offenses long after they've been committed, not the newest saint or the oldest. If you see their faces in your mind's eye right now, the voice of honesty within you says, I can't say 'I forgive you' because that would not be truthful. God tells me to. I believe I should. Maybe it would even be better for me if I did. But I know I haven't forgiven you for what you did to me. Right now I'm not sure I know whether I can, or how."[65]

3. It is difficult to remove shame if there is guilt at the root.

Guilt will destroy our soul if we do not deal with it. Listen to David explain what guilt did to him:

> "My guilt has overwhelmed me, like a burden too hard to bear, my wounds fester and are loathsome because of my sinful folly. I am bowed down and brought very low; all day long I go about mourning. My back is filled with searing pain; there is no health in my body, I am feeble and utterly crushed; I groan in anguish of heart" (Psalm 38:4-8 NIV).

He knew that confessing his sin was the only way he could find freedom from his anguish: "I confess my iniquity; I am troubled by my sin" (Psalm 38:18 NIV).

I went through a period in my own life when I began to know the power of freedom from guilt over sin in my life. With each step of forgiveness, I experienced just a little more taste of the abundant life and freedom from shame. The more I experienced it, the more I wanted it. I discovered that each time I forgave someone who had hurt me or rejected me; I felt less anger and shame and more peace and joy. I went through a mental inventory of all the people who had hurt me, including teachers, pastors, and girlfriends in my growing-up years. I began to believe and experience the divine power of forgiveness. In my encounters with women whom I teach and mentor, there is no greater power I can offer them in their lives than God's gift of *forgiveness.* Guilt is a soul matter, so we need a soul antidote. God gave us that authoritative power through forgiveness.

FORGIVENESS

Forgiveness does not mean that we let the other person off the hook so they can get away with what they did to us. It involves letting you and me off the hook and freeing us from *our pain and anger* which will, in turn, give us indescribable peace. Forgiveness is the gift of grace that God gave us when His Son died on the cross for our sins. In order for it to work, however, we have to exercise it. This is not a nice option, but a command. Jesus told us: "For if you forgive men when they sin against you, your heavenly Father will also forgive you. But if you do not forgive men their sins, your Father will not forgive your sins" (Matt. 6:14-15 NIV).

Forgiveness:

- Is not forgetting;
- Does not mean you are a doormat for their continued sinful abuse;
- Is required by God;
- Means you resolve not to live with the consequences of another person's sin;
- Is our key to removing the guilt for our wrongdoing;
- Is hard;
- Is healing, which can take a long time;
- Is an act of faith;
- Does not make you feel better when the person who hurt you is punished;
- Is the key to handling hurt and betrayal;
- Is our ticket to freedom.

We need to forgive because it is the only thing that will release us from our feeling of guilt and, ultimately, shame. It is also important to ask God to forgive us for our sins that we have committed. We need to pray something like this: "God, I confess that I sinned when I stole from the video store. I repent of that sin and ask that You forgive me. Free me from feelings of guilt and shame and cover me with Your forgiveness and righteousness. Thank You."

Repenting from our sin means that we confess our sin and *turn away* from doing it again.

An article in the July/August 2006 issue of *Today's Christian Woman* explains our confusion about forgiveness:

"Our human mind yearns to make all the confusing puzzle pieces fit together neatly before we forgive. However, the truth is we can forgive an offender even if we never discover the reasons for the inflicted pain. Author Philip Yancey writes in *What's So Amazing About Grace,* 'Not to forgive imprisons me in the past and locks out all potential for change. I thus yield control to another, my enemy, and doom myself to suffer the consequences of the wrong.'" [66]

Forgiving others who have hurt us and even forgiving ourselves for things we have done can be the hardest steps of faith we will ever take; however, it will be the greatest encounter of freedom and healing that you and I will ever experience. James, the brother of Jesus, tells us: "Therefore, confess your sins to each other and pray for each other *so that you may be healed*" (James 5:16 NIV).

EMBRACING SHAME AND FINDING FREEDOM

Dealing with our guilt through the power of forgiveness removes the *cloak of shame.* Unlike guilt which says, *I have done something wrong,* shame says, *I am wrong.* How do we get rid of this *feeling of shame?* We can correct faulty actions, but how do we fix *being wrong?*

Reveal

In order to allow God to remove our weight of shame, we have to bring it out of its secret hiding place. Whenever I speak to women about shame, I tell them that we have to open their box of shame to see what it looks like. I don't understand how this works, but I know that it does because I have experienced it. I am like the blind man who was healed and replied to the Pharisees' questioning: "I don't know. One thing I do know. I was blind but now I see!" (John 9:25 NIV). *I do know this: that once the ugliness of our secrets is brought out into the light, they lose their power.*

If we are honest about what we find, we see that most of our shame-induced experiences occurred during childhood. This was a time in our lives when we were little, and our parents and authority figures made our decisions for us. We also have to recognize that we were too young to have the knowledge or ability to establish for ourselves what was right and wrong, or good and bad. We were too young to understand that we live in a sinful, dysfunctional world where other people's failures or morally wrong deeds were not our burden of shame to wear.

As I began to look at my own childhood shame, I was afraid to let it go because I had been wearing it for so long that I didn't know what it would be like if I released it, or even if I had the right to do so. Shame was part of my identity, and what would happen to me if I no longer owned it? I was also very fearful of how it would look if I verbalized it and someone else saw it. Would it bring me even more shame?

Empathy and love will diffuse the power of shame. Some of our shame can be dealt with between just us and God, but we will also need help with others to deal with the rest of it. This is when we need to call upon a trusted counselor or friend. We need to be very careful about our choice because this person needs to be empathetic and not judgmental in any way. If they don't love us through the process, they will heap more shame on us, which would certainly crush us.

But we have to let shame out of our box, face it, and then begin to own it. It is a part of us that we have been wearing which does not belong to us, so we need to *surrender it* to God.

Restore

God is a restorer. When a fire destroys a forest, the trees grow back. When we cut our finger, it heals. Our God, who made the heavens and the earth, is a restorer, as well as a creator. He can only begin to heal our pain, however, when we give it to Him. This process is called *surrender,* a word that we often cringe from. We think this means that because we have to give something away, it is going to be painful and a lot of hard work. Let's allow God to change that word in our minds so that it can be the means to finding our true self—the one that God created.

Rick Warren puts it this way:

"Surrendering to God is not passive resignation, fatalism, or an excuse for laziness. It is not accepting the status quo. It may mean the exact opposite: sacrificing your life or suffering in order to change what needs to be changed....Likewise it does not mean giving up rational thinking. God would not waste the mind he gave you! God does not want robots to serve him. Surrendering is not repressing your personality. God wants to use your unique personality. Rather than its being diminished, surrendering enhances it. C.S. Lewis observed, 'The more we let God take us over, the more truly ourselves we become—because he made us. He invented all the different people that you and I were intended to be....It is when I turn to Christ, when I give up myself to His personality that I first begin to have a real personality of my own.'" 67

The first time I experienced a true sacrificial surrender was the period in my life when my children were teenagers. I understood the concept that our children are a gift from God, and they are on loan from Him for us to love and treasure during our lifetime. When they were small, I would go through the motions of agreeing with God that, yes, they were really His because He, in fact, created them. I have found that everything in life looks easy when we say the right words and simply give God lip-service. It is a completely different matter when He beckons to us and tells us He is actually going to teach us how to live this out.

My superb children were brilliant, fun, and accomplished during what were supposed to be the difficult teenage years. I took great pride in their accomplishments, so ultimately that made me look like a great mother. We hit a difficult period toward the *end* of the teen-age years when all of a sudden our perfect life was turned upside down. For a period of time, it felt as though my world had collapsed. My pride was crushed when my hopes and dreams for my son went flying out the window. All of our pleading, crying, and praying could not change the situation we were in. I felt as though my whole life was spinning out of control, but I didn't know how to fix it. This is when I heard God telling me to surrender my children to Him—not just with my lips, but also my heart. I hung on as long as I could, but I finally reached the point of exhaustion and came to the end of any resolve I had mustered. I recall very clearly in the middle of the night when I said,

"Okay, Okay, I give up. I give both of my children to You. This situation is so hard that I can't do it any longer. I know that I gave birth to them and love them with all of my soul, but I know that You created them and are the one who has a plan for their lives. Obviously, my plans are not working, so I trust You to look after them and shape them into who you created them to be." Afterward, I cried myself to sleep.

The next morning I woke up completely exhausted, but I felt more peace than I had known for months. I recognize that, as mothers, we want our children to experience the very best that this life has to offer, but we must realize that we have to allow them to become the people God designed them to be. I had wonderful plans for my children, but I know God's plans are so much better. Whenever we surrender something to God, we are releasing it so that God can *restore* it to what it was designed to be. New life comes out of every surrender.

In Katie Brazelton's book, *Pathway to Purpose for Women,* she devotes an entire chapter to surrender. She offers this enlightening insight:

> "Surrender is one of the greatest challenges of faith you will face, but step by step God will prepare you to be completely his, to be totally engaged in his purposes for your life. As you walk with God more closely every day, you will be increasing your trust in the Lord of lords, and Jesus will become totally sufficient for you. Eventually the day will come, if it has not already, when the Holy Spirit taps you on the shoulder and asks, 'Will you now give your entire life to Christ? Will you submit to the plan the Lord lovingly crafted for you?' What a humbling privilege it is to be asked to give your all for Christ right in the midst of life circumstances."[68]

When we surrender our failures, inadequacies, which are the root of *shame* to God, He can and will *restore* all that has been taken from us. He can take our shame and turn it into beauty. The very thing that caused us the most excruciating pain and disappointment can strengthen our spirits and enable us to find the greatest peace and joy.

How Do We Surrender?

Surrendering is not something we do once and then we are finished. After I surrendered my children to God, I wanted to take back my ownership over and over again. I had to keep reminding myself that even though it was my responsibility to love them and pray for them, I had to let God work out their plans and purposes.

Whether we realize it or not, there is a great deal of shame in all of our lives. The surrendering process can take a long time, but it will be worth it. Here are some steps to get you started:

- Open your box of secrets.
- Ask God to tell you what you need to give to Him.
- Ask God to tell you the truth in that situation.
- Make a conscious choice to surrender by saying, "God, I ask that You give me the strength and power to surrender the shame of _____. I give it to You, asking that You take away my shame and pain and restore it with your peace and new life."
- Each time the issue comes up, give it back to God until you feel the release from that shame.
- Always thank God for loving you enough that He wants you to live a joyous life of freedom.
- Wait with anticipation for what God will do to replace what you have surrendered.

We know that God is in the business of restoring lives. He took the prostitute Rahab and restored her life so that she could become a part of the genealogy of Jesus Christ. He took Esther, a Hebrew slave, and made her a queen. He took the barren Hannah and gave her a son. He took Ruth and gave her a husband. Likewise, God can take our lives and not only remove our shame, but also restore those things in our lives that have either been taken from us, or that we feel have been robbed from us.

The Phantom of the Opera hid in the underground cellar of Paris and did not allow the world to enjoy his beautiful music. In the same way, our shame can also be viewed as a masked apparition that is causing us to hide our beauty from the world.

Unleashing the Beauty of Victory

I admire the words of wisdom of the beautiful Maya Angelou, who said, *"I can be changed by what happens to me, I refuse to be reduced by it."*[69]

Shame is part of our human repertoire, but it does not have to become part of who we ultimately become or reduce us as human beings. When shame is taken away from us, we begin to radiate and sparkle from the inside out. Imagine a beautiful crystal goblet that has dirt and mud inside of it. Now, take that goblet and begin to wash the dirt out until it is clean. Then, hold that goblet up to the light and watch how the crystal sparkles and the light brings out radiant and brilliant colors.

When we allow God to remove our shame through forgiveness and surrender, we will begin to radiate with a beauty that we could never have believed or dreamed possible. We need to allow God to reframe us.

Reframe

I am going to ask you to take out the picture of who you are *with shame*, and replace it with the picture of who you can be *without shame*. This means that you will have to picture yourself differently. Sometimes, I use the following illustration to show women how beautiful and precious they are to God. I take two goblets and stand them side by side. One is a cheap water goblet that I bought with one dollar. I use this water goblet every day and often stick it in the dishwasher, or throw it into the sink. I treat it for what it is—a cheap piece of glass that has no value. I probably wouldn't even care if it broke, since it has no value and can be easily replaced. The other goblet is a beautiful Waterford crystal goblet. I take this one out of the china cabinet only for special occasions and tenderly place it on the dining room table. Each time I place the glass in its proper place, I stand back and admire its beauty, which never ceases to stir and amaze me. After the meal is over, I personally remove the goblets from the table and put them in their separate spot on the kitchen counter because I do not want them to end up in the dishwasher. These crystal glasses get their very own special sink filled with clean, hot water and soap. Then, they are carefully dried with a clean linen towel. Before they go back into the dining room cabinet, I hold them up to the light to make sure there are no fingerprints on them or other grease marks. When I am satisfied that they are spotless, I gently place them into their special spot in the cabinet.

Begin to reframe the picture of who you are in light of how God sees you. You may see yourself as the cheap water glass that is inadequate and shameful, without any value, but God sees you as the stunningly beautiful crystal water goblet. You have value and significance, so you are not full of dirt and shame. You need to reframe the picture of yourself as one who is being lavished with love by a holy God who created you to be lovely. You also need to learn to love yourself the way God loves you. You are no longer a *victim,* but a *victor.*

What kind of beauty can we possibly derive from shame?

- We receive a heart that is full of compassion for other people who struggle with shame.
- We become less critical of the world around us.
- We can learn to love ourselves.
- As we become beautiful on the inside, our whole body will become more beautiful. Our eyes will be brighter and not downcast with shame. We will walk with confident boldness, and our shoulders will not be so hunched over. Our smile will erase the scowl and furrows on our brow.
- It will be easier for us to forgive other people when we realize how God forgives us and removes our shame.

While I was sitting at a conference, I watched a woman being interviewed.

Throughout the entire interview, her face was downcast, and she could not make eye contact with her interviewer. I wanted to run up to her, lift her chin, and look into her sad eyes. I longed to proclaim to her that she did not have to live in shame. I wanted her to know that God can lift off her shame and thus lift her head. We are given this hope and promise in the Psalms: "But you are a shield around me, O Lord; you bestow glory on me and lift up my head" (Psalm 3:3 NIV).

When Adam and Eve hid in the Garden of Eden, they started the domino effect of sin and shame throughout all of the following generations to come. Jesus Christ came to the world to become the catalyst for change. He died to put an end to the toxic effects of sin and shame in our lives. God's love and grace are big enough to cover every one of your sins and all of your shame—every last bit of it—so that you can see your great worth and live a *victorious, abundant* life.

Stop and ask God to Unleash Your Beauty

Begin by asking: God, what shame do I have that is preventing me from being all that You created me to be?

S—Scripture: "If you put away the sin that is in your hand and allow no evil to dwell in your tent, then you will lift up your face without shame; you will stand firm without fear" (Job 11:14, 15 NIV).

T—Thanksgiving: I praise You, God for sending Your Son to die on the cross so that I can live without shame. Thank You for the tools of forgiveness and surrender that enable You to be the "lifter of my head." I long to see the world around me through the eyes of beauty and not self-condemnation. Thank You that when I stay close to You, You teach me to stay away from any sin that will cause further shame.

O—Observation: God sent His Son to die so that I can live— free from shame and condemnation. To live a life free from fear and shame, I need to make a deliberate effort to "put sin away."

P—Prayer: God, sometimes Your love and goodness seem almost too good to be true. Help me to look into my life and reveal my shame to You. I long to be a woman of beauty who walks through this life with a confidence that comes from knowing Your love. Thank You that Your love covers my shame. Show me how to let go of something that has been a part of me for so long. Help me to live out of the framework of being a beautiful Waterford crystal goblet that shines and radiates Your beauty. With Your help, show me how I can clean the dirt out of myself so that I *feel* clean, restored, and glorious. Thank You for being the "lifter of my head." God, when I am downcast, remind me that my help and power comes from above, and by lifting my head to look up, I will encounter a loving and compassionate God. Thank You for coming into this world—not to condemn me, but to free me from the prison of my own shame. Amen.

13

UNLEASHING THE BEAUTY OF GRATITUDE
Ubuntu

God has two dwellings: one in heaven and the
other in a meek and thankful heart.

—IZAAK WALTON (1593-1683), BRITISH WRITER

THE BLAST OF HEAT from the open oven door quickly mingled with the hot air in the rest of the house on July 17, 2004. Sweat was pouring down my face and burning my eyes as I reached into the oven to baste the turkey one last time. All of the exquisitely prepared dishes were almost ready to be carried to the dining room table. We were having a Thanksgiving dinner on this excruciatingly hot and humid summer day. This unusual meal was the celebration and highlight of our family's Conley-McLaughlin Summer Reunion. Since my wedding to Jack, this was the first time that every one of our children and grandchildren had come home from all their different homes throughout western Canada and the United States. Jack and I had been anticipating and planning this event for over a year; and now we had almost come to the end of our activities. The prior days of the reunion had been filled with family golf tournaments, scavenger hunts, creating arts and crafts with the children, and cooling off at the beach. In the evenings, we ate our meals on the patio deck that overlooked the spectacular Okanagan valley. At the end of each day, as the sun went over the mountains and the warm evening air ushered in the darkness, we lingered on the deck over dessert and coffee, telling stories. All of our preparations could not have anticipated the comfortable rhythm and laughter in all of our meals and games. Now it was almost over, but not quite: we still had our Thanksgiving dinner to share with each other.

As all eighteen of us stood around the dining room table, my eyes looked around at our huge blended family. In my wildest dreams, I could never have imagined that I would be so blessed to be the mother and stepmother of such a loving, generous, and funny family. As I looked at the table centerpiece, my eyes lingered over every decoration. I had asked my daughter Michelle to arrange the centerpiece, so she asked everyone to bring an item to represent the places where they lived. There were seashells from the Pacific Ocean; jars with colorful seeds from Alberta; roses from Roseville, California; an American flag and top hat from Las Vegas; and driftwood from Vancouver Island. These items represented the homes of our five children and grandchildren who became part of a blended family when my husband Jack and I were married in 1996. We all realized that a signed contract cannot make people love each other. That love rather comes from accepting each other, overlooking difficulties and faults, spending time together, and being grateful for what has taken place in our lives today.

Even though all of these children did not have my blood, they had every piece of my heart and soul. My words were chocked with emotion, and tears flooded my eyes as I offered up a Thanksgiving prayer. I thanked God for this gift: my family. When we stop and let our eyes see what God has loaned to us while we are in our earthly existence, we begin to see the ordinary as something that needs to be recognized and cherished.

The Power of "Thank You"

My children often remind me about the times when they were little and the discomfort they felt when I made them say, "Thank you." When we were invited to someone's house for dinner, or if they received a gift, their "thank you's" often didn't come as fast as I expected them to. I recall whispering to them, "What do you say to that nice lady?" They would stand by my side with their heads down and mutter their forced and stiff "thank you". Afterwards, they always reassured me that they would have said "thank you" if I would have just given them more time. Yet, I felt it was so important for them to show gratitude that I wasn't going to take that chance. As they grew older, their gratitude naturally emerged out of a genuinely grateful heart—not one that was always prompted by their mother. Now that they are adults, they take every opportunity to show their gratitude through words, hugs, cards, e-mails, and phone calls. They have learned the power of *sincere* gratitude.

There is great power in those two words of "thank you." When we hear them directed toward us, it is as though someone has recognized and acknowledged our value. In my supervisory role at the car dealership, I have many opportunities to conduct interviews and do employee evaluations. Each time I talk to an employee, I am reminded that the number-one thing they are looking for in their jobs is *appreciation* and someone saying "thank you" for what they are doing. They rank it above increased salaries, a comfortable work space, the number of holidays they can take, and even titles.

Everyone wants to be acknowledged and thanked for what they do. When any of us have given up our time and energy to make an effort to assist someone, we love to hear those two words that give us a stamp of approval, acknowledging what we have done. We pretend that it doesn't matter if we are not thanked, but I believe that our ears are tuned in for that coveted "thank you."

"Thank you" seems to be a very common phrase these days, but I consider it be more lip- service than sincerity. When I am flying, the airline attendant thanks me for flying with them. (I had no choice because their fares were the cheapest.) When I call a large company, a synthesized voice thanks me for calling. Much of our world has learned to say "thank you" out of a sense of obligation and propriety, in the same way I made my children mouth those words. For some people it is hard to express those two words, and many times the phrase is uttered in a very mechanical way out of a sense of duty. The words of gratitude are important, but they need to be offered with a sincere motive behind them. That is where the power comes in.

As Jesus traveled to Jerusalem along the border of Samaria and Galilee, He came across ten men who had leprosy. In that day, lepers were considered unclean, so their access to other people was severely restricted. When they saw Jesus, they kept their distance and cried out to Him, "Jesus, Master, have pity on us" (Luke 17:12 NIV). Jesus saw them, healed them, and off they went—except for one:

> "One of them, when he saw that he was healed, came back praising God in a loud voice. He threw himself at Jesus' feet and thanked him. Jesus asked, 'Were not all ten cleansed? Where are the other nine? Was no one found to return and give praise to God except this foreigner?' Then he said to him, 'Rise and go; your faith has made you well'" (Luke 17:15 NIV).

Only one leper went back to say "thank you." First, he shouted out to Jesus, "Help me", but then after his healing, he shouted out, "Thank You." Sincere gratitude makes us *go back* and acknowledge that we have received something. It makes us want to *shout,* "Thank you."

As little children being told by our parents to say "thank you", we don't understand the whole concept of gratitude. When I prompted my children to express their heartfelt thanks, I can just imagine what went through their minds: "*I'd better say 'thank you' or I'll probably never get anything again.*"

Gratitude is not a natural inclination; instead, it comes as a result of discipline and acknowledgment that what people have given us is a valuable gift to be received and enjoyed. When gratitude becomes sincere, however, it not only empowers us to receive further blessings, but it also can even heal our soul. To the only one (a Samaritan, no less!) who came back, Jesus said, "*Your faith has made you well.*"

We read frequent proclamations of praise and thanksgiving to God in the Psalms, as well as warnings against ingratitude. Throughout Psalm 107, the psalmist strongly encourages us to give thanks, reminding us not to defraud God by taking honor for what we have and consider to be our accomplishments: "For God pours contempt upon the *haughty* and causes princes to wander among ruins" (v. 40 TLB). It is almost as though he wants to pull us over to his side, like I did with my little children, and prompt us, "*What do you say to that man for the present?*" When we remember a word that has lifted our spirits, a relationship that has changed us, a gift that was meant to bring us joy, or a prayer that has brought healing, I invite all of us to always go back and shout, "Thank you!"

Gratitude Expands Our Vision

My husband Jack and I often talk to people about ways to live out their lives in the "Upper Room." We explain to people the difference between living their lives with a *poverty consciousness* and an *abundance consciousness*. I believe that what distinguishes the two is an attitude of gratitude.

Poverty consciousness

This poverty attitude warns us to hoard things because there may never be enough. It also tells us that whatever we need or want depends on our ability to get it, constantly reminding us at the same time that other people have more than we do. We are afraid that we will not be taken care of, be overlooked, or ever measure up to society's standards. Poverty finds it hard to say "thank you" or acknowledge that God is our abundant provider. This attitude closes the door on us, making it difficult to receive any further blessings from God for our lives.

People who live with this mentality have a vision that I call *basement living*. They tell themselves that this is the life that has been allotted to them; they do not deserve more and they can't afford any better. They still have old boxes packed away in every corner of their basement that are labeled *Fear, Guilt, Shame, Anger, Rejection, Poor Me,* and *"I have been overlooked."* The "Upper Room" is prepared and waiting for them, but they are unwilling or afraid to unpack their boxes and live in the glorious, luxurious, freedom style of living.

Fears of failure, as well as those of success, stop all of us from receiving all that God wants to bless us with. Fear closes our minds into tight little balls and stops us from seeing the bigger picture of God's generosity and abundance. The amount of money or material possessions has nothing to do with this mentality. We can have money tucked away in the bank or investments, but a poverty mentality still goes out and buys day-old bread at half price and a pair of shoes that are on sale, even though they don't fit.

Abundant consciousness

I implore all of us to come and live in the splendor and magnificence of the "Upper Room." We don't get to live there because we have worked hard or deserve it because of our wealth. Even though we realize that we don't own it, we love living there and thank God for it every day. Just as everything else in this life, the "Upper Room" belongs to God, but He allows us to live in His lavish and luxurious presence. In fact, everyone in this world receives the invitation to live there. When we accept Jesus Christ as our personal Savior, we are given the invitation to live in glorious freedom and abundant joy. Once we accept the fact that we are free from the sins and shame of our past, we can give Him all of our old ugly, dusty boxes labeled *unworthiness, rejection, guilt, betrayal, depression, shame* and *unforgiveness*, get out of the basement, and move upstairs.

Abundant consciousness has its basis on two pillars. The first pillar involves the principle that our heavenly Father has infinite resources at His disposal:

> "For all the animals of field and forest are mine! The cattle on a thousand hills! And all the birds upon the mountains! If I were hungry, I would not mention it to you—for all the world is mine, and everything in it" (Psalm 50:10, 11 NIV).

The second pillar is based on the fact that God is always giving, without any limits. The apostle Paul assures the church of God's generosity:

"You will be made rich in every way so that you can be generous on every occasion, and through us your generosity will result in thanksgiving to God" (2 Cor. 9:11 NIV). God doesn't just give; He "scatters abroad" (v. 9). We, in turn, receive every blessing in abundance for ourselves and have plenty to give away.

This "Upper Room" mentality is acquired through an understanding of these two pillars. Gratitude is the pleasure and contentment we feel when we realize that someone loves us enough to give us a gift. We also have to recognize that a gift always has a person attached to it. A gift says, "When you take my gift, you take a part of me." God wants to give us the gift of Himself and all the blessings that go along with that. He freely gives us freedom, joy, laughter, peace, generosity, and kindness.

When we live in freedom from fear and unworthiness, we see each surprise in life as a gift from God. We are not afraid of what may be lurking in secret, dark, and evil places because those ugly boxes have all been unpacked and given to God. We understand that our worth is not something that we have to work for or deserve, but that it is a free gift to us from our generous heavenly Father. We receive God's gifts with a gracious "thank you" for His generous blessings in every area of our lives. We don't need to hang our heads, look down, and say, "*Oh no, I can't accept that; I don't deserve it. You shouldn't have.*" We can't claim credit for anything or take ourselves too seriously because we realize that everything, including every breath we take, is a perfect gift from God to use while we live in this existence called earth.

Ellen Vaugh says in her book, *Radical Gratitude*:

"How many times have I done the same thing, over and over, vainly hoping that it would bring different results? How many times have I started a stressful day determined that it would turn out differently than the bad day before, even though I haven't changed my strategy? Living with a habitually grateful heart requires that we change strategy. It requires us to change how we respond to life's stimuli."[70]

No matter what our circumstances tell us, if we want to live with an *abundance consciousness*, we have to make a deliberate choice to change

the way we think about how we are going to live. We have to be determined to no longer fearfully live in the basement:

> "It's in Christ that we find out who we are and what we are liv-
> ing for. Long before we heard of Christ and got our hopes up, he
> had his eye on us, had designs on us for glorious living, part of
> the overall purpose he is working out in everything and everyone"
> (Eph. 1:7, 8 MSG).

God tells us that we can enjoy *glorious living.* Your "Upper Room" is
waiting, ladies. What is holding you back?

GRATITUDE UNVEILS MIRACLES

When we offer up our gratitude to God, it opens the door to praise and
worship. Praise is gratitude in action, along with the offering of ourselves
and our feeble love to an almighty God. Praise is a choice that we make,
not a feeling that awaits recognition. The more we become grateful
people, the easier our praise will flow from our lips. Once we begin to
understand that God has designs on us for glorious living, we can
respond with offerings of praise. Here is the best part: when we can run
back to God and shout "thank you" for everything He does for us, He
bestows even more blessings on us.

The older I get, the more I am beginning to understand the concept
of why God wants us to say "thank You" and praise Him for everything
in our lives. When I give someone presents and they never acknowledge
receiving them, or thank me for them, my natural inclination is to stop
giving them anything else. It is not that I am even looking for a "thank
you," but in the back of my mind there is this human voice reminding
me that if they are not grateful for what I have done for them, why
should I want to do any more?

When we ask God for something and He answers our prayer, if we
don't thank Him for what He has done in our lives, why should He want
to give us more? I believe that thanklessness closes the door on any more
abundant blessings. It is the simple concept of sowing and reaping. If we

offer gratitude, blessings will be showered back on us. The more grateful we become, the more God will open our eyes to see the miracles that He ushers into our lives. We have to keep our eyes wide open because some of His most extravagant gifts come in plainly wrapped packages. If we don't have grateful hearts, we won't be able to see them. We may have become so accustomed to blessings that we feel we deserve them, so we no longer recognize them.

Creation and our existence itself are full of beauty and wonder. Look at the splendor of a new birth, the sun coming up each morning in all its majesty, and the mystery of our seasons. Each time we gather to eat at a table with loved ones, read a good book, or shampoo our hair, we ought to think about the miracle of having all those benefits at our fingertips. When we are able to cherish and praise God in the everyday occurrences in our lives, our whole perception changes.

Stormie Omartian tells us in her book, *The Prayer That Changes Everything*:

> "When we praise and worship God, His presence comes to dwell with us. And the most amazing thing about that is when it does, things change. Always! You can count on it. Hearts change. Situations change. Lives change. Minds change. Attitudes change. Every time you praise God, something changes within you, or your circumstances, or in the people or situations around you."[71]

When our attitudes change from ingratitude to gratitude, our eyes will be receptive to acknowledging God's miracles all around us.

GRATITUDE IN EVERYTHING

We translate the Greek noun *Eucharisteo* as "thanks or thanksgiving. It is the expression of joy Godward, and is therefore the fruit of the Spirit. Believers are encouraged to abound in it."[72] In other words, God wants us to be thankful in everything and for everything: "Be joyful always; pray continually, give thanks in all circumstances, for this is his will for you in Christ Jesus" (1 Thess. 5:16-18 NIV).

God never tells us to do something unless it is for our benefit. I have gone through difficult times in my life when I have felt as though I was floating helplessly in dark, murky waters. During those times, I was not able to be thankful for anything, let alone praise God, but I did learn that I *needed* Him to keep me afloat during the times when I felt like I was drowning. God does not say to give thanks *for* the circumstances; He says to give thanks *in* the circumstances. The longer I live and see Him at work in my own life, the more I am able to understand that through all circumstances God does work everything out for my good. Sooner or later, I am able to look back and see what He was able to accomplish while I felt so helpless and alone. I need for God to be *with me* in the turbulent waters, and He promises in His Word to do that.

Some of you will find it difficult to thank God for anything right now. You may have experienced some horrible atrocity that you cannot even comprehend. You may be wondering if there is a God who even cares about the job that you just lost, your husband who keeps beating you, your child who has cancer, a friend who has betrayed you, or bankruptcy that is just around the corner. I pray that you will be able to grasp that powerful truth of knowing that God is *with you* in absolutely everything. He promises, "Never will I leave you, never will I forsake you" (Heb. 13:5 NIV).

Most of us who live in western countries are materially blessed compared to those who live in "have-not" nations. For those of us who live in countries of the world where we have enough food to put into our bellies each day and milk in our fridge, we are a very, very blessed people. In short, we are rich.

Lately, I have been watching documentaries and newscasts about the AIDS epidemic that has left millions of children in Africa without their mommies and daddies. I have also watched little African boys being taught to hold a gun and kill other people. I have eight grandchildren who have loving parents and all the comforts of home. My heart aches for the children that do not have someone to tuck them into bed at night or enough food to satisfy their hunger. My tears flow for their pain. I wonder how they are able to thank anybody, let alone God, for the circumstances that they are in. The more I pray about this and ponder their horrible plight, the more I believe that, as neighbors in the world community, we have a responsibility to become more caring and loving with one another. Once we learn to exercise a grateful heart, we should allow God to let that abundance of blessings pour out on the rest of humanity.

When I was the keynote speaker for the city of Kelowna, British Columbia, for the World Day of Prayer in 2006, I learned a new word, *ubuntu*, which the Zulus in South Africa use to describe *humanity towards others*. It carries many dimensions of meanings related to humility, sharing, caring, helping as much as you can, and working with others. In the Bible, it is referred to in this verse: "Love your neighbor as yourself" (Mark 12:33b NIV).

What does this mean for you and me—to show *ubuntu* to those around us? Perhaps we are to be the hands and feet of God by helping those who are unable to help themselves. How can we be a conduit of God's blessings to others so that they will be able to recognize a loving heavenly Father and give thanks to Him?

St. Basil the Great wrote these thought-provoking words in the fourth century:

> "The bread which you do not use is the bread of the hungry. The garment hanging in your wardrobe is the garment of one who is naked. The shoes you do not wear are the shoes of one who is barefoot. The money you keep locked away is the money of the poor." [73]

God pours out His blessings freely, and for those of us who receive them, I believe it is our responsibility to share with those who do not have them. God's blessings need to keep flowing so that *all* of humanity is able to shout, "Thank you!"

HINDRANCES TO GRATITUDE

1. Regrets
While Jesus was walking on this earth, He tried to teach us everything so that we could be able to live a life without regrets. When we live our lives

looking backwards and recounting all our misgivings, our eyes will be focused on everything that is wrong, instead of that which is good and right. Regret is so painful: it is like a dull knife that keeps stabbing at us and reminding us of what we did wrong. When we live in a state of regret, we live in sorrow, not gratitude.

It is painful for me to listen to women when they tell me that their lives are filled with regret. They look back and only see their mistakes, shame, and missed opportunities for God to use them. Now that they are older and wiser, they realize what their lives could have been like. Did God overlook them? Did they not hear from God during their younger years? Were many of their years simply wasted?

I believe that everything in our lives has been perfectly orchestrated by God. Even if it doesn't looks like it, nothing in our lives is wasted. *Today* is the place where we need to be grateful to God for everything in our past. He will use all of it to make us wiser, stronger, and more aware of the world around us so that we can really make a difference *today.*

Jesus also tells us that in order to live a joyful life, we need to be obedient to His Word: "When you obey me you are living in my love, just as I obey my Father and live in his love" (John 15:10 TLB).

When we live in the boundaries that God has given us, we are aligned with His will. He created a beautiful world for us; we agree with it. He died for our forgiveness; we receive it. He tells us to pray, and when we do it, we find peace. He tells us to think on things are good and beautiful; when we do so, we see beauty. He tells us to speak words of love, and when we do, we receive love back.

Aligning ourselves with His plans and purposes give us freedom, joy, and purpose—not regret. There may be failures at times, but they can be viewed with gratitude as stepping stones to implore us to be wiser for the future.

In the Psalms, David learned that his delight came from his obedience to God: "And I delight to do your will, my God, for your law is written upon my heart!" (Psalm 40:8 TLB).

The more we learn to be obedient to God, the more we will live with delight flowing from our lips, praising Him for His wonderful patience and loving kindness toward us.

2. Self-Absorption

A prime example of self-absorption, King Nebuchadnezzar was so prideful that he built a golden statute of himself, ninety feet high and nine feet wide. Once, He even commanded his subjects that when his band started to play, they were to fall on the ground and worship him. Those who disobeyed would be thrown into a fiery furnace. One day as he was strolling on the roof of his royal palace in Babylon, he exclaimed, "*I,* by my own mighty power, have built this beautiful city as *my* royal residence, and as the capital of *my* empire" (Dan. 4:30 TLB). Notice two specific words in this verse: *I* and *my.*

Self-absorption is all about "what *I* have done," and "everything that I have is *mine.*" When we see life from this angle, we pat ourselves on the back and congratulate ourselves for our success and accomplishments. Everything we do is focused on accumulating more, and we are grateful only when we succeed. That kind of gratitude is *all about me,* and it is never enough.

David Foster explains this attitude so well in his book, *The Power to Prevail:*

> "Think of the attitude of entitlement like an old, rusty anchor chained to a proud and arrogant man. It reveals a hollow heart that can never be filled and will never be satisfied. It prompts the insatiable drive for more and fosters the almost incurable belief that no matter what you have, it will never be enough. Though you have all the trappings of success, you still feel empty. The most miserable people in the world are not those who have suffered great losses, but those who have everything they've ever wanted—except the power to enjoy it." [74]

Self-entitlement says, "*I deserve it.*"

- My new promotion *entitles* me to a company car, a corner office, my private secretary, and other special perks.
- I *deserve to* cheat on my expense account; after all, I worked hard while I was away.

- I paid for this expensive meal and *I will not settle* for anything less than the very best food and service.
- I *expect* others to treat me with respect.

Yes, we probably should get a decent meal if we paid a good price for it. What makes it self-entitlement is our selfish, arrogant attitude which says we've earned it, so we deserve the best. Never satisfied, we will begin to want more and more other things that we are not even entitled to. It is difficult for us to extend any gratitude to God that He allowed us to have all of those things in the first place. After all, we feel that we *deserved* it.

Let's find out what happened to King Nebuchadnezzar, who looked over his kingdom and was *proud* of his accomplishments. God abhors pride, so He will not let us get away with a haughty spirit. As the king was walking and admiring his kingdom, he heard a voice that said,

> "Oh, King Nebuchadnezzar, this message is for you: You are no longer ruler of this kingdom. You will be forced out of the palace to live with the animals in the fields, and to eat grass like the cows for seven years until you finally realize that God parcels out the kingdoms of men and gives them to anyone he chooses" (Dan. 4:31, 32 TLB).

That was pretty harsh punishment for worshipping himself and taking pride in his beautiful kingdom and gardens. He was too proud of what he had accomplished.

Pride separates us from our loving and caring heavenly Father. We must always remember that every object we "own" has been bestowed to us, not because we are *entitled* to it, but because it is a gift of God's *grace*. He truly is the owner of all things, but He lets us use and enjoy them while we're on earth.

When we live our lives in self-absorption, our pride will eventually cause us to trip over our own ego. King Solomon must have had that experience because he tells us: "Pride goes before destruction, a haughty spirit before a fall" (Prov. 16:18 NIV).

Let's raise our eyes upwards to give praise to the One who holds the whole world in His hands. He is the one who knows the stars by name and causes the sun to rise each morning. He tells the oceans how far they can go and waters the earth to make it fertile. He crowns the mountains with snow in the winter and bursts forth flowers with an explosion of color in the summer. He owns the cattle on the thousand hills. He is the God Almighty. There is none before Him and there will be none after Him (Isa. 43:10 NIV). He is to be praised and worshipped and no one can take His glory away from Him.

3. Break-neck speed

We miss the mysteries and wonders of our world when we are too busy to notice them. We live in an environment of so much noise, confusion, and activity that we have lost our sense of observation. Everything around us is designed to stimulate us and catch our attention. In the movie theaters, the color, sound, and speed of even the children's movies is so overwhelming that it feels like we are riding the crest of a roller coaster. Faster and louder motion and color are moving all around us. With this much noise and speed, we miss the intricacies of the beauty and miracles around us. There is no time to be grateful for the beauty of a raindrop running down the window pane. We don't stop and marvel at a rainbow or watch the full moon come over the mountaintop. We forget about gazing at the beauty of the May flower and the delicacy of the daisies in a field. We need to stop, observe, and recognize the Creator of this amazing beauty.

When our family was traveling through Switzerland in 1998, we decided to take a hike up Mount Wengen. As we climbed higher and higher, my eyes were riveted on the most magnificent beauty I had ever beheld. It was a tough hike, so my husband Jack, my son Donovan, and I would take regular rest stops to catch our breath. Each time we stopped, we saw a new waterfall, wildflowers, a canyon, or a different mountain peak. It was so amazing that I wanted to fall on my knees and worship God for lavishing us with such a beautiful world. My heart was overflowing with such gratitude and joy that at times it brought tears to my eyes. It was when we *stopped* and separated ourselves from the noise and speed of this world that we were able to recognize the handiwork of our great Creator. That kind of recognition shouts a "thank you" that echoes throughout creation for a long time.

Unleashing the Beauty of Gratitude

It is true that women who are loved radiate beauty from the inside out. One of the ways that we feel loved is when we know someone is looking after us and providing for us. The most magnificent woman is the one who is *grateful* to the One who loves her and provides for her.

Gratitude accepts imperfections

Let's face it: life is not perfect and never will be, until we get to heaven. I think there is a yearning inside all of us to find the perfect Garden of Eden. We would like everything in its place, a perfect husband, beautiful yard, satisfying career, and adorable children. A grateful woman, however, looks at all the imperfections in her life and accepts them for what they are. (This includes her body when she looks in the mirror.)

This is how author John Ortberg describes contentment:

> "I must learn to be grateful for all the 'slightly imperfect' gifts in my life. If I withhold my gratitude in hopes of receiving the perfect spouse, child, body, or birthday present, I will never be grateful at all." [75]

If we wait for gratitude to kick in when life reaches our expectations of our perceived perfection, we are setting ourselves up for disappointment. Let's be grateful and enjoy what is right in front of us.

Gratitude is contagious

There is a contagious energy coming from a woman with a heart of gratitude. From her grateful spirit, a joy bursts forth that exudes confidence. She accepts everything in her life as a gift from God. She knows that God created the heaven and earth, and that He is the owner and provider of everything we have. (Even if we feel it is ours because we have worked hard for it, the fact remains that God gave us the physical body, energy, wisdom, and abilities to earn it.) She knows that she does not have to hoard things because her heavenly Father is her provider, and His storehouse will never run out. When we live out of this abundance consciousness, no one can intimidate us, and we can walk with our heads held high. This attitude gives us a confidence that draws others to us like a magnet.

Gratitude overflows into generosity

People who perceive life as a gift to be enjoyed want to share that joy and blessing with other people. Consequently, it is as though they are so full of gratitude that their blessings pour out wherever they go. Their spirit is one of *ubuntu,* which gives them the freedom to joyfully share what they have with the rest of the world. Their gratitude overflows into generosity, giving the word "re-gifting" a whole new meaning.

God tells us that *if* we are generous and feed the poor and hungry, *then* our soul will be even more beautiful: "and *if* you spend yourselves on behalf of the hungry and satisfy the needs of the oppressed, *then* your light will rise in the darkness, and your night will become like noonday" (Isa. 58:10 NIV).

There is a reason that God tells us to feed the hungry and take care of the needy: He knows that because we are selfish, we need an antidote for self-absorption. He knows that generosity will release more beauty in us.

Gratitude knows what is real

I love being around a woman who doesn't take life too seriously. She is free to give, because she realizes that she is not responsible for how the recipient uses that gift. In the same way, she knows that she is responsible for gifts that are given to her. She freely receives and uses all the gifts of freedom and forgiveness of her sins in her own life and enjoys living in the "Upper Room."

Beauty is unleashed when we loosen our grip on the things of this world and accept the truth that our value is not measured by how much we own. This type of woman doesn't even know what the word *self-absorption* means because her eyes focus on what really matters: God, friends, family, and the poor and needy in the community.

Stop and ask God to Unleash Your Beauty

Begin by asking: God, show me the areas in my life where I have an ungrateful attitude.

S—Scripture: "Rejoice in the Lord always, I will say it again: Rejoice! Let your gentleness be evident to all. The Lord is near. Do not be anxious about anything, but in everything, by prayer and petition, with thanksgiving, present your requests to God" (Phil. 4:4-6 NIV).

T—Thanksgiving: Thank You, God, that You are my provider and are always near to me. Thanksgiving is in my heart, and my lips declare praise to You. You want me to pray to You whenever I need help. I do rejoice in You because You provide me with everything that I need. Thank You for being my Abba Father and Provider.

O- Observation: It is impossible to be anxious and thankful at the same time. I need to pray about everything so that I can be free from an anxious spirit.

P- Prayer: When I stop and look around, I stand in awe of the beauty of Your creation. I have only my mouth to declare Your praises and my voice to shout "Thank You!" I see the mountains that are so glorious and strong, with their peaks reaching up into the heavens. I thank You that they are part of the powerful foundation of this earth. I watch the full moon rising over the horizon and see the sparkling trail of light that it leaves on the rippling waves in the ocean. I look up at the tall redwood trees that clap their hands as the wind sweeps over them. I thank You for dolphins that jump out of the water in all their majesty and the pearls that silently grow in their protected oyster shells. I see new birth and death all around me. I am grateful that all existence is in Your hand and that You know the time and day of each of our arrivals and departures. I thank You that all of this was created for mankind to use and enjoy. I ask You to open my heart so that I can see Your miracles around me every day. I praise You, God. Amen.

14

UNLEASHING THE BEAUTY OF TRUTH
Beauty and the Beast

Beauty is power; a smile is its sword.

—CHRISTOPHER MORLEY

"WE HAVE RECEIVED an order to evacuate the building," uttered the master of ceremonies. These few words put an end to a wonderful wedding reception.

A fire which began with a lightning strike had spread so much that it consumed thousands of acres of valuable timber and was now entering our community, destroying everything in its path. It was Friday, August 23rd, 2003. This night, dubbed "Firestorm," would be etched forever in the memories of everyone living in Kelowna, British Columbia.

The previous Saturday, as Jack and I sat on the deck of our home looking at the mountains across the lake, we noticed a relatively small and seemingly containable fire. By the time fire-fighters were able to reach the flames, however, the fire had spread out of control. In the days which followed, we watched from our patio deck as water bombers and planes dropped fire retardant and flew out on hundreds of sorties On the ground, brave firefighters fought valiantly over craggy, mountain terrain to control the ever-increasing inferno. It was difficult to think that all this had started from a spark igniting a fire in a single tree.

Each day we were glued to the television, expecting good news that the fire was now under control. We desperately hoped that the fire guards which had been built to control the flames from coming closer to the residential areas were doing their job. Major news and television networks from across Canada and the United States, including CNN, had picked up the story and the unfolding events could be seen around the world. It was said to be the largest fire disaster in the history of Canada. I thought that surely in the 21st century we had enough man-power, heavy- duty equipment, water bombers, and technology to stop this consuming monster, but the fire raged on hour after hour and day after day. It did not know night from day and had a life and mind of its own.

The great fire devoured the mountain like a hungry beast that would not stop. Finally, the military was called in, and a temporary village was set up in an old football field within a central part of the city. Once all the tents were up, it looked like a war zone. All day long, we could hear the sound of helicopter blades chopping in the air above us. Heavy machinery was brought in to plow down trees so they could build a "fire guard," which is a large clearing of land that prevents the flames from spreading.

Every morning after we got up, the first thing we did was look outside. On most days, we could see nothing because of all the smoke. It felt like we were in the midst of an all-consuming fog that would not lift. The smoke was so thick that we could not see traffic in front of us, and it was so intense that it burned our eyes. Although my workplace was miles from the fire, I could still go outside and catch ashes and small pieces of wood. The thrust of the flames was so powerful that at times it sounded like a 747 airplane leaving the ground. Men and machinery were in a fierce battle against a red-hot monster that was more powerful than anything human beings could control.

Just when we thought it could not get any worse, the television stations announced that the historic railway trestles were burning— trestle #1, then #2, and on it went until we knew that 12 of the 18 were gone.

Over a hundred years of memories on those historic walking trails went up in flames and turned into a black, scarred mess.

Finally, with manpower and help from a little rain, the ordeal was over. At times, there were up to 1,300 sweaty, sleep-deprived men and women battling the flames. The mountain burned from August 16th to September 9th, 2003, and the fire had consumed over 75,000 hectares of our beautiful mountains, parks, and residential areas. Two hundred and thirty-eight homes had burned to the ground and over 30,000 people were evacuated.

As I looked at the mountain from our patio deck, my heart ached over all the brown, empty patches. In my lifetime, I know I will never again see it lush and green.

"Evacuation Alert" and "Evacuation Order" had become familiar phrases that struck unrelenting fear into the hearts of thousands of Kelowna residents for almost a month.

As soon as people were given the evacuation order, they had to leave their homes within the hour. Thousands of lives were literally torn apart. Television cameras showed us pictures of people grabbing their pets, pictures, and ornaments as the fires came closer to their homes. In an instant, they lost the familiarity of their comfortable lives. Everything was destroyed; nothing was left.

"Evacuation Order" was the phrase that ended the beautiful marriage ceremony on the night of the Firestorm. That night as guests streamed out of the reception hall, Jack and I stayed to say our good-byes to a tearful bride who stood there stunned. Her wedding day was over. This special day had been planned for months, but it ended with those two words. In this particular case, however, the evacuation order had been misinterpreted. The reception hall was not close enough to be in grave danger from the fire that night. Nevertheless, because of the fear factor involved and the fact that we could see the flames in the distance through the window, as soon as we heard the word "evacuation," it was assumed to be the *order*. In fact, it was only the alert. The word *alert* meant "be *ready* to be evacuated."

Fear often causes us to jump to conclusions by misinterpreting words and situations. This can ultimately cause a lot of unnecessary pain and disappointment.

The Beauty of a Flame

Flames have tremendous power. From the beginning, fire has helped man in many ways, such as keeping him warm and allowing him to cook his food. Today, flames still have the power to:

- Heat glass to the point where it can be shaped into beautiful beads or other magnificent ornamental creations;
- Cook our food in a barbecue, grill, or stove top;
- Roast marshmallows over a campfire;
- Keep our homes warm in the winter;
- Light candles to gives our homes beauty and ambience;
- Ignite a torch so that it can melt metal to build bridges, buildings, or spaceships.

There is a hypnotic beauty in flames. When my children were younger, we would go on camping trips during which the fire pit created our most memorable moments. As soon as it got dark, the campfire was lit, and the crackling of the logs prepared the ambience for the evening. The guitar would come out, and the singing and festivities would begin. Around the dancing, mesmerizing flames, we felt free to tell stories or share burdens that we would not normally feel comfortable talking about. For us, there was great power and comfort in the seductive colors and warmth of the flame.

The Destruction of the Flame

An unguarded flame is like a beast that has the power to destroy everything in its path. I watched a tiny spark destroy a mountain, reaping absolute devastation, heartache, and destruction. The Bible tells us about the flames in the supernatural battle that we are in. Fiery darts are being aimed at us by Satan that are intended to destroy their target—our soul—through deception and accusations.

The apostle Paul must have been in a few battles. He warns us: "In every battle you will need faith as your shield to stop the fiery arrows aimed at you by Satan" (Eph. 6:16 TLB). In verse 12, we are told that "our battle is against evil rulers and authorities of the unseen world, against those mighty powers of darkness who rule this world, and against wicked spirits in the heavenly realms."

You and I need to aware that we are in a battle with unseen forces intent on destroying our souls. The most dangerous thing we can do is go on with our Christian lives, ignoring the messages that our souls are sending us. We are in grave danger when we allow only our sight, touch, hearing, smell, and taste to be the motivators for guiding us through our lives. It is actually the things we cannot see—those that occur in the supernatural—that will determine the course of our lives. In order to live an abundant, powerful Christian life, we need discernment and wisdom to know that when our perception is blurry and wrong, it is because of the lies of Satan.

In military strategy, one must never underestimate the power and strength of the enemy. When we are engaged in battle, we need to find out all that we can about the enemy so that we can prepare ourselves with the proper equipment, tools, and weapons. Our battle is not against each other (flesh and blood), but rather against the unseen supernatural powers of darkness, such as evil, wickedness, and accusations. The powers of evil will try to rob us of all our spiritual possessions that we gain when we receive Christ as our personal Savior. These include the fruits of the Holy Spirit, which are love, joy, peace, patience, kindness, goodness, faithfulness, gentleness, and self-control. The tactics of the enemy are very deceptive and subtle, so we need to guard ourselves from them. In this type of battle, we need to put up our supernatural "shield," which is the truth found in the Word of God.

Who Is the Enemy?

If we are in a battle, there is obviously an enemy. Who is an enemy in your life? Is it someone who has hurt you by lying to you or saying hurtful things about you to other people? Is it a friend or family member who has disappointed you? Is it a lost job, opportunity, or dream?

Our greatest enemy can be the way we *perceive* life around us or *interpret* what someone says or does to us. It can involve fear, our insecurities, our feelings of rejection, or lack of self-worth, which can make us react in a hurtful way by responding in anger or defeat. Satan uses this unseen enemy—our perception of life and misinterpretation of words spoken to us—to destroy our souls.

Neil T. Anderson, the author of *The Bondage Breaker,* is very candid about this:

> "How important is it that we learn to resist the persistent accusations of Satan? It is absolutely vital to our daily victory in Christ. We have all felt like worthless nobodies from time to time. And when we feel like worthless nobodies we act like worthless nobodies, and our lives and ministries suffer until we repent and choose to believe the truth. But Satan never gives up. He will try to get us down more often and keep us down longer by hurling one false accusation after another."[76]

There are days when I feel insecure and vulnerable the minute my feet hit the floor. I don't understand this, but I do know it is true because I have experienced it. I am confident in who I am, but for some reason doubts start to play around in my mind: *I'm not smart enough. I'm not young enough. I'm not good at anything. I don't spend enough time with people I love. I won't have enough money when I retire.* It takes an intentional effort to say, *NO, that is not the truth.*

Over the years, I have learned to how to catch those darts when they start flying at me by detecting their pattern. It is usually when I am overtired, I have made a mistake at work, and I feel that I have let someone down, or I feel the flu or a cold coming on. It happens more often during the winter months when the sky is overcast for days at a time, and my spirit becomes heavy. Do you see a pattern here? Satan gets us when we are already down, in those times when we are the most vulnerable and feel too tired or dejected to protect ourselves. This is when we need to put up a shield to protect our bodies, hearts, and minds from his relentless attacks.

Putting Up the Protective Shield

We need to take up the "shield of faith" to ward off the flaming, accusing arrows of Satan. I have seen many movies such as *Troy* in which soldiers fought side by side with a solid wall of a large shield protecting them. The shield was called a "scutum" that covered almost their whole bodies. It was so large that even a single solider could protect himself sufficiently. Darts were often dipped in pitch and then set on fire, but the wooden shield was covered with leather to quench them quickly. In our lives, I believe "fiery darts" are Satan's ways of condemning us and accusing us. He does this by:

- Making us think people are slandering us.
- Making us feel that we have been selfish.
- Playing on our insecurities by implanting fear.
- Causing us to gossip or believing other people's gossip about us.
- Misinterpreting things that are said or done to us.
- Making us feel that we are unlovable.
- Making us think we are stupid.
- Making us think we are unattractive.
- Making us think we only deserve to be poor.
- Getting us discouraged when disappointments come along.

The apostle Paul knew that the only way to quench these fiery darts is by lifting up the *shield of faith* and bringing God's truth into the picture.

The beauty of the shield

There is such comfort to know that we have the power to deflect the slander of our enemy, which are the *fiery darts,* by lifting up our *shield of faith* to protect us as we bring God's truth into the battlefield.

As I write this, I am at a family camp retreat in the beautiful Rocky Mountains with my husband, who is the keynote speaker at this event. My daughter Michelle and her husband Tim, along with their adopted son Matthew are also here, and we are relishing our precious family time.

There is, however, a shadow lurking around us. The enemy is subtly and slyly slipping discouragement and fear into our minds as we discuss more of the adoption proceedings. This will be Tim and Michelle's second adoption, but this time things are not going well. The due date keeps getting moved around because the young, teen-age birth mother keeps changing her mind. We are all doubtful that the adoption will not go through at all. It is almost as if Satan can smell the fear and discouragement in Michelle's mind. I have found in my own life that fear and discouragement opens the door to fiery darts that have the ability to destroy hope.

We sat there with our arms around each other, talking and crying about the whole adoption situation. Suddenly realizing that our doubts and fears were allowing our spirits to be crushed, we chose to stop that way of speaking. We knew that in order to find comfort and truth, we had to let go of our human, distorted perceptions by taking up the *shield of faith*. We had a choice—to either allow the enemy to keep crushing us, making us cry and lose sleep, or apply God's truth to the situation. We decided to choose God's truth.

Months later, I looked into the eyes of a dear friend over a cup of steaming, freshly brewed coffee. Tears were streaming down her cheeks as she shared some fears in her life. I knew the situation and people in her life that she was talking about, so I could tell by her words that fear was distorting her perception. I said, "Let's just stop a minute and bring God's truth in the picture." Over the next few minutes, we reminded each other of God's words of encouragement and how His perfect love drives out fear. We looked at the situation realistically, not out of fear or from what happened in the past, but through our steadfast belief that God would make all things work together for everyone's good (Rom. 8:28). I had to remind her that even if the results did not work out perfectly, God would give her the courage and strength to accept the way this would all unfold. By the time we finished our coffee, her tears were dried, and there was a new light in her eyes and a smile on her face. God's Word is so powerful that it can take a perceived situation and turn it into a completely different picture. We just have to trust that God knows what He is doing, even though we have an enemy that wants us to believe otherwise.

God reminds us:

"For I know the plans I have for you, says the Lord. They are plans for good and not for evil, to give you a future and a hope" (Jer. 29:11 NIV).
* Truth: *Everything God does in our lives is to give us a good future.*

"For the Lord your God is the one who goes with you to fight for you against your enemies to give you victory" (Deut. 20:4 NIV).
* Truth: *God is always available to help us against our enemies.*

"How priceless is your unfailing love. Both high and low, men find refuge in the shadow of your wings" (Psalm 36:7 NIV).
* Truth: *We will find comfort in God's Word.*

As we speak these verses and pray, God will change our perception of our circumstances and lift our spirits. We will be reminded that God is with us *through* our pain: He will protect and love us *in* our trials and give us hope *for* tomorrow. By reminding ourselves of the promises which are God's words of truth, we are able to quench the *fiery darts* of doubt and discouragement from the enemy. Oh, what power there is when truth changes our perspective of our feeble, distorted, human thoughts.

UNLEASHING THE BEAUTY OF TRUTH

When I go white-water rafting, I have to put on a life jacket and follow precise instructions. When you or I decide to go mountain climbing, we have to buy all the proper equipment for climbing. We need the right shoes, ropes, hooks, and clothes. No one would ever think to go scuba diving without a scuba diving suit and air tank. When we go skiing, we need to wear a helmet and goggles, and our safety release must be working properly on our skis. We must always be wise in preparing for the possibility of danger by having all the right equipment. If we spend so much time and careful consideration on other things in our lives, why do we so often neglect the most important part—our soul?

We are human beings; therefore, we are visual. We react to life around us through our human eyes and ears, taste, smell, and touch. We perceive what people say and do to us through our human perception which has been marred by sin. Satan knows this, and he will use our misperceptions to deceive us in his endeavor to destroy our souls. We need God's protection of the *shield of faith* to be the constant truth in our lives so that we can life a victorious, abundant Christian life.

To unleash the beauty in our souls, we need to be able to identify the *fiery darts* of the enemy. A woman who is pursuing beauty needs to be alert to this and able to acknowledge them as an attack from Satan rather than a personal affront to her. There is great power when we align our thinking with truth from God's perspective. Every woman needs to recognize that:

- She in a spiritual battlefield.
- Words and situations are all assessed through human perception.
- Satan can use her emotions to give her false messages.
- When she is going through a difficult time in her life, her emotions are vulnerable, so the enemy has a clearer firing line.
- She needs to stop and use the *shield of faith* to assess truth.
- The Bible is filled with promises of hope and peace, so she needs to take the time to find them and read them.
- Fear and insecurity are two of the enemy's most powerful tactics.
- She needs to make sure to seek God's truth.
- God has given her everything she needs to win the supernatural battle.
- She should never be too afraid or prideful to ask for help.
- There is great protection from many shields placed side by side, just like in the battlefield. She can visualize the power of a community of shields when she knows she cannot stand alone.

Recognizing mesmerizing, deceptive darts

I wrote earlier how flames can be very soothing, beautiful, and mesmerizing. For a woman to unleash beauty, she must also be able to identify *beautiful, deceptive* flames from Satan. This may come from time to time in words that are soothing to our soul, such as:

- "You did such a great job teaching that new course."
- "You always look like a million bucks."
- "Nobody can do it like you."
- "If you left, this place would fall apart."
- "I don't know how you do it; you must be superwoman."
- "This world would be a better place if everyone was like you."

There is nothing wrong with those words, and we love to hear them. They can encourage us to identify our gifts, passions, and abilities that God has given us, but they become *deceptive fiery darts* if we let them mesmerize us into thinking that they are the words that shape our identity. When we *need* those phrases and words to soothe us, make us happy, and give us our identity, then we run into grave difficulty when they stop. Our identity is shaped through the truth in who we are in Jesus Christ, not through words spoken by other people.

If we rely on those words to shape our self-worth, what do we do when those words stop being beautiful and encouraging? We may overhear someone saying unkind or untruthful words about us, or we may even be confronted by someone who is angry and lashing out at us. How about those times when we mess up, and they approach us with critical and slanderous expressions? When we feel unsure of ourselves, we begin to question ourselves and even become depressed when we haven't heard good words for a long time.

In the same way that we have to take up the shield of faith to quench the *fiery* darts, we also need to put up the shield to absorb the beautiful, mesmerizing darts. A woman of beauty cannot depend on words spoken by other people to shape her identity. She can and should enjoy hearing them, be thankful for them, seek out the wisdom in them, and then let them go.

A small, unguarded spark from a lightning storm caused "Firestorm" in Kelowna in 2003 and destroyed mountains and many homes, shattering many lives. If we don't guard ourselves from the small, deceptive flames that the world hurls at us, they will continue to grow, consume us, and eventually destroy us. If we want to be women who live victorious, vibrant, beautiful lives, we must be able to identify misinterpretations and accusations by catching those fiery darts from the enemy, who is like a ravaging beast intent on destroying our souls.

The place where all of our misinterpretations and accusations take place is in the battlefield of our minds. This is where we process all the messages that we receive, and we continue to act out from what we believe from them. The words we heard as little children shaped us then and continue to reverberate in our head. If they were messages of love, affirmation, and laughter, they shaped our mind to believe that we have value and the world is a safe place to be. If we heard words to belittle, devalue, or condemn us, we continue to feel angry and worthless. Here is the crucial part. If we heard a lot of condemning, negative words, they will continue to play in our head and keep us a prisoner within our own soul. I could probably ask you right now: "What painful sentences and words do you keep hearing in your mind?" Those accusations will be like a tape that keeps repeating itself and condemning us over and over again. They sound like this:

- "You're pudgy. You don't want to be fat when you get older, do you?"
- "You come back and try on some dresses when you put some meat on those bones."
- "How will you ever get anywhere if you don't buckle down?"
- "Look at how pigeon-toed he is."
- "You just can't seem to get anything right."
- "You think you know everything…well, you don't."

Every time we do something wrong, the enemy will be there to play those tapes for us to remind us how worthless and stupid we are. He knows when we are vulnerable, along with all of our weaknesses and mistakes that we have made. Those negative messages will be the beast that can literally cripple us from succeeding in life. We have to know how to fight those self-defeating, worn-out tapes.

As confident Christian women, we don't go looking for Satan behind every bush with every sentence or every little thing that goes wrong in our lives. We walk in the boldness and power of being a child of God. Satan was disarmed when Christ died on the cross for you and me. He still likes us to think that he has power in this universe and tries to deceive us into believing it. We know that as Christians we are not defeated by that, but we have the same power and authority that raised Christ from the dead available to us:

"I pray also that the eyes of your heart may be enlightened in order that you may know the hope to which he has called you, the riches of his glorious inheritance in the saints, and his incomparably great power for us who believe. That power is like the working of his mighty strength, which he exerted in Christ when he raised him from the dead and seated him at his right hand in the heavenly realms" (Eph. 1:18-20 NIV).

When we continue to walk in victory and not defeat, our shoulders will be straight, we will have confidence in what we do, and we will not cower in fear when words are spoken against us or when we fail at something.

Fear and insecurity cause us to misinterpret words and people's intentions. In the same way that "Evacuation Order" was misinterpreted for "Evacuation Alert" and ruined a beautiful wedding, our misinterpretations of words that are said can ruin many things in our lives. We live in an age of uncertainty, confusion, and anxiety, and on many days we are moving so fast, we don't even have time to think. But if we want to live with joy, we have to take time to believe that Christ's power is in us for those who believe—one that will stop any demonic flame in a heartbeat.

Let's ask God for wisdom and a discerning spirit that will help us to identity and separate God's truth from the enemy's accusations and lies. A woman of beauty recognizes small flames that are hurled at her and knows how to put them out quickly. She runs to God for comfort by searching for His truth to receive powerful and beautiful words for her life.

Stop and ask God to Unleash Your Beauty

Begin by asking: God, what is causing me pain as a result of a wrong perception?

S—Scripture: "No weapon forged against you will prevail, and you will refute every tongue that accuses. This is the heritage of the servants of the Lord" (Isaiah 54:17 NIV).

T—Thanksgiving: Thank You, God, that You are my protector and that accusing words will be refuted by You. Thank You for Your wonderful promises in the Bible that can bring about an instant paradigm shift.

O- Observation: I need to be aware of the power of destructive, false perceptions and accusations. I need to be reminded daily that my enemies are not human beings, but supernatural forces. I also need to be aware that when I am not feeling well, or going through a difficult and vulnerable time, I will be more open to Satan's deception.

P- Prayer: Thank You, precious Jesus, for the *shield of faith* that stops the fiery darts of the enemy. Even though I understand the concept of this shield, I ask for Your wisdom and discernment in knowing when I need to put up the shield. Teach me when to stop, put up the shield, and bring truth into the situation. Teach me the truths of God so that I can apply them to my life. God, You know that we are such visual human beings. Teach me that the battle is in the supernatural, and that the only way I can truly discern it is through my spirit. Make me wise and discerning in recognizing the promptings of the Holy Spirit when I am in the midst of danger or a battle but don't even know it. Give me an even greater measure of discernment to recognize the *beautiful, mesmerizing* flames. I don't want to go through life waiting and listening for words that will make me feel better or proud. Teach me who I am in Jesus Christ, and remind me that I have the authority in You to rebuke the enemy. Show me all that You want me to be through Your words of truth. Thank You for giving us all the tools we need to guard ourselves from the enemy of our soul, and teach me how to use them every day. Help me not to just think about them or talk about them, but apply them to every aspect of my life. Amen.

EPILOGUE

*A*T THE END of every chapter, I pray with you to ask God to unleash all the beauty in your life. There is no greater passion or desire for me than to see all women walk in the fullness of their beauty in which they were created.

Yet, there is one prayer that I have not prayed with you yet, and that is the prayer to receive Jesus Christ as your personal Savior. What would that prayer do? That prayer would re-connect you back to your creator: God.

Every single one of us has sinned against God, and this sin has caused all our beauty to be hidden. Jesus Christ died on the cross so that we could get free from this sin, connect us back to God, and begin to live the glorious abundant life that I talk about throughout the entire book.

It says in 1 Peter 3:18 (TLB) that "Christ also suffered. He died once for the sins of all us guilty sinners, although he himself was innocent of any sin at any time, that he might bring us safely home to God."

When we confess our sins to God, He forgives them. We can then begin to live a new life out of a cleansed heart and begin our lifelong journey of becoming more magnificent and free each day. It is not so much the words that we say, but the attitude in our hearts that says, *"From this day forward, I choose to let go of my sin and acknowledge God in every area of my life."*

Pray this simple prayer with me:

> *Lord Jesus, please come into my life and be my Savior and Lord.*
> *I acknowledge that I have sinned, and I ask You to please*
> *forgive me for my sins. Please fill me with the Holy Spirit*
> *and give me the gift of eternal life. Start me on the road to*
> *living the glorious life that You have created me for.*
> *Be my power and helper in every step of my journey.*
> *Thank You that You will. Amen.*

When you give God your sin, it will initiate the process of giving Him access and permission to begin unleashing you into your true, magnificent self.

NOTES

Chapter 1—Unleashing the Beauty of Purpose

1. Barbara Moss, "Career Intelligence: Burnout singes more workers", *The Globe and Mail*, Globe Careers, Section C-Academic, C8, Friday, September 22, 2006, C1.

2. Katie Brazelton, *Pathway to Purpose for Women* (Grand Rapids, Michigan: Zondervan, 2005), 153.

3. Nancy Leigh DeMoss, *Lies Women Believe and the Truth That Sets Them Free* (Chicago: Moody Press, 2001), 120, 121.

4. Gordon MacDonald, *Ordering Your Private World* (Nashville: Thomas Nelson Publishers, 1985), 184.

5. Mark Buchanan, *The Rest of God Restoring Your Soul By Restoring the Sabbath* (Nashville: W Publishing Group, A Division of Thomas Nelson Publishers, 2006), Front cover flap.

6. A.W. Tozer, *The Pursuit of God* (Camp Hill, PA: Christian Publications, 1982, 1993), 17, 18, 19.

Chapter 2—Unleashing the Beauty of Friendship

7. "Melissa Kaplan's Chronic Neuroimmune Diseases", *UCLA Study on Friendship Among Women: An Alternative to Fight or Flight, 2002 Gale Berkowitz,* Information on CFS, FM, MCS, Lyme Disease, Thyroid and more, (Last updated December 19, 2005), http://www.anapsid.org/cnd/gender/tendfend/html

8. *Vine's Expository Dictionary of New Testament Words* (Iowa Falls, Iowa: Riverside Book and Bible House)

9. Quote from http://www.transcendentalists.com/emerson_quotes.htm

10. Dee Brestin, *The Friendships of Women* (Minneapolis: Cook Communications Ministries, 1997), 90.

11. Ibid, p. 91.

12. *UCLA Study on Friendship.*

13. Alan Loy McGinnis, *The Friendship Factor* (Minneapolis: Augsburg Publishing House, 1979), 100.

14. Random House College Dictionary, Revised Edition, ©1975 by Random House, Inc.

15. David Foster, *The Power to Prevail: Turning Your Adversaries into Advantages* (New York: Warner Books, Inc., 20030, 48, 49.

16. John Ortberg, *Love Beyond Reason* (Grand Rapids, Michigan: Zondervan Publishing House, 1998), 161.

Chapter 3—Unleashing the Beauty of Love
17. Story of Kathy is used by permission.
18. *Vine's Expository Dictionary of New Testament Words.*
19. Rick Warren, *The Purpose-Driven Life: What on Earth Am I Here For?* (Grand Rapids, Michigan: Zondervan Publishing House, 2002), 127.
20. John Ortberg, *Love Beyond Reason: Moving God's Love from Your Head to Your Heart,* 14.

Chapter 4—Unleashing the Beauty of Hope
21. Vine's Expository Dictionary of New Testament Words.
22. Carol Kent, *Tame Your Fears and Transform Them into Faith, Confidence, and Action* (Colorado Springs: NavPress, 2003), 113.
23. Rick Warren, *The Purpose-Driven Life: What on Earth Am I Here For?,* 29.
24. Ibid., 110,111.
25. Larry Crabb, *Shattered Dreams,* (Colorado Springs: WaterBrook Press, 2001), 74.
26. Carol Kent, *When I Lay My Isaac Down: Unshakable Faith in Unthinkable Circumstances,* (Colorado Springs: NavPress, 2004), 108.
27. Nancy Leigh DeMoss, *Lies Women Believe and the Truth That Sets Them Free,* 85.

Chapter 5—Unleashing the Beauty of Godly Desires
29. Thomas K. Grose, "What Makes us Buy?", *Time (Canadian edition),* September 26, 2006, Vol. 168, No. 13, A11.
30. *Vine's Expository Dictionary of New Testament Words.*
31. Nancy Leigh DeMoss, *Lies Women Believe and the Truth That Sets Them Free,* 85.
32. James Strong, *Strong's Exhaustive Concordance of the Bible* (McLean, Virginia: MacDonald Publishing Company)
33. John Piper, *When I Don't Desire God: How to Fight for Joy* (Wheaton, Ill.: Crossway Books, 2004), 166.
34. Ibid., 147.

Chapter 6—Unleashing the Beauty of My Name
35. John Maxwell, *Dare to Dream...Then Do It* (Nashville: J. Countryman, a division of Thomas Nelson, Inc., 2006), 69.
36. *Strong's Exhaustive Concordance of the Bible.*

Chapter 7—Unleashing the Beauty of Adventure
38. David Foster, *The Power to Prevail: Turning Your Adversities into Advantages,* 6.

39. John Maxwell, *Dare to Dream...Then Do It*, 113.
40. David Foster, *The Power to Prevail: Turning Your Adversities into Advantages*, 10, 11.

Chapter 8—Unleashing the Beauty of My Home
41. Robert J. Morgan, *Nelson's Complete Book of Stories, Illustrations & Quotes: The Ultimate Contemporary Resource for Speakers* (Nashville: Thomas Nelson Publishers, 2000), 452.
42. Nancy Gibbs, *"The Magic of the Family Meal"*, Time Magazine (Canadian edition), Vol. 167, No. 24, June 12, 2006, 30.
43. Robert J. Morgan, *Nelson's Complete Book of Stories, Illustrations & Quotes: The Ultimate Contemporary Resource for Speakers*, 452, 453.
44. Nancy Gibbs, "The Magic of the Family Meal", 30.

Chapter 9—Unleashing the Beauty of God's Glory
45. Strong's Exhaustive Concordance of the Bible.
46. Stormie Omartian, *The Prayer That Changes Everything: The Hidden Power of Praising God* (Eugene, Oregon: Harvest House Publishers, 2004), 106.
47. Ibid., 105.
48. Vine's Expository Dictionary of New Testament Words
49. Stormie Omartian, *The Prayer That Changes Everything: The Hidden Power of Praising God*, 108.
50. Ibid., 109.

Chapter 10—Unleashing the Beauty of Pure Motives
51. Strong's Exhaustive Concordance of the Bible.
52. Carol Kent, *Tame Your Fears and Transform Them into Faith, Confidence, and Action*, 34.
53. Vine's Expository Dictionary of New Testament Words.
54. A.W. Tozer, *The Pursuit of God* (Camp Hill, Pennsylvania: Christian Publications, 1982, 1993), 97.

Chapter 11—Unleashing the Beauty of Prayer
55. Used with permission from Beth Hanishewski, September, 2006.
56. T.W. Hunt, *The Life-Changing Power of Prayer* (Nashville: LifeWay Press, 2003), 17.
57. The Random House College Dictionary, Revised Edition, 1975.
58. Gordon MacDonald, *A Resilient Life* (Nashville: Nelson Books, 2004), 193.
59. Patricia Raybon, "Mountain Mover", *Today's Christian Woman*, September-October, 2006, 60. Gordon MacDonald, *Ordering Your Private World*, 149.

61. Bill Hybels, *Too Busy Not to Pray: Slowing Down to Be with God* (Downers Grove, Illinois: Intervarsity Press, second edition 1998 by Bill Hybels), 88.

62. Gordon MacDonald, *Ordering Your Private World*, 150.

63. Mme. Guyon, *Experiencing the Depths of Jesus Christ* (Gardiner, Maine: Christian Books Publishing House, 1975), 88.

64. Used with permission from Beth Hanishewski, e-mail, September 13, 2006.

Chapter 12—Unleashing the Beauty of Victory

65. Grace Ketterman, M.D. and David Hazard, *When You Can't Say I Forgive You* (Colorado Springs: NavPress, 2000), 13.

66. Denise George, "Today's Christian Woman", *Christianity Today International*, July/August 2006, 40.

67. Rick Warren, *The Purpose-Driven Life: What on Earth Am I Here For?*, 80.

68. Katie Brazelton, *Pathway to Purpose for Women*, 168, 169.

69. Maya Angelou, *Maya Angelou Quotes*, http://en.thinkexist.com/quotation.

Chapter 13—Unleashing the Beauty of Gratitude

70. Ellen Vaugh, *Radical Gratitude* (Grand Rapids, Michigan: Zondervan, 2005), 172 ,173.

71. Stormie Omartian, *The Prayer That Changes Everything: The Hidden Power of Praising God*, 10.

72. *Vine's Expository Dictionary of New Testament Words.*

73. Message by Linda C. Loving, "Random Acts of Kindness", Program 3729, First air date May 1, 1994 from http://www.csec.org/csec./sermon/loving_3729.htm (accessed August 21, 2006).

74. David Foster, *The Power to Prevail: Turning Adversities into Advantages*, 26, 27.

75. John Ortberg, *Love Beyond Reason: Moving God's Love from Your Head to Your Heart*, 109.

Chapter 14—Unleashing the Beauty of Truth

76. Neil T. Anderson, *The Bondage Breaker* (Eugene, Oregon: Harvest House Publishers, 2000), 158.